Leading Systemic School Improvement Series

...helping change leaders transform entire school systems

This Rowman & Littlefield Education series provides change leaders in school districts with a collection of books written by prominent authors with an interest in creating and sustaining whole-district school improvement. It features young, relatively unpublished authors with brilliant ideas, as well as authors who are cross-disciplinary thinkers.

Whether an author is prominent or relatively unpublished, the key criterion for a book's inclusion in this series is that it must address an aspect of creating and sustaining systemic school improvement. For example, books from members of the business world, developmental psychology, and organizational development are good candidates as long as they focus on creating and sustaining whole-system change in school district settings; books about building-level curriculum reform, instructional methodologies, and team communication, although interesting and helpful, are not appropriate for the series unless they discuss how these ideas can be used to create whole-district improvement.

Since the series is for practitioners, highly theoretical or research-reporting books aren't included. Instead, the series provides an artful blend of theory and practice—in other words, books based on theory and research but written in plain, easy-to-read language. Ideally, theory and research are artfully woven into practical descriptions of how to create and sustain systemic school improvement. The series is subdivided into three categories:

Why Systemic School Improvement Is Needed and Why It's Important. This is the *why*. Possible topics within this category include the history of systemic school improvement; the underlying philosophy of systemic school improvement; how systemic school improvement is different from school-based improvement; and the driving forces of standards, assessments, and accountability and why systemic improvement can respond effectively to these forces.

The Desirable Outcomes of Systemic School Improvement. This is the *what*. Possible topics within this category include comprehensive school reform models scaled up to create whole-district improvement; strategic alignment; creating a high-performance school system; redesigning a school system as a learning organization; unlearning and learning mental models; and creating an organization design flexible and agile enough to respond quickly to unanticipated events in the outside world.

How to Create and Sustain Systemic School Improvement. This is the *how*. Possible topics within this category include methods for redesigning entire school systems; tools for navigating complex change; ideas from the "new sciences" for creating systemic change; leadership methods for creating systemic change; evaluating the process and outcomes of systemic school improvement; and financing systemic school improvement.

The series editor, Dr. Francis M. Duffy, can be reached at 301-854-9800 or fmduffy @earthlink.net.

Leading Systemic School Improvement Series

Edited by Francis M. Duffy

POWER, POLITICS, AND ETHICS IN SCHOOL DISTRICTS

Dynamic Leadership for Systemic Change

Francis M. Duffy

Leading Systemic School Improvement Series, No. 6

Rowman & Littlefield Education
Lanham, Maryland • Toronto • Oxford
2006

Published in the United States of America
by Rowman & Littlefield Education
A Division of Rowman & Littlefield Publishers, Inc.
A wholly owned subsidiary of
The Rowman & Littlefield Publishing Group, Inc.
4501 Forbes Boulevard, Suite 200, Lanham, Maryland 20706
www.rowmaneducation.com

PO Box 317
Oxford
OX2 9RU, UK

British Library Cataloguing in Publication Information Available

Library of Congress Cataloging-in-Publication Data

Duffy, Francis M. (Francis Martin), 1949–
    Power, politics, and ethics in school districts : dynamic leadership for
systemic change / Francis M. Duffy.
        p. cm. — (Leading systemic school improvement series ; no. 6)
    Includes bibliographical references and index.
    ISBN 1-57886-322-8 (hardcover : alk. paper) — ISBN 1-57886-318-X
(pbk. : alk. paper)
    1. Educational change—United States. 2. School districts—United
States—Administration. 3. School-based management—United States.
I. Title. II. Leading systemic school improvement ; no. 6

LB2817.3.D842 2006
371.2'00973—dc22

                                                          2005018977

Cowardice asks the question, "Is it safe?" Expediency asks the question, "Is it politic?" Vanity asks the question, "Is it popular?" But, conscience asks the question, "Is it right?" And there comes a time when one must take a position that is neither safe, nor politic, nor popular, but one must take it because one's conscience tells one that it is right.

—Dr. Martin Luther King Jr.

This book is dedicated to those courageous, passionate, and visionary change leaders in school systems throughout the world (teachers, school district administrators, building-level administrators, and school board members) who are using their power and political skills in ethical ways to "do the right thing" to create unparalleled opportunities to improve student, faculty and staff, and whole-district learning. May God bless and guide their important work.

CONTENTS

PROLOGUE: DYNAMIC LEADERSHIP FOR SYSTEMIC CHANGE IN SCHOOL DISTRICTS

The term "systemic change" has many definitions. So it is important for you to know right at the start that when "systemic school improvement" is used in this book it refers specifically to transforming an entire school district and its relationship with its external environment. This kind of transformation requires dynamic change leadership that is colored brightly by the ethical use of power and political skills.

It is also important to define the term "dynamic leadership." In this book, dynamic leadership means leading with courage, passion, and vision. Dynamic leadership means doing the "right thing" even when the right thing is politically incorrect or unpopular. Dynamic leadership requires a change leader to step out in front of her colleagues and lead. Dynamic leadership is about influencing relationships between and among individuals, teams, schools, and clusters of schools within a school district. Dynamic leadership is partially a function of a change leader's ability to earn and maintain the trust and respect of his colleagues. Dynamic leadership is exercised with technical knowledge and skills for leading change and turbocharged by using power and political skills in ethical ways. Dynamic leadership means orchestrating change much like a conductor arranges and manages a symphony orchestra.

Yet despite the significant need for dynamic leadership for systemic change in school districts and despite what we know is needed to provide dynamic leadership for that kind of change, there remains a leadership conundrum that blocks the emergence of effective dynamic change leadership. This conundrum can best be characterized as a failure of leadership.

A LEADERSHIP CONUNDRUM

We all know them. They are our colleagues who move into leadership positions and then become intoxicated with their new authority and power (see Marshall's chapter in part III for a more elaborate discussion of this phenomenon). What is it about a leadership position that inebriates practitioners with their newfound power? What is it about leaders drunken with their power that brings them to use negative political acts to hurt others and ultimately hurt their school systems? Where and when in their careers do some education leaders lose their moral compass, their personal code of ethics—or worse yet, did they ever have one? And what is it about leadership for change that magnifies these negative leadership dynamics? These questions, and others like them, present a leadership conundrum—a failure of leadership. Let's see if we can unravel this mystery to understand why it exists.

One of the answers to the above questions lies in preparation programs for education leaders. The premise for the existence of these programs is that leadership can be taught. Cook (2000), Block (2003), Farson (1996), and others (including Ackoff and Rovin in their essay in part III) believe leadership *cannot* be taught. Leadership, they believe, is a matter of who a man or woman is as a person. Therefore, how a person behaves in a leadership role may be more a function of *who she is* rather than of *what she knows*.

The "who, not what" conceptualization of leadership suggests that there is a set of qualities that are somewhat analogous to human personality. People are born with their core personalities in place. Over time, personality qualities are refined until the personality is relatively unchangeable. These personality qualities cannot be taught or trained, but they can be enhanced. Leadership qualities, like personality qualities, are not trainable, but they can be enhanced. Therefore, leadership behavior emerges as leaders act in ways that are congruent with their core values and beliefs. They behave this way almost unconsciously. Therefore, the content and orientation of their core values and beliefs will define how they lead.

The answers to the above questions must also include a variation of the adage, "Teachers teach the way they were taught." Education leaders probably lead the way they were led. Thus, another way to understand the leadership conundrum is to suggest that some education leaders are probably significantly influenced by negative role models for leadership in school districts.

A more cynical explanation of why an education leader may use power and political acts in negative ways is that this behavior works. It produces results. Ethical behavior, however, never gets applause, because it's tacitly expected. Even though ethical behavior can positively affect one's reputation over the long run, short-term praise and rewards for being ethical are not forthcoming.

Since unethical behavior creates results, it is sometimes tolerated. It is punished only when it is unashamedly and unskillfully used. When tolerated unethical behavior produces valued results it is rewarded with extended contracts, merit pay increases, and promotions. Experience shows, however, that unethical behavior works only for the short run. In the long run, there are negative consequences, such as the destruction of trust, the decline of morale, and the withdrawal of commitment. A more personal side effect of the unethical use of power and political behavior is that the reputation of the unethical leader can be permanently damaged for the remainder of her career within a school district. When this happens a "damaged" leader may quit or be fired, but then, quite disturbingly, he gets hired by another school district, where he repeats his patterned unethical leadership behavior. (I often wonder about how and why this happens.)

The organization design of school systems also contributes to the unethical use of power and political acts. The dominant organization design in school districts is a mechanistic hierarchy organized as a bureaucracy. Leadership in bureaucratic hierarchies aims to enforce rigid chains of command, control resources tightly, and exercise strict command and control. This kind of control is not necessarily a bad thing, but it can be if people in the power positions fall victim to its temptations—the temptations associated with power and ego gratification.

While rigid chains of command worked well in the past, when organizations like school systems required stability and little change, this design seems not to work in organizations within complex, rapidly changing environments and staffed with highly educated, semi-autonomous workers. These kinds of organizations are called "knowledge organizations" (Duffy, 2003). In knowledge organizations, leaders need commitment from followers, not compliance.

Negative leadership dynamics also are magnified during times of great change. This may happen because education leaders sometimes do not know how to lead large-scale change. They learned old-fashioned, outdated change theories that no longer work. In fact, these old theories probably never consistently produced desired outcomes. Then, repeatedly frustrated in their efforts to lead change with nonexistent or outdated change leadership skills, they resort to the negative use of power and political acts to force change—which, of course, fails more often than not.

TRANSFORMING LEADER AND FOLLOWER ROLES

I am not suggesting that education leaders should avoid using power and political behavior—they should, and they must. What I am suggesting is that power and political behavior must be used in ethical ways to create good outcomes for entire school systems.

Furthermore, I am not suggesting that leadership positions should be abolished and transformational change turned over to a leaderless "mob." The voice of leadership is needed and will continue to be needed to guide whole school systems along winding paths toward desirable new futures. Instead, the roles of leaders and followers must be transformed. This transformation will redefine leader and follower roles in ways that allow each to act differently toward each other as they collaborate to improve student, faculty and staff, and whole-system learning in their school districts.

The transformation of leader and follower roles will not automatically create desirable and effective behavior. A school system's reward system will also need to be retooled to reinforce desirable behavior. Edward Thorndike (1966) taught us that behavior that is rewarded is repeated and behavior that is repeated is learned. This principle is reinforced by Richard Farson (1996), who suggests that people do not learn from their failures—they learn from their successes (because success is rewarded and therefore the behaviors that created success are repeated and learned). Unfortunately, this principle applies to bad behavior as well as good. So, it is important to reinforce the right behaviors. The right behaviors will be those that support a district's code of ethics, its grand vision, and its strategic direction.

The reshaping of leader and follower roles must begin at the level of a school district's school board. Superintendents won't change their leadership behavior unless their school boards change how superintendents are evaluated and rewarded. Central-office staff won't change their follower behavior unless their superintendents change how they evaluate and reward their staff. Principals won't change their leadership behaviors until their superiors change how they evaluate and reward the principals. Teachers won't change their follower behaviors until building principals change the way they evaluate and reward teachers. Unlearning dysfunctional and ineffective leader and follower behaviors must start at the top of a school system.

Changing school board members' behavior is difficult. Often, people in these positions have political aspirations beyond the school board meeting room. These aspiring politicians have goals that create short-term wins for them, sometimes at the expense of their school systems. In creating their short-term political wins school board members of this class sometimes use their school districts and its leaders as scapegoats. In responding to or anticipating scapegoating, district leaders can fall into one of two response modes: they either become defensive or they take aggressive preemptive actions. In either mode, district leaders can easily find themselves using power and political skills in unethical ways—for example, using their language skills to spin mendacious webs to destroy or sully someone's reputation.

Another reason why changing school board behavior is difficult is the necessity of finding a lever to motivate them to change. This lever is not easy to find. Who evaluates school board members? To whom are school board members accountable? Some would argue that voters hold elected school boards accountable by periodically going to polling booths. Despite the prospect of being voted out of office, however, experience shows that some school boards thumb their collective noses at the voters and their communities. They, too, are drunk with their power. We see this behavior in how they treat people who show up at public meetings. We see it in their arrogance and condescension. We see it in the controversial decisions they make in closed executive sessions. And then they are reelected—more often as the result of their election campaign rhetoric than of the outcomes of their work. Fortunately, this is not true for all school boards.

What about appointed school boards? Who holds them accountable—the person who appoints them? Political appointees hold their positions because they kowtow to their benefactors' political agendas. As long as appointed school board members are in good favor with their benefactors, they stay on the board regardless of the kind of leadership they provide.

Teacher unions are another reason why education leaders sometimes fall into using power and political acts in unethical ways. Good and decent leaders descend into frustration and desperation in the face of failed attempts to convince teacher union leaders to collaborate for change. Out of frustration and desperation, education leaders can resort to using power and political acts in unethical ways. The two teacher unions in the United States are infamous for their recalcitrance and negative political behavior. Instead of acting as partners for change, teacher union leaders occasionally act as combative adversaries who put the union's interests above those of children (for a real-life example of this, please read Gil's essay in part III).

EVERY LEADERSHIP ACT IS A POLITICAL ACT

In the world of change leadership, every act is a political act. A political act is one that uses power to achieve some aim—either personal or for the benefit of an entire school system. Sometimes these political acts are ethical, and sometimes they are not. To act in a political way that is also ethical, change leaders must strive to make sure people fit appropriately

into the power structures of their school systems. Fitting people appropriately into the power structure means making sure that the right people are in the right positions, have the right amount of power to do their
jobs well, and have the capacity to use their power effectively.

Speaking of capacity to use power effectively, the concept of empowerment is insufficient. It is not enough to empower people. People need
to have the *opportunity* to use their newly bestowed power, the *capacity* (i.e., knowledge and skills) to use that power, and the *willingness* to
use it. Therefore, people need to be not just empowered but enabled to
use power.

Some leaders are reluctant to share their power because of the mental model in their heads about the nature of power. They think their
power is like the money in their wallet: if they share some of that money
with others, they have less money and the others have more—a win/lose
relationship.

Power is more like the knowledge we have in our heads. When we
share our knowledge with someone, that knowledge interacts with the
other person's knowledge, and the potential to improve both the quantity and quality of the shared knowledge increases. Power sharing works
the same way as knowledge sharing. But this is a hard sell for some folks
in managerial and leadership positions who hang on to the win/lose
mental model as if it was their dying breath.

Although we all are familiar with power abusers who use their political skills negatively, the more pernicious power players are those warm-
hearted, touchy-feely, fuzzy-wuzzy huggy bears and the "father knows
best" types who are absolutely convinced that you do not know what's
good for yourself *but that they do!* And by God, they are going to lead
you to their worldview, with their warm smiles, their gentle hugs, and
their granite-hard dogmatism.

We also need protection from these good people, who think they
know what's good for us. As Paterson (1993, 1943) observes, "Most of
the harm in the world is done by good people, and not by accident, lapse
or omission." Paterson's quote is from her book originally published in
1943, a devastating critique of collectivism and a staunch defense of in-
dividualism. The quote is a searing indictment of those with a deep-
seated Maslovian need to act "in the best interests" of others.

POWER AND POLITICAL BEHAVIORS ARE NEEDED
TO REINFORCE DISEQUILIBRIUM

Discontent or discomfort with one's current situation does not by itself
stir a desire for change. In the language of systems theory, discontent or
discomfort create disequilibrium. Disequilibrium is a necessary precon-
dition of change. Kurt Lewin (1951) referred to the creation of disequilibrium as "unfreezing." However, if disequilibrium were the only ingredient needed to motivate educators in school districts to change,
there would be a lot more change. A critical factor must reinforce
disequilibrium—changing leaders' willingness to use power and political behavior in ethical ways.

Change leaders who feel powerless and in a state of stupefaction
about their situations cannot lead change, no matter how unhappy they
are with the current state of their school systems. When change leaders
feel powerless, when they feel they have no influence, they predictably
persist in what they know. They establish routines and habits of the
mind that wrap them in the comforting delusion of being in control of
their situations, a perception fed by their nearly obsessive need to manage the minor details of other people's work.

To create and sustain whole-system change, change leaders must believe as a matter of deep faith that they have the power to lead their
school districts' transformation journeys. Then, they must use their
power, because power held unused is remarkably useless. Furthermore,
the use of power necessitates political behavior. Political behavior can
be negative and destructive, or it can be positive and constructive. Thus,
the intent of political behavior depends on the ethics of the power user.
This dependency is analogous to a double-edged sword lying on a table.
The sword is neutral—it is neither good nor bad. It is the ethics of the
swordsman that will make the sword an instrument for good or one for
evil. It is the ethics of the power user that will make her political behavior an instrument for good or for evil.

Positive political behavior benefits individuals, groups, and whole organizations. Destructive political behavior injures people, groups, and
organizations; it is intended to benefit the power users. Although destructive political behavior benefits the power user in the short term, in
the long term he will suffer from the consequences of that famous cir-

cular karmic dynamic that is so familiar to many of us: "What goes around comes around."

THE CONTEXT FOR THE ETHICAL USE OF POWER AND POLITICAL SKILLS

The concept of "systemic change" provides the context for the kind of change leadership described in this book. Because the term has different meanings, I need to clarify exactly which meaning I will be using. Squire and Reigeluth (2000) identify four distinct meanings of the term:

Statewide policy systemic change: this meaning focuses on statewide changes in tests, curricular guidelines, teacher-certification requirements, textbook adoptions, funding policies, and so forth. These changes are supposed to be coordinated to support one another (Smith & O'Day, 1990). This meaning is frequently used by policy makers when they talk about systemic change.

Districtwide systemic change: educators subscribing to this meaning see systemic change as any change, including new programming, intended to spread across an entire school district. This is the meaning often held by pre-K to 12th-grade educators.

Schoolwide systemic change: using this meaning, educators see systemic change happening inside single school buildings. It typically involves "a deeper (re)thinking of the purposes of schooling and the goals of education" (Squire & Reigeluth, 2000, p. 144). This is the meaning that seems to inform the work of such groups as the New American Schools, Inc., and the Coalition of Essential Schools.

Ecological systemic change: this meaning sees systems as rich networks of interrelationships and interdependencies within the system and between the system and its "systemic environment" (the larger system of which it is a part, its peer systems within that larger system, and other systems with which it interacts outside of its larger system). This perspective recognizes that a significant change in one part of a system requires changes in other parts of the system. It also recognizes the need for changes in three interconnected aspects of a system: its core and supporting work processes, its internal social architecture, and its relationships with its environment (Duffy, Rogerson, & Blick, 2000).

This view of systemic change subsumes the other three meanings, and it is how "systems thinkers" view systemic change (e.g., Ackoff, 1981; Banathy, 1996; Checkland, 1984; Emery & Purser, 1996; Senge, 1990). This is the definition used in this book.

THE ORGANIZATION OF THE BOOK

The interplay of power, political behavior, and ethics in organizations has been the subject of many books and articles so when conceptualizing this book I didn't want to go down those same paths. Instead, you will examine these dynamics from the perspective of change leaders in school systems who want to help their districts create and sustain ecological systemic change (hereafter called whole-system change).

The book is organized using three sections. Part I describes the context for the ethical use of power and political skills to transform entire school systems. Chapters 1 through 4 are in part I. Part II dives deeply into the use of power, political behavior, and ethics to lead change. Chapters 5 through 7 are in this section. Finally, part III offers a collection of essays written by invited authors who share their personal perspectives on power, politics, and ethics in relation to change leadership.

Ecological systemic change (defined earlier) provides the theoretical context for expressing my views on powerful, political, and ethical change leadership. Ecological systemic change is complex. Complex, however, doesn't mean it is impossible or extraordinarily difficult. It means that there is a lot to think about and a lot that must be done. In chapter 1 you will examine some of the basic concepts for understanding this complexity and for seeing how your school district functions as a system.

Systemic change must also be informed and guided by a superordinate goal—a vision of a desirable future for a district. This vision must be supported by a well-designed strategic plan that is aggressively deployed. Together, the superordinate goal and the strategic plan are called a "strategic framework," and it guides strategic change. Chapter 2 provides detailed information about change leadership for strategic change.

In leading change, change leaders will encounter challenges that are problems and predicaments. Problems can be solved. Predicaments cannot be solved; they can only be coped with, according to Abraham Kaplan (1964). Predicaments worsen if perceived as problems to be solved. Problem solving requires analytical thinking. Predicaments require interpretive thinking that puts a larger frame around the situation so its complexity can be understood. Change leaders in school systems experience predicaments more than they solve problems. Chapter 3 highlights several key challenges (problems as well as predicaments) that change leaders probably will encounter as they lead their school systems on a transformation journey.

To facilitate leadership for ecological systemic change, change leaders must use a methodology and a set of tools specially designed to support that kind of change. In chapter 4, you will find one example of a methodology and tools that fit this purpose. Only highlights of the method are presented in chapter 4, because it has been described in great detail in other publications (Duffy, 2003; Duffy, 2004). Another example of a methodology for creating and sustaining whole-system change is the Guidance System for Transforming Education (GSTE), created by Charles Reigeluth of Indiana University, Bloomington, Indiana.[1]

If change leaders in school systems want to engage their districts in ecological systemic change, that engagement will require the skillful and ethical use of power and political skills. Chapter 5 presents information about the use of power and political skills to lead ecological systemic change.

Power and political skills are neutral dynamics. They can be used destructively for selfish purposes, or they can be used constructively for the good of the whole system. Whether they are used destructively or constructively is a function of the heart and soul of the user. In chapter 6, I explore the ethical use of power and political skills to lead change in school systems.

Individuals and groups will resist your efforts to lead whole-system change—count on it. You will need to use power and political skills in ethical ways to respond to and manage this resistance. The way in which you handle the resistance will affect the degree to which people will trust you. Chapter 7 offers some insights to managing resistance to change.

I first started studying large-scale approaches to organization change back in 1975, as a graduate student at the University of Pittsburgh. My understanding of these approaches deepened in 1980 when Chris Argyris offered me an honorary faculty position in the Harvard Graduate School of Education to study his and Donald Schön's ideas about organizational learning. Over the years since then, one of the things that I've learned about teaching people how to improve school systems is that it is important to expose them to examples of what others are thinking about leading change—thus the rationale for the seven essays you will read in part III. Some of the essay writers are education leaders, others are systemic-change experts.

Drs. Russell L. Ackoff and Sheldon Rovin lead off with an essay titled "On the Ethical Use of Power and Political Behavior to Lead Systemic Change." The second essay, titled "Decisions, Dilemmas, and Dangers," is written by Richard Farson. Dr. Michael E. Hickey presents his views on change leadership in the third essay, "Parents, Power, and the Politics of School Reform." Dr. Libia S. Gil shares her personal experience with leading change using power and political skills in the fourth essay, "Disrupting the Status Quo: A Case for Empowerment." Art Kleiner offers a unique perspective on the consequences of misused power and political skills in the fifth essay, "Schools and the 'Hidden Curriculum.'" The sixth essay, "The Power of an Idea: New American Schools and Comprehensive School Reform," was written by David T. Kearns, John L. Anderson, and Nelson Smith. The seventh and final essay was written by Dr. William J. A. Marshall. His essay is titled "Lessons in Power Sharing and Leadership Shaping Within the Forums of Campus Governance: A Concerto in C Minor."

CONCLUSION

The challenges, paradoxes, problems, and predicaments you will face as a change leader while planning and implementing complex, systemwide change in your school district require you to have the will and capacity to use power and political behavior in ethical and skillful ways. Without political awareness and skill, you will predictably become caught up in bureaucratic infighting, selfish politics, and destructive power struggles, which will greatly impede your district's transformation journey. If you use your power and political skills in unethical ways, you will almost certainly damage your reputation and injure your school system.

Transforming your school system so it can create and sustain innovations that improve student, faculty and staff, and whole-system learning requires focusing on a number of issues emerging from the interplay of power and politics. The way you respond to these issues should be based on a personal and systemwide code of ethics. The issues will have a direct and powerful influence on your efforts to create requisite changes in three key areas: your district's relationships with its external environment, its core and supporting work processes, and its internal social architecture. The way in which you resolve these issues will affect your system's overall performance in the three areas just listed. Examples of these issues include:

- Implementing transformational change when people want your system to maintain its status quo
- Fostering innovative thinking and puzzle solving despite resistance to new ideas
- Acquiring resources and political support from individuals and groups who may have a political agenda different than yours
- Managing conflict with others whose help and cooperation are needed
- Diagnosing power relationships so you can anticipate and countervail negative politics by others.

This book provides you with an opportunity to think differently about power, politics, and ethics to provide dynamic leadership for systemic change in school districts. The key to successfully implementing transformational change in your school district and improving the long-term performance of your district will undoubtedly lie in your dynamic leadership for whole-system change—leadership driven by the ethical use of power and political behavior.

NOTE

1. The GSTE methodology is being used to guide the transformation of the Metropolitan School District of Decatur Township in Indianapolis, Indiana. The website is found at www.indiana.edu/~syschang/decatur/change_process.html.

REFERENCES

Ackoff, R. L. (1981). *Creating the corporate future.* New York: John Wiley & Sons.

Banathy, B. H. (1996). *Designing social systems in a changing world.* New York: Plenum.

Block, P. (2003). *The answer to how is yes: Acting on what matters.* San Francisco: Berrett-Koehler.

Checkland, P. (1984). *Systems thinking, systems practice* (reprinted with corrections February 1984 ed.). Chichester Sussex. New York: John Wiley & Sons.

Cook, Jr., W. J. (2000). *Stragtegics: The art and science of holistic strategy.* Westport, CT: Quorum Books.

Duffy, F. M. (2004). *Courage, passion and vision: A guide to leading systemic school improvement.* Lanham, MD: Rowman & Littlefield Education and the American Association for School Administrators.

Duffy, F. M. (2003). *Step-Up-to-Excellence: An innovative approach to managing and rewarding performance in school systems.* Lanham, MD: Rowman & Littlefield Education.

Duffy, F. M., Rogerson, L. G., & Blick, C. (2000). *Redesigning America's schools: A systems approach to improvement.* Norwood, MA: Christopher-Gordon.

Emery, M., & Purser, R. E. (1996). *The Search Conference: A powerful method for planning organizational change and community action.* San Francisco: Jossey-Bass.

Farson, R. (1996). *Management of the absurd.* New York: Simon & Schuster.

Kaplan, A. (1964). *The conduct of inquiry: Methodology for behavioral science.* San Francisco: Chandler.

Lewin, K. (1951). *Field theory in social science.* New York: Harper & Row.

Paterson, I. (1993, 1943). *The god of the machine.* New Brunswick, NJ: Transaction.

Senge, P. M. (1990). *The fifth discipline: The art and practice of the learning organization* (1st ed.). New York: Doubleday.

Smith, M. S., & O'Day, J. (1990). Systemic school reform. In S. Fuhrman & B. Malen (Eds.), *The politics of curriculum and testing* (pp. 233–267). Philadelphia: Falmer.

Squire, K. D., & Reigeluth, C. M. (2000). The many faces of systemic change. *Educational Horizons, 78*(3), 145–154.

Thorndike, E. H. (1966). *Human learning.* Cambridge, MA: Massachusetts Institute of Technology Press.

ACKNOWLEDGMENTS

Russell Ackoff, Sheldon Rovin, Libia Gil, Art Kleiner, Richard Farson, Michael Hickey, David Kearns, John Anderson, Nelson Smith, and William Marshall either authored or coauthored the seven essays that are presented in part III of this book. These people are very busy professionals with superior reputations in their fields. Their willingness to write an essay for this book is a powerful testimony to their commitment to helping people know and understand an important force affecting change leadership in school systems—the dynamic interaction of power, politics, and ethics. I offer my heartfelt thanks to these essayists for sharing their thoughts and beliefs with me and you.

I

THE CONTEXT FOR THE ETHICAL USE OF POWER AND POLITICAL SKILLS

Part I provides the context for the ethical use of power and political behavior to lead whole-system change—that is, ecological systemic change—in school districts. In chapter 1, you will learn some of the basic concepts about what systems are and how they function. Chapter 2 discusses change leadership for strategic change, including what it takes to transform an entire organization. Chapter 3 identifies several key challenges that change leaders face when attempting to lead whole-system change. Finally, chapter 4 lays out the essential elements of a methodology specially designed to help change leaders create and sustain whole-system change in their school districts.

1

A CHANGE LEADER'S GUIDE TO SYSTEMS THINKING

Piecemeal change to improve schooling inside a school district is an approach that at its worst does more harm than good and at its best is limited to creating pockets of "good" within school districts. When it comes to improving schooling in a district, however, creating pockets of good isn't good enough. Whole school systems need to be improved.

To transform an entire school system, change leaders in that system must know what a system is and how it functions, and they must be skillful in using a set of systems thinking tools. This chapter introduces you to both of these competency sets.

WHAT A SYSTEM IS AND HOW IT FUNCTIONS

The nature of systems has been described in great detail over the past 50 years—for example, von Bertalanffy (1950), Katz and Kahn (1978), Squire and Reigeluth (2000), and Wheatley (in Duffy, 2001). Another significant contributor to this literature is Russell Ackoff.

Ackoff (1999, pp. 6–8) adds depth and breadth to our understanding of organizations as systems. He says a system is a whole entity consisting of several parts with the following properties, which were edited to fit school systems:

- The whole school system has one or more defining properties or functions; for example, the defining function of a school district is to educate children and teenagers.
- Each piece of a school system can affect the behavior or properties of the whole; for example, a couple of low-performing schools in a district can drag a whole district into low-performing status.
- There is a subset of school system components that are essential for carrying out the main purpose of the whole district, but they cannot, by themselves, fulfill the main purpose of a school system; for instance, teachers and classrooms in a single school building are essential elements of a school system and are necessary for helping a school system fulfill its core purpose, but these classrooms and schools cannot and never will be able to do what the whole school system does.
- There is also a subset of components that are nonessential for fulfilling a school system's main purpose, but are necessary for other minor purposes—for instance, school public relations, secretarial work, and pupil personnel services.
- A school system depends on its environment for the importation of "energy" (i.e., human, technical, and financial resources). A school district's external task environment (the environment it interacts with on a daily basis) consists of individuals and groups identified as customers, critics, competitors, suppliers, and stakeholders. Because of this kind of relationship, a school district is an open system.
- The way in which an essential element of a school system affects the whole system depends on its interaction with at least one other element; for instance, the effect a single school's performance has on the whole district depends on the interaction that the school has with at least one other school in the system.
- The effect that any subset of a school system has on the whole system depends on the behavior of at least one other subset of elements. For example, let's say that a school district is organized prekindergarten to 12th grade. This means the core work process for that district is 13 steps long (pre-K to 12th grade).

Now, let's say that district leaders are concerned about the performance of their high school (which is a subset of the whole system). This high school contains grades 9–12. It would be a mistake to focus improvement efforts only on that high school, because its performance is affected by at least two other subsets of schools (i.e., the elementary and middle schools that "feed" into the high school).

Since all essential elements of a school system interact, it would be wise to examine and determine how the elementary and middle schools are affecting the performance of the high schools. Focusing improvement only on the high schools would be a nonsystemic and, therefore, piecemeal approach to improvement.

- A school system is a whole entity that cannot be divided into individual components without losing its essential properties or functions. For example, the dominant approach to improving schooling in the United States is called "school-based" or "site-based" improvement. This approach divides a school system into its aggregate parts—individual schools. Then, it is assumed that improving these individual schools will somehow improve the whole system. When attempts are made to improve a school system in this way—by disaggregating it into its individual schools—its effectiveness as a system deteriorates rapidly.
- Because a school system derives its effectiveness from the interaction of its elements rather than from what the elements do independent of the system, efforts to improve the individual elements as if they were not part of a whole system (as in school-based improvement) causes the performance of the whole system, according to Ackoff (1999), to deteriorate and the system to be significantly weakened.

SYSTEMS THINKING

"Systems thinking" is a popular concept. It has many meanings. It can refer to a set of specific tools (such as causal loop diagrams or systems archetypes); it can describe a unique perspective on how organizations function as systems; or it can refer to a lexicon of terms of art for the field of systems dynamics. Below, I talk about systems thinking tools that require practice and patience to develop and use.

Richmond (2000) presents an in-depth description of seven different intellectual skills collectively known as "systems thinking" skills. These skills complement each other but are used at different times during a systemic change effort. These seven systems thinking skills constitute a four-step systems thinking method: (1) describe the problem, (2) state a hypothesis explaining the problem or develop a model to explain the problem, (3) test the hypothesis or model, and (4) implement high-leverage changes and communicate results.

The seven systems thinking skills can be organized using the four-step systems thinking model. The thinking skills of dynamic thinking (1), system-as-cause thinking (2), and forest thinking (3) are part of step one of the method. Operational thinking (4), closed-loop thinking (5), and quantitative thinking (6) are all used during step two of the method. Finally, scientific thinking (7) is used during step three of the four-step systems thinking method. Each skill is briefly described below.

Dynamic Thinking

Events in school districts are often viewed as unconnected events. One way to improve your response to these events is to begin identifying how they are connected. You do this by observing the events to see if they fall into patterns of behavior. Dynamic thinking skills help you cluster events into patterns. For example, one troublesome event in school districts is the low performance of particular schools. If this low performance persists over time for the same schools, it is a significant pattern of behavior.

Static thinking, which is the opposite of dynamic thinking, influences change leaders in school districts to focus only on the low performance of single schools rather than thinking about how that low performance is part of a larger pattern of interconnected cause-and-effect relationships. However, dynamic thinking skills help change leaders identify the underlying pattern of cause-and-effect relationships (often called closed loops) that contribute to low performance within several schools and then help identify ways to make important changes.

System-as-Cause Thinking

When you use dynamic thinking (described above), you begin to see your school system's problems organized into patterns of events rather than as unconnected events. Given those patterns, you now have to start thinking about why those patterns exist; in other words, you have to develop hypotheses to explain these patterns.

In the development of hypotheses to explain your school system's performance problems, the operating principle is this: include only those variables that are under your control and that are capable of generating the events you are trying to explain. The relevant diagnostic question, therefore, is: "In what ways are we 'doing it to ourselves'"? (Richmond, 2000, p. 6). In other words, you need to focus on variables and factors inside your district that are under your control and that may be causing the troublesome patterns of events.

The opposite of system-as-cause thinking is "system-as-effect" thinking. This more common perspective entices change leaders to look outside their districts to explain their problems, as in "No Child Left Behind is doing this to us." The system-as-effect perspective creates too many variables for you to consider when you are trying to explain and understand your district's performance problems. Because external variables are part of your district's external environment, they are, by definition, beyond your control. So there is little benefit to considering them, because there is almost nothing you can do about them. System-as-cause thinking, in contrast, "places responsibility for the [troublesome performance problems] on those who manage the processes, policies, strategies, and structure of the system itself" (Richmond, 2000, p. 6).

If you want to develop your system-as-cause thinking skills, try changing the diagnostic statement "It's their fault" (external blame) to "How do we contribute to this problem?" (internal responsibility). Certainly, external pressures and requirements exist and have an effect on your system, but you don't have the power to change them. In contrast, it is almost always possible and beneficial to ask, "What are we doing as a school system to magnify or exacerbate these external pressures to make things worse for ourselves?"

Forest Thinking

The old saw cuts like this: "He couldn't see the forest for the trees." In other words, when people focus too intently on the details of a situation they lose sight of the big picture—the forest. This "tree-by-tree" thinking is the opposite of forest thinking.

If you use the tree-by-tree approach to develop hypotheses to explain your school system's performance problems, you quickly become overwhelmed and perhaps obsessed with "the details." Forest thinking, on the other hand, asks you to step back from the details to see the big picture. With this thinking skill, you organize patterns of events into broad categories. These categories are used to create an "on average" view of your system's performance problems. By analogy, tree-by-tree thinking creates a detailed, 90-minute movie, while forest thinking gives you snapshots.

To develop forest thinking skills you need to get into the habit of identifying patterns of events and then organizing those patterns into categories. For example, if you identify patterns of events related to your faculty and staff's knowledge and skills instead of delineating those patterns for each role (e.g., master teacher, teacher, beginning teacher, speech and language specialist, resource room specialist, reading specialist, and so on), you could clump the patterns into two categories— teaching staff and support staff. A tool that helps you do this is called the "ladder of inference" (Argyris, 1990; Argyris, Putnam, & McLain Smith, 1985; Senge, Roberts, Ross, Smith, & Kleiner, 1994).

Operational Thinking

If you want to identify possible "causes" of your system's performance problems, you need to develop operational thinking skills. Operational thinking focuses on the causes of performance problems. The opposite of operational thinking is "correlational," or "factors" thinking.

Factors thinking is characterized by lists of "factors" (as in critical success factors) or "drivers" (as in what factors drive success in our district) that are assumed to cause behavior. Any time you create a list of factors purportedly explaining the causes of behavior, you are using factors thinking.

The main problem with factors thinking is that it doesn't explain how each factor actually causes behavior. For example, you might develop a list of critical success factors that you think affect your district's performance. How these factors actually affect performance, however, is left to your imagination. These critical success factors might influence performance, but that doesn't mean that they cause performance. For example, job performance is influenced by three critical factors: opportunity to perform, willingness to perform, and ability to perform. But none of these factors in isolation explains how they collectively work their magic.

To develop a deeper and richer understanding of your district's performance problems, you could use operational thinking. For example, if you want to identify what's causing problems in your pre-K-to-12 instructional program, you would construct a visual representation (a map) illustrating the "flow" of the instructional program. The map would visually depict the instructional program, its major components, resources that are poured into it, and its expected outcomes, among other things. Then you would ask, "Given our map of how we do our work, what actually causes effective teaching and learning (or any work process) in our district?" instead of asking, "What are all the factors that influence teaching and learning?"

You would also do this kind of mapping for other supporting work processes in your system, processes that are in fact the rich interactions of individual and team knowledge and skills, sets of policies and procedures, and so on. All of these variables are interconnected, woven into a web of dynamic cause-and-effect relationships that produce behavior. By mapping the various activities associated with the core and supporting work processes in your school system you can develop a deep and profound understanding of how your system functions, why it functions the way it does, and possible errors that interfere with your system's overall effectiveness.

Closed-Loop Thinking

Imagine you are in an in-service session discussing your district's performance. The facilitator divides you into small discussion groups and asks each group to discuss your district's performance. More than likely, each group would develop lists that include curriculum, instruction, classroom management, instructional methods, state and federal legislation affecting education, among other items, and would discuss each as if it were unrelated to the others. Then, you would probably rank these variables in terms of their importance as "drivers" of performance in your system. If you were to list these factors on a piece of paper and then try to relate them to your district's performance, you might use a straight line with one arrowhead on it pointing to your district's performance—one arrow for each factor.

Making a list like the one suggested above is an example of "straight-line" thinking, which is the opposite of "closed-loop" thinking. Straight-line thinking leads to the assumption that the factors you listed somehow caused your district's performance. Systems thinkers, however, know that system performance is not determined by factors operating in isolation of each other. Instead, system performance is determined by a complex network of multiple cause-and-effect relationships. If you were to draw these networked relationships on a piece of paper, you would have a set of closed loops, one for each factor, with arrowheads at each end, each leading to the other, and all leading to your system's performance. Closed-loop thinking creates a more accurate picture of reality whereby observed "effects" feed into other variables to create "causes" that create additional effects that in turn feed into other variables to create yet more causes, thereby weaving an elaborate web of cause-and-effect relationships.

Quantitative Thinking

"Quantitative" is not a synonym of "measurable." This confuses people, because both concepts involve numbers. The data-based decision-making movement seems to be founded on the premise that to know something you must be able to measure it, and measuring requirements compel educators to seek the Holy Grail of measurement—perfectly accurate numerical data. Measurement thinking is the opposite of quantitative thinking.

Notwithstanding the drive for measuring performance to acquire perfectly accurate numerical data, aren't there things in our school systems that we can never measure accurately? Can you ever accurately measure motivation, attitudes, beliefs, or resistance to change? Yet these variables, sometimes called "soft variables," are important to individual, team, and organization performance. Do you agree with the premise that one's motivation has an important influence on job performance? Do you agree that the overall level of resistance to change in your school system can make or break your district transformation effort? These are important variables, but they cannot and never will be measured accurately. But if you ignore these variables when planning your district's transformation because you can't measure them, you are surrendering to the belief that because you don't have perfect numerical data about them that they are unimportant. But they *are* important, and they *can* be quantified, although not measured.

To quantify "soft," indeterminate variables, you create numerical metrics using a Likert Scale; for example, you might set zero to represent a total lack of motivation and 10 as representing high motivation. You could then survey a sample of your faculty and staff with a set of questions related to motivation, compute an average score of all respondents, and then plot that average score on a scale of zero to 10. This scale and the numbers on it are, of course, arbitrary, but they are not ambiguous. Given the average score on the motivation scale, you could factor into your thinking about your district's performance a variable called "strength of motivation." All "soft" variables can be quantified in this way, even though they cannot be precisely measured.

To develop your quantitative thinking skills, the next time you have a set of data in front of you that were collected through measurements (e.g., student test scores on achievement tests), invite your colleagues to start thinking about key "soft" variables that might be affecting the test scores but were not included in the data set—for example, student motivation to perform well on the tests. Then think about what would happen if you quantified those variables and factored them into your data analysis.

Scientific Thinking

Scientific thinking skills are most important for system thinkers who strive to develop computer models to describe and explain the performance of their organization (system). Those who develop these models are often pressured to validate or "prove the truth" of their models. Instead of "proving" the validity of their models, model builders aim to identify the point at which their models become inadequate for guiding decision making. This approach is based on the fact that scientific progress is made by discarding falsehoods, not by discovering truths. Proving-truth thinking is the opposite of scientific thinking.

Scientific thinking requires you to avoid using complex numerical data to understand the performance of your system and focus instead on using numbers that are simple and understandable. You should seek to identify and understand the relationship between and among these numbers. These relationships, rather than the numbers themselves, are very important for understanding your system's performance.

CONCLUSION

Systems thinking is a popular topic in the practice of school district improvement. Many people talk about the need for change leaders in school districts to be systems thinkers. But, as you can imagine from reading the above descriptions of the seven systems thinking skills, applying systems thinking is not easy.

Part of our challenge in striving to become systems thinkers is the dominant mental model embedded in our brains about how to identify and solve problems in school systems. This traditional mental model characterizes thinking skills that are the opposite of systems thinking skills. These opposites were identified when the systems thinking skills were described—for instance, dynamic thinking (systems skill) versus static thinking (traditional skill) and system-as-cause thinking (systems skill) versus system-as-effect thinking (traditional skill).

To learn systems thinking skills, you need to study them more deeply and practice each set one at a time. Then, as you gain mastery over each set you can begin to combine them to create a powerful set of thinking skills to help you create and sustain systemic school improvement in your district.

Although systems thinking skills are important for the success of your efforts to transform your entire district, they are not the only systems tools you need to know, understand, and apply; for example, you also need to identify and understand underlying dynamic structures called "system archetypes" (e.g., see Kim, 2000) in your system that may be affecting human behavior. It is at this deep structural level that you can find significant leverage for transforming your system. These other systems tools are not presented in this chapter, but you should make an effort to learn more about them from other sources (e.g., Kim, 2000; Richmond, 2000) before engaging your school system in transformational change.

REFERENCES

Ackoff, R. L. (1999). *Re-creating the corporation: A design of organizations for the 21st century*. New York: Oxford University Press.

Argyris, C. (1990). *Overcoming organizational defenses*. Boston: Allyn & Bacon.

Argyris, C., Putnam, R., & McLain Smith, D. (1985). *Action science*. San Francisco: Jossey-Bass.

Bertalanffy von, L. (1950). An outline of general systems theory. *British Journal of the Philosophy of Science, 1*, 134–165.

Katz, D., & Kahn, R. L. (1978). *The social psychology of organizations* (2nd ed.). New York: John Wiley & Sons.

Kim, D. H. (2000). *Systems archetypes I: Diagnosing systemic issues and designing high-leverage interventions*. Toolbox Reprint Series. Williston, VT: Pegasus Communications.

Richmond, B. (2000). *The "thinking" in systems thinking: Seven essential skills*. Toolbox Reprint Series. Williston, VT: Pegasus Communications.

Senge, P., Roberts, C., Ross, R., Smith, B., & Kleiner, A. (1994). *The Fifth Discipline fieldbook*. New York: Doubleday.

Squire, K. D., & Reigeluth, C. M. (2000). The many faces of systemic change. *Educational Horizons, 78*(3), 145–154.

Wheatley, M. (2001). Bringing schools back to life: Schools as living systems. In F. M. Duffy & J. D. Dale (Eds.), *Creating successful school systems: Voices from the university, the field and the community* (pp. 3–19). Norwood, MA: Christopher-Gordon.

2

CHANGE LEADERSHIP FOR
STRATEGIC CHANGE

The triple societal engines of standards, assessments, and accountability have increased the instability and complexity of school districts' environments to extraordinary levels. Add to this frenetic mix a mobile society with transient families who expect that their children's education in their next hometown will be at least as good as, or better than, the education they receive in their current hometown, even if the new school system is 3,000 miles away. Then the federal government pours into this roily cauldron a catalytic piece of legislation known as No Child Left Behind (NCLB). This complexity and instability puts significant demands on change leaders with responsibility for leading their school districts toward desirable futures.

Responding effectively to the increasingly complex demands placed on school systems requires change leadership to transform entire school systems, not pieces of school systems. Change leadership for whole-system change also requires the skillful and ethical use of power and political skills. This chapter examines critical elements of change leadership and school district transformation. Subsequent chapters will provide more in-depth coverage of the ethical use of power and political skills.

THE CONTEXT FOR SCHOOL DISTRICT TRANSFORMATION

Many authors writing about organization transformation (e.g., Hock, 1995; Wheatley, 1993) rightly point out that those who manage organizations and try to improve them are locked inside an ineffective mental model—a mental model often characterized as Newtonian or mechanistic. Yesterday's organizations were able to use and benefit from the mechanistic organization design, because the environments within which they existed were relatively stable and simple. Today's organizations, including school systems, find themselves in environments that are "VUCA"—volatile, uncertain, complex, and ambiguous (Murphy, 2002). Organization designs best suited for unstable and complex environments are those using contemporary designs often characterized as "organic" (Daft, 2001).

Authors like Dee Hock (1995) characterize a VUCA environment as "chaordic." He coined the term by combining the words "chaos" and "order." If transformation-minded change leaders want to provide strategic leadership to transform their school systems using a conceptual framework like Hock's notion of chaordic organizations situated in VUCA environments, they must accept the premise that their school systems are self-organizing, adaptive, nonlinear, complex systems that exhibit characteristics of both chaos and order.

Leadership within a chaordic, VUCA environment occurs within a strategic arena. The strategic arena for transforming school systems extends over at least three levels—local, state, and federal. Strategic leadership to transform a school system must focus on anticipating, identifying, and coordinating hopes, aspirations, policies, and legislation at and from all three levels. At the local level, strategic leadership to transform entire school systems responds to a community's hopes and aspirations for educating its children. At the state level, strategic leadership to transform a school system considers the policies and requirements of state departments of education. At the federal level, strategic leadership to transform a school system interprets and responds to the requirements of federal legislation affecting education. If change leaders are blind to the requirements of this three-level strategic arena, they will fail to transform their school systems effectively.

The turbulent environments within which many school districts exist create metaphorical "white water" (Vaill, 1991). To navigate this white water, some change leaders[1] are awakening to the need to transform their school systems in fundamental ways by creating simultaneous changes in three key areas: the core and supporting work of their systems, their systems' internal social architecture (which includes organization culture, power and political dynamics, organization design, job descriptions, and the district's reward system), and how their systems interact with the outside environment (Duffy, 2003a; Duffy & Dale, 2001; Duffy, Rogerson, & Blick, 2000). Fundamental changes in these three areas are the result of examination and redefinition of a district's basic purpose; its identity as an agency of its community; and its relationship with parents, community members, and other external stakeholders.

Fundamental, transformational change is required to navigate environmental "white water." Incremental change—or as it is sometimes called, "continuous improvement"—is grossly ineffective within this kind of environment (see Farson's essay in part III, where he comments on the difference between gradual, incremental change and big change). It is ineffective because the focus of continuous improvement is on tweaking the status quo to make it incrementally better. Beckhard and Pritchard (1992) also comment on the difference between incremental and fundamental (i.e., transformational) change when they say, "If an incremental change strategy is chosen, it is likely to deal with 'first things first' and to make necessary changes in sequential order. If a fundamental change strategy is chosen, the implications for the organization are that the organization itself, its parts, and their relationships will simultaneously change" (p. 3).

There is, however, a role for incremental continuous improvement in a transformation process: it must follow, not precede or substitute for, transformation.

WHAT IT TAKES TO TRANSFORM ORGANIZATIONS

Organization transformation is often required in response to complex and unstable environments. This kind of fundamental change is associated with significant modifications in an organization's grand strategy, which, in turn, require changes in an organization's core and supporting work processes, its internal social architecture (which includes culture, power relationships, policies, structures, and processes), and in its relationships with its external environment. Deep and broad fundamental change requires a new mental model for organizing and managing organizations, a model that leads to qualitatively different ways of perceiving, thinking, and behaving (Cummings & Worley, 2001, p. 498). Since organization transformation requires fundamental and radical changes in how people in organizations perceive, think, and behave at work, tweaking the organization and continuously improving the status quo won't help create fundamental, transformational change.

Transformation requires tools and techniques different from those used for incremental change, or continuous improvement (Burke, 2002). These special tools include total system, large-group events, such as the Community Engagement Conference and District Engagement Conference, that are part of a school district transformation methodology highlighted in chapter 4 (and described in detail in Duffy 2002, 2003a, 2004). Transformation also should occur rapidly, so that it doesn't get bogged down in organizational politics, individual resistance, or other forms of organizational inertia (Tushman, Newman, & Romanelli, 1986). In making the same point, Cummings and Worley (2001, p. 500) say, "The faster an organization can respond to disruptions, the quicker it can attain the benefits of operating in a new way."

Because a school district is a system, all of its features and components are connected to each other through complex system dynamics that reinforce and maintain themselves as a function of balancing equilibrium (a system force that keeps an organization stable and resistant to change). These complex and mutually reinforcing system dynamics make it difficult to improve a system in a piecemeal manner (Cummings & Worley, 2001, p. 500). All of these dynamics significantly affect three broad categories of school system performance variables, categories that I refer to as "change paths" (environmental relationships, core and supporting work processes, and internal social "architecture"). These three sets of variables must be improved simultaneously and in a coordinated fashion (Duffy, Rogerson, & Blick, 2000; Miller & Friesen, 1984). Chapter 4 presents a methodology designed to make simultaneous changes along these three paths.

Transformation Requires Second-Order Change

Changing an entire school system is a complex endeavor. Because of this complexity, it is helpful to think strategically about orders of change. "Order" refers to the system level at which particular changes will occur.

Cummings and Worley (2005) discuss two orders of change. "First-order" changes focus on improving pieces of the whole system—for example, a curriculum, a department, or an individual school building. Change occurs as the result of working on those isolated processes or with people in targeted schools. Further, as Meyer, Goes, and Brooks (1993) say, first-order change focuses on making changes in an organization's internal processes, systems, and structures that are planned to occur gradually over time during periods of relative stability; that is, first-order change focuses on incremental change (continuous improvement). Although first-order change might result in immediate improvements in the targeted process, department, or school building, they will likely fail if complementary and supplementary changes are not made in other parts of a school system.

"Second-order" (or "gamma") change focuses on the entire system (Cummings & Worley, 2005, p. 481). Change at this level takes into consideration multiple system factors influencing a school system's overall performance. Second-order change is transformational, radical, and complex; it involves fundamental shifts (Newman, 2000). For school systems, these fundamental changes are gathered into the three broad categories of district variables identified above (i.e., environmental relationships, core and supporting work processes, and internal social architecture). Therefore, transforming an entire school system requires second-order change, which cannot be achieved through incremental, continuous improvement.

Transformation Requires a New Organizing Paradigm

A paradigm well suited to transformational change in school districts is marked by such features as high participation of faculty and staff in determining the future of their district; a central office that functions as a central service center rather than as a central command center; leadership roles that are less complex, less stressful, and more focused on transformational leadership than in less successful situations; and an organization design that is more participative, more agile, and more flexible, thereby creating a school district that has the capacity to seize opportunities at the intersection of anticipatory planning (strategic plans) and unanticipated events (reality) (Duffy, 2003a).

A paradigm for transformational change in school districts also should focus on changing the entire school system, not just pieces of it. However, the dominant paradigm for improving schooling in districts is the "one school at a time" approach. Acting within this paradigm, educators focus on improving pieces of their school system (e.g., some school districts launch "high school reform" initiatives). The problem with this approach can be drawn from Russell Ackoff's systems principles presented in chapter 1; for example, although individual schools are important to the overall success of a school district, these schools by themselves cannot and never will be able to do what an entire school system does. Said another way, a child's education is more than what he or she learns in a school building or at a particular grade level. His or her education is the cumulative effect of what is learned over 13 or more years of schooling (in a pre-K-to-12 school system).

Transformation is driven by senior and line managers. The literature about and real-world experience with transformational change is clear: senior executives and other line managers must drive transformation (Pettigrew, 1987; Waldersee, 1997). In school districts, the senior executives comprise the superintendent and her immediate assistants. The other line managers are building principals. Without the unequivocal and visible leadership of these leaders, transformational change in school districts will fail.

Transformation requires innovation and learning. Transforming a school system means that the way a district will be organized and how it will operate in the future will be significantly different than in the present or past. To create this kind of transformation, significant innovation and learning is required. One of the most insidious obstacles blocking innovation and learning involves mental models.

In organizations, there are generally two broad categories of mental models—personal and organizationwide (Duffy, 2003b). A school district's organizational mental model is articulated in its vision and experienced directly through the district's organization culture. To transform a district, educators in that district have to change their district's mental model, because every key decision and action in a district is influenced by that model.

In many ways, a district's controlling mental model is like the autopilot on an airplane. Imagine that a plane is stuck on autopilot and the pilots want to change direction. The pilots can wrestle the steering yoke toward the direction they want to go, but eventually they will tire and release their grip. The autopilot will then retake control of the plane and move it back to its original flight path—the one that was internally programmed into the plane's computer.

This is what happens when educators try to transform their school districts without changing their district's defining mental model. The mental model is the district's autopilot. Educators can wrestle with change until they tire; when they surrender to their fatigue, their district will move back to its original flight path—the one effectively programmed into their district's culture.

There is a more effective way to transform a district. This is done by initiating the resetting of a district's autopilot, its mental model, before launching the district's transformation journey. This timing is important because transformational change starts first in our minds—because the way we think determines how we feel, the way we feel determines how we act, and the way we act significantly determines whether or not transformation is achieved. Of course, working to change your district's mental model doesn't end quickly—it continues for the entire transformation journey.

Transformation requires a reshaping of a school district's culture. Transforming a school district requires a change in a district's culture. Changes in the culture support changes in a district's strategic direction, mission, and vision. Cultural change focuses on the "people" part of a school system—the part called the internal social "architecture." The internal social architecture supports (or constrains) people doing their work. It is composed of organization design, policies, procedures, job descriptions, and so forth, all of them linked to a district's culture.

Culture change is one of the most important outcomes of transformational change. In fact, if educators cannot change their school district's culture (which is part of its internal social "architecture"), their transformation effort will fail—no culture change, no transformation.

Transformational change requires courageous, passionate, and visionary leaders. Courageous, passionate, and visionary leadership must begin at the highest level of a school system—with the school board and superintendent—and then spread throughout a school district. Courage helps a leader stand his ground in the face of adversity. Passion gives her the emotional energy she needs to persevere toward the goal of transformation. A vision marks a desirable destination to move toward. It is the flame from which the lamps of hope are lit.

Courage, passion, and vision are useless in isolation. They must be simultaneously present in a district's change leaders. A leader can have courage but not passion or vision. A passionate leader might lack the courage of his convictions and cave in to political pressure to give up the dream. A visionary leader without courage and passion is a man or a woman with a dream but without the strength of character or emotional energy to make that dream real. Courage, passion, and vision are powerful when they are stitched together and worn as a mantle.

STRATEGIC CHANGE LEADERSHIP

School district transformation is not a quick fix for a school system. It probably cannot be managed directly. This suggests that school district transformation must be navigated over time by change leaders who truly are strategic thinkers and who fundamentally understand both the visible and invisible effects of change within their systems as well as the dynamics that maintain their school districts in a state of balancing equilibrium (i.e., system forces that work to keep things just as they are).

Cook (2000) contends that strategy is set only for an entire organization—not for pieces of it. The leaders who are correctly positioned to lead strategic planning, therefore, are the leaders at the very top of an organization. In school systems, these senior-level leaders are the superintendents.

Because many school superintendents, especially urban superintendents, do not remain in their positions very long, certainly not long enough to transform their current school systems, they must deploy a transformation strategy that does not require their sustained direct influence. Instead, strategic leaders who are looking out for the best interests of their current school system, rather than their own personal careers, need to deploy a transformation strategy that will be deployed with or without them (Murphy, 2002). This means that a current school superintendent who wishes to transform her school district must develop a transformation strategy that her successors can continue to deploy.

Developing a transformation strategy with successors in mind requires all the technical, interpersonal, and conceptual skills that a school superintendent can muster. In particular, he must develop a profound understanding of the dynamics of his school district's culture that tend to block change, as well as the various cause-and-effect loops that characterize and drive his school system's behavior.

Superintendents should not be expected to resolve this issue alone. Their school boards need to be proactive in creating policies that will protect their school systems from the "new broom sweeps clean" phenomenon—where a new superintendent, the "new broom," enters a district and sweeps away all changes made by her predecessor. Here are some ideas that a school board can use to accomplish this task.

1. When they hire a new superintendent they must be sure to make it clear to him that they do not want good, effective, and valuable improvements made by his predecessor swept out in favor of a brand-new change agenda.

2. Number one, above, implies that the board members know which improvements are "good, effective, and valuable." To do so, they have to create an evaluation process that will evaluate the overall effectiveness of their change process and its outcomes. It is advisable to have a neutral third party do the evaluations, to remove the temptation on administrators to "cook" the evaluation data in their favor.

3. They should consider adopting a single change methodology for their district. If they do, their district will have a single change process that all superintendents are required to use but that allows each to launch new change initiatives that support the district's grand vision and strategic direction. By requiring all superintendents to use the same process to create change, the board will create a culture of transformational change followed by periods of continuous improvement within their district, in a cycle

that engages faculty and staff in ongoing conversations about how to improve the performance of their district.

TRANSFORMATIONAL LEADERSHIP

A specific type of leadership is required to create and sustain school district transformation. In the past, leadership was associated with "getting things done" or "leading people somewhere." To transform a school district, leadership must change simultaneously three sets of key school system performance variables: its relationship with its environment, its core and supporting work processes, and its internal social "architecture." This kind of leadership is called "transformational leadership" (Burns, 1978; Leithwood, 1992).

School district transformation requires leaders who can stimulate motivation in their followers to work for long-term goals instead of short-term self-interests and to work toward achievement and self-actualization instead of emotional security (Avolio & Bass, 1988). Transformational leadership is inspirational, because it redirects the energies and potential of people to achieve a vision. Transformational leadership taps into the emotional energy of people and provides them with meaning and a sense of personal value. People inspired by a transformational leader no longer "go to work"; instead, they work for a "cause." A sense of excitement, adventure, and enthusiasm emerges as people realize they can do more than they had ever thought possible.

Dimensions of Transformational Leadership

Bass's (1985) research identified five factors that describe transformational leaders. These are:

- *Charisma*: the ability to instill values, respect, and pride and to articulate a vision.
- *Individual attention*: paying attention to followers' needs and assigning meaningful projects so followers grow personally.
- *Intellectual stimulation*: helping followers rethink rational ways to examine situations and encouraging followers to be creative.

- *Contingent reward*: informing followers about what must be done to receive the rewards they prefer.
- *Management by exception*: permitting followers to work on tasks without being interrupted by the leader unless goals are not being accomplished in a reasonable time and at a reasonable cost.

Avolio, Waldman, and Yammarino (1991) described the "Four I's of Transformational Leadership": (1) idealized influence, (2) inspirational motivation, (3) intellectual stimulation, and (4) individual consideration. Bass and Avolio (1993) added depth to these "Four I's." They explained that "transformational leaders integrate creative insight, persistence and energy, intuition and sensitivity to the needs of others to 'forge the strategy-culture alloy' for their organizations" (p. 113).

An essential element of transformational leadership is its focus on vision. Making explicit the core values that support the vision, modeling behaviors, and attitudes that reflect those core values, and coaching and facilitating the development of individuals in adopting these core values are important tasks of transformational leadership.

Another fundamental aspect of transformational leadership is an astute understanding of the interconnectedness of all aspects of a school system. This understanding is a hallmark of systems thinking (see chapter 1). Transformational leaders who want to transform school systems into high-performing organizations of learners must be well versed in the subtleties of systems thinking. Systems thinking helps leaders see the school system as a whole, to see their interrelationships, interdependencies, patterns, and relationships. Leaders also use systems thinking to determine where small changes in the district might be leveraged to create great improvements.

Transformational leaders also have an informal, personal style with people. They approach their tasks from a collaborative perspective reflected in statements such as, "We are in this together, so let's see what we can do to be creative and solution oriented." Transformational leaders see their role focusing on coaching and facilitating rather than on directing or commanding. Building relationships, inspiring creativity, using humor appropriately, demonstrating optimism, finding solutions to puzzling situations, and steadfastly persisting toward transformation goals are important characteristics of those who want to transform entire school systems.

Eight Reasons Why Transformational Change Fails

Transformation is change—revolutionary change. Transformational change often fails. Kotter (1996) describes eight "errors" made by change leaders that contribute to this failure. While describing these errors he reminds readers of an important lesson about change—it is important not to skip steps in the change process. Skipping steps brings about the illusion of speed but only slows down the process in the long run and often results in failure.

Kotter (1996) converted the eight "errors" into positive statements describing what change leaders can do to increase the effectiveness of their organization improvement efforts. These statements were adapted for school district transformation.

Create a sense of urgency. People need a good reason to change. Kotter recommends that leaders identify a rallying point around which people can coalesce. This sense of urgency is created prior to beginning your district's transformation effort.

Create a powerful, guiding coalition. For the change methodology presented in chapter 4, a "strategic leadership team" is needed to guide school district transformation (Duffy, 2002, 2003a, 2004). This team is the guiding coalition for transforming a school system. It is powerful because it is staffed with the superintendent, one or two of his or her trusted subordinates, influential building-level administrators and teachers chosen by their colleagues to serve on this team, and others.

Develop and recognize the power of a vision and a strategy. A district's new strategic direction and vision emerge while preparing to engage in whole-system transformation. It becomes the task of leaders to articulate this vision clearly to people throughout the school system and the community.

Communicate the new vision. Kotter believes that there can never be too much communication about vision and strategy. Every channel of communication must be engaged, including face-to-face, written, video, and electronic communications. Kotter, however, suggests that people often underestimate by a factor of 10 the time needed to communicate the vision. Kotter also emphasizes the importance of the adage, "Walk your talk." He says, "Nothing undermines change more than behavior by important individuals that is inconsistent with the verbal communication" (Kotter, 1996, p. 10).

Remove obstacles (systems or people) that act as barriers to the new vision. "Whenever smart and well-intentioned people avoid confronting obstacles, they disempower employees and undermine change" (p. 10). People in leadership roles must learn how to identify and evaluate the nature of the obstacles that prevent progress toward the vision. Obstacles to innovation are removed continuously throughout the life of a school system. Removing obstacles often requires change leaders either to circumvent rules or to break them.

Generate short-term wins. Creating early success during your transformation journey is very important. Early success generates the energy and enthusiasm needed to continue onto more challenging puzzles, predicaments, and problems. Short-term wins must be created early in the transformation, because they provide emotional "fuel" to keep the transformation moving forward.

Consolidate gains and produce more change. Kotter warns against declaring victory too soon in your entire transformation journey; people will lose their edge and stop pushing toward the vision. Early improvements must be consolidated and used as a springboard for further innovation.

Anchor changes firmly into the corporate culture. Leaders must understand the puissant role that organization culture plays in inhibiting or enhancing opportunities for innovation and change. In addition, change leaders must have the ability and the courage to reconstruct and redirect organization culture in ways that support desired changes.

CONCLUSION

As society changes, so do the expectations for educating children entering a school system. What was considered a "good education" in the past may not be viewed the same way today. Yesterday's solutions for improving schooling may be insufficient for tomorrow's children. Yesterday and today's solutions for improving schooling also bring with them, by way of unintended consequences, tomorrow's problems and predicaments. A school system will only spiral upward toward higher and higher levels of student, faculty and staff, and whole-system learning, through repeated cycles of transformational change followed by relatively stable periods of continuous improvement. It is the power of dynamic leadership for whole system change that will help school districts build internal capacity to invent, reinforce, and sustain important improvements throughout their systems.

NOTE

1. For example, Richard DeLorenzo, the superintendent of the Chugach School District in Anchorage, Alaska—one of the first two school districts in America to win the prestigious Baldrige National Quality Award.

REFERENCES

Avolio, B. J., & Bass, B. M. (1988). Transformational leadership, charisma, and beyond. In J. G. Hunt, B. R. Baliga, H. P. Dachler, & C. A. Schriesheim (Eds.), *Emerging leadership vistas* (pp. 29–49). Lexington, MA: Lexington Books.

Avolio, B. J., Waldman, D. A., & Yammarino, F. J. (1991). The four I's of transformational leadership. *Journal of European Industrial Training, 15*(4), 9–16.

Bass, B. M. (1985). *Leadership performance beyond expectations.* New York: Academic.

Bass, B. M., & Avolio, B. J. (1993 Spring). Transformational leadership and organizational culture. *Public Administration Quarterly, 17*(1), 112–122.

Beckhard, R., & Pritchard, W. (1992). *Changing the essence: The art of creating and leading fundamental change in organizations.* San Francisco: Jossey-Bass.

Burke, W. W. (2002). *Organization change: Theory and practice.* Thousand Oaks, CA: Sage.

Burns, J. M. (1978). *Leadership.* New York: Harper.

Cook, W. J., Jr. (2000). *Strategics: The art and science of holistic strategy.* Westport, CT: Quorum Books.

Cummings, T. G., & Worley, C. G. (2005). *Organization development and change* (8th ed.). Cincinnati, OH: South-Western College.

Cummings, T. G., & Worley, C. G. (2001). *Organization development and change* (7th ed.). Cincinnati, OH: South-Western College.

Daft, R. L. (2001). *Organization theory and design* (7th ed.). Cincinnati, OH: South-Western College.

Duffy, F. M. (2004). *Moving upward together: Creating strategic alignment to sustain systemic school improvement*. Leading Systemic School Improvement Series, No. 1. Lanham, MD: Rowman & Littlefield Education.

Duffy, F. M. (2003a). *Courage, passion, and vision: A guide to leading systemic school improvement*. Lanham, MD: Rowman & Littlefield Education and the American Association of School Administrators.

Duffy, F. M. (2003b Winter). I think, therefore I am resistant to change. *Journal of Staff Development, 24*(1), 30–36.

Duffy, F. M. (2002). *Step-Up-to-Excellence: An innovative approach to managing and rewarding performance in school systems*. Lanham, MD: Rowman & Littlefield Education.

Duffy, F. M., & Dale, J. D. (Eds.) (2001). *Creating successful school systems: Voices from the university, the field and the community*. Norwood, MA: Christopher-Gordon.

Duffy, F. M., Rogerson, L. G., & Blick, C. (2000). *Redesigning America's schools: A systems approach to improvement*. Norwood, MA: Christopher-Gordon.

Hock, D. W. (1995). The chaordic organization: Out of control and into order. *World Business Academy Perspectives, 9*(1), 5–18.

Kotter, J. P. (1996). *Leading change*. Boston: Harvard Business School Press.

Leithwood, K. (1992). The move toward transformational leadership. *Educational Leadership, 49*(5), 8–12.

Meyer, A. D., Goes, J. B., & Brooks, G. R. (1993). Organizations reacting to hyperturbulence. In G. Huber & W. Glick (Eds), *Organizational change and redesign* (pp. 66–111). New York: Oxford University Press.

Miller, D., & Friesen, P. (1984). *Organizations: A quantum view*. Englewood Cliffs, NJ: Prentice Hall.

Murphy, C. (2002). VUCA. Retrieved on June 25, 2003, from carlisle-www.army.mil/usawc/dclm/MurphyChapters%5 CMurphyChapterFeb02B.pdf.

Newman, K. (2000). Organisational transformation during institutional upheaval. *Academy of Management Review, 25*(3), 602–619.

Pettigrew, A. (1987). Context and action in the transformation of the firm. *Journal of Management Studies, 24*(6), 649–670.

Senge, P. (1990). *The fifth discipline: The art and practice of the learning organization*. New York: Doubleday.

Tushman, M. L., Newman, W. H., & Romanelli, E. (1986 Fall). Convergence and upheaval: Managing the unsteady pace of organizational evolution. *California Management Review, 29*(1), 29–44.

Vaill, P. (1991). *Managing as a performing art: New ideas for a world of chaotic change.* San Francisco: Jossey-Bass.

Waldersee, R. (1997). Becoming a learning organization: The transformation of the workforce. *Journal of Management Development, 16*(4), 262–274.

Wheatley, M. (1993). *Leadership and the new science: Discovering order in a chaotic world* (2nd ed.). San Francisco: Berrett-Kohler.

3

CHANGE LEADERSHIP CHALLENGES

Navigating large-scale, districtwide change is challenging work. Yet there are examples of it happening; for example, in the Chugach School District in Alaska, one of the first two school districts in the United States to win the prestigious Baldrige National Quality Award (2003), and in the Metropolitan School District of Decatur Township in Indianapolis, Indiana,[1] facilitated by Dr. Charles Reigeluth from Indiana University. Navigating change at this scale requires change leaders who are courageous, passionate, and visionary, using power and political skills in ethical ways.

Change leaders focusing on whole-system transformation, however ethical their use of power and political skills, will inevitably face significant challenges during their districts' journeys toward a desirable new future—a future that captures extraordinary opportunities to improve student, faculty and staff, and whole-system learning. In this chapter, 21 key challenges that change leaders may face while leading transformational change in their districts are presented. The challenges are described below.

LEARNING CHANGE LEADERSHIP KNOWLEDGE AND SKILLS

One of the key reasons why large-scale change fails is that those trying to lead it are sometimes not well versed in the theoretical knowledge and practical skills they need to lead this kind of change. Graduate programs preparing future school administrators ought to develop a specialty area in change leadership. For example, at Gallaudet University the faculty in the Department of Administration and Supervision recently retooled its Education Specialist program to offer an Education Specialist degree in Change Leadership in Education; its Doctor of Philosophy Program in Special Education Administration has a set of five courses focusing on organization improvement.

In the absence of formal graduate programs focusing on change leadership, educators (teachers as well as administrators) with an interest in leading change in their school systems could design and implement personal learning plans. These plans would bring them to books, articles, and perhaps courses in graduate schools of business where they could learn what they need to know to lead change effectively.

Because foundational knowledge and skills are so important to effective change leadership, it would be a serious mistake for change leaders to launch a large-scale change effort without that knowledge and those skills. In fact, it can be predicted that if these leaders do not have prerequisite change leadership knowledge and skills, their change effort will fail.

BECOMING SYSTEMS THINKERS

To transform an entire school system, change leaders in that system must know what a system is and how it functions; they must understand what it means to be a systems thinker; they must be able to define the system to be improved; they must understand the dynamics of critical system archetypes; and they must be skillful in using a set of systems thinking tools. Chapter 1 provided an overview of systems thinking skills.

Systemic school improvement has a mysterious sound to it. Some people have a hard time getting their minds around the idea and cannot envision a school district as a system. All they see is a collection of un-connected individual schools. Some people catch a glimpse of a district as a system but cannot hold onto the image. Still others define a school system as a classroom inside a school inside a cluster of schools inside a district inside a community inside a state inside a region inside the country inside the world inside the universe. This mental model is often referred to as a "nested system" (Bronfenbrenner, 1977, 1979). Though theoretically correct, this model is notably useless for informing the practice of school district improvement. How can anyone improve a system that complex?

Emery (in Emery & Purser, 1995) gave a more actionable definition of a system. She said that the system to be improved is that collection of people, processes, and tools that must collaborate to deliver a product or service to a customer. To define that system, people literally make a map of all those interrelated elements and draw a circle around them. Everything inside the circle is the system to be improved. Everything outside the circle is that system's external environment.

For improving school systems, the circle goes around all the people, processes, programs, buildings, and so forth inside a school district. That's the system to be improved. Within the system to be improved, there are smaller subsystems that can be used to kick-start and sustain districtwide change. These smaller subsystems are called "clusters." A cluster is a set of interconnected schools that must collaborate to educate children. A cluster must contain a school district's entire instructional program. For example, in many school districts, the instructional program is pre-K to 12th grade. In other districts, the instructional program is pre-K to 6th, pre-K to 8th, or 9th–12th. The length of the instructional program is irrelevant. The relevant principle is that regardless of the length of the instructional program, to engage in whole-system change the clusters must capture the entire work process of a school district.

OVERCOMING THE SYSTEM'S HISTORY WITH CHANGE

The field of education is littered with the debris of failed change efforts. When people working in a school district repeatedly experience failed change efforts, they become cynical at best about the newest change proposal. At worst, they become hard-core guerrillas working to under-mine the latest "fad" that change leaders are trying to introduce to their systems.

A system's history with change might not be just of failure; it can also be colored by the experience of "new brooms sweep clean." This experience goes like this. The current superintendent is either fired or quits after a couple years on the job. This superintendent brought his or her change agenda into the system and started making changes. Some of the changes were starting to work just as the superintendent left. Then, in comes a new superintendent—the new broom—and with him or her comes a brand-new change agenda. Then, as they say (in the tradition of mixing metaphors), in with the new and out with the old and there goes the baby with the bath water. This cycle is repeated in urban districts on average every 2.8 years. Nationally, the average tenure for a superin-tendent is six years. I recently met a former superintendent at a national conference from a district where the average tenure for superintendents is 1.8 years—no, 1.8 is not a typographical error!

When educators experience either a pattern of failed change efforts or frequent change brought on by successive new superintendents, they become resistant to change, angry, depressed, burned out, or a combi-nation of these emotions. If change leaders are in a system where these kinds of emotions are prevalent, they must take time to work with peo-ple to help restore hope and optimism and ultimately strengthen com-mitment to the change process that is being proposed—*before* launch-ing the change effort. If change leaders try to launch a change effort without identifying these emotions and then taking steps to work through them, the change effort will fail.

BECOMING WILLING TO BREAK OR BEND RULES

Rule breaking or bending is one of the hallmark characteristics of effec-tive change leaders. It is only through the circumvention of rules that true innovation can happen, because the rules almost always protect the status quo.

The only rules that I know of that were sent directly from God are the Ten Commandments. All other rules were created by people to protect their self-interests, their ideas, and their turf. Of course, not all rules should be broken or bent, because the consequences of breaking or bending some of them are severe. For instance, it is probably unwise to break rules associated with local, state, and federal laws, although there may be laws that should be protested and perhaps disobeyed if they are seriously flawed or inherently unfair.

Even though it is important to identify rules that can be circumvented, it is challenging for change leaders to do so. It is especially challenging for change leaders who like rules and believe in them. These people can make rule breaking easier by using the principle of "outside-in analysis" (Beckhard, 1983). With outside-in analysis, change leaders identify those rules that are not required by law and that are defined instead as policies. They search for policies, especially within their school district, that are potential obstacles to change. Then they figure out ways to change the policies or to circumvent them. If these policies are not changed or circumvented, when change ideas are proposed people will say, "We can't do that, because the policy says. . . ."

Another way to get around rules that are imposed by an external organization like a state department of education is to ask for a waiver. The Chugach School District in Anchorage, Alaska approached its state department of education to seek waivers from specific policies and rules so as to allow it to transform its system in ways that helped it win one of the first two Baldrige National Quality Awards in education.

UNFREEZING MENTAL MODELS[2]

One of the central challenges for change leaders in the present environment for school districts is creating and sustaining systemic school improvement. Systemic school improvement focuses on making three sets of districtwide simultaneous improvements (see chapter 4 for more about how to do this): improving a district's relationship with its external environment, improving how educators do their core and supporting work, and improving a school district's internal social "architecture." This kind of whole-system change requires educators to unlearn and learn mental models that inform their work, influence their internal social architecture, and affect their external relationships.

Mental models are extraordinarily resistant to change. In support of this assertion, consider what Kegan and Lahey (2002) say:

> If we want deeper understanding of the prospect of change, we must pay closer attention to our own powerful inclinations not to change. This attention may help us discover within ourselves the force and beauty of a hidden immune system, the dynamic process by which we tend to prevent change, by which we manufacture continuously the antigens of change. If we can unlock this system, we release new energies on behalf of new ways of seeing and being. (p. 1)

The "hidden immune system" they are talking about comprises our mental models. Since all mental models are resistant to change and since they often can obstruct efforts to make and sustain improvements, unlearning and learning mental models is a kind of professional learning that is crucial to the success of any school-district improvement effort.

CREATING DISEQUILIBRIUM IN THE SYSTEM

It's a fact—when a system is in a state of balance or stable equilibrium, not much is changing. To create change, especially whole-system change, that stable equilibrium must be disrupted and replaced with reinforcing, or unstable, equilibrium. With reinforcing equilibrium change happens and happens quickly. The danger is that reinforcing equilibrium is like a neutral third party—it doesn't care if the change is positive or negative.

Using principles of statistical quality control, educators can plot a school district's performance on a graph (see figure 3.1). Here's a simple explanation of the concept illustrated in that graph. The graph has a floor and a ceiling. A lot of activity in the name of improvement happens within the upper and lower limits of the graph as educators work to create change in their school systems. The results of these activities are marked as points on the graph. As long as the plotted points for these changes stay between the lower and upper boundaries, no real change occurs—only the appearance of change. In other words there is a lot of activity in the name of change but no real change occurs. To experience real positive change, people need to create breakthrough change—that

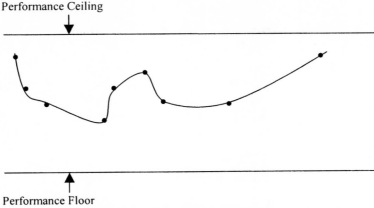

Figure 3.1. Plotting a School District's Performance

is, change resulting in plotted points that break through the upper limits of the graph, as illustrated in figure 3.2.

Because change leaders in school systems are so accustomed to frenetic activity in the name of change within the boundaries of the graph, they are sometimes blind to the significance of and need for creating breakthrough change; breakthrough improvement is not part of their mental models for creating change. To create breakthrough change they need to change their mental models from the dominant one-school-at-a-time change paradigm to one of whole-system change.

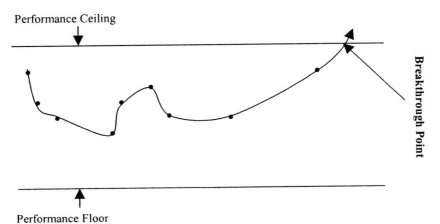

Figure 3.2. Breaking Through the Performance Ceiling

MANAGING ORGANIZATIONAL ENTROPY

Entropy is a law of physics. Systems of all kinds, including our human bodies, consume energy. The "energy" used by school systems includes human energy, equipment, money, books, furniture, and other supplies. The depletion of this energy is called "entropy."

In living systems, entropy cannot be stayed; it always results in death. In organizations, entropy can lead to figurative death. However, in organizations entropy can be slowed or reversed by replenishing resources and human energy. This replenishment process is called negative entropy, or "negentropy." Change leaders must be aware of entropy and know how to create negentropy if they want to lead their school systems effectively toward desirable futures (see Duffy, 2004, for more about entropy and negentropy while changing school systems).

ACKNOWLEDGING THAT THE BEST TIME TO CHANGE AN ORGANIZATION IS WHEN IT'S DOING WELL

"Deeply troubled companies don't usually seek help. And when they do, they have a hard time benefiting from it" (Farson, 1996, p. 95). Burke (2002) says that "a paradox of organization change is that the peak of success is the time to worry and to plan for and bring about significant change" (p. 1). This suggests that the best time to transform a school system is when it is "healthy" and doing well and that the worst time to do this is when a school system is failing. Healthy, well-functioning school systems are often easier to improve than failing ones.

It is important to recognize the difference between "successful" and "healthy" school systems. Being successful doesn't mean being healthy. School systems that are emotionally "unhealthy" can still be successful in achieving their goals. Healthy school systems, on the other hand, are not only successful but capable of conducting in-depth self-evaluations and then taking action to improve. Success by itself is not the best climate for school systems to engage in self-evaluation, because success creates a perceptual blindness as to where improvements can be made. It is important to know, however, that though it is often relatively easy to change successful school systems, they often are resistant to change.

Why? Because success becomes an obstacle to change, as in, "If it ain't broke, don't fix it."

Shaping a school district's future must be guided by the knowledge that good school districts must also move toward higher levels of performance. There are many good school systems in the United States. At the dawn of the 21st century, however, good is not good enough if we are to bring to our children the knowledge to which they have a right and with which they will bring us and themselves to the future. Not only is good not good enough, but as Collins (2001) says,

> Good is the enemy of great. And that is one of the reasons why we have so little that becomes great. We don't have great schools, principally because we have good schools. We don't have great government, principally because we have good government. Few people attain great lives, in large part because it is just so easy to settle for a good life. The vast majority of companies never become great, precisely because the vast majority become quite good—and that is their main problem. (p.1)

LEARNING THAT THE PATH TO THE FUTURE IS NOT A STRAIGHT LINE UPWARD AND FORWARD

The traditional approach to change management assumes that change rolls out according to a rational plan that is relatively straightforward and sequential. Experience, however, serves as a powerful counterpoint: change rolls out in illogical, paradoxical ways that rather resemble winding paths coursing their way toward a future (the concept of winding paths to a future is discussed in chapter 4). Burke (2002) provides examples of why change is nonlinear and messy: "The implementation process is messy: Things don't proceed exactly as planned; people do things their own way, not always according to the plan; some people resist or even sabotage the process; and some people who would be predicted to support or resist the plan actually behave in just the opposite way. In short, unanticipated consequences occur" (p. 2).

Also, these consequences are made even more complex by the fact that they often appear as paradoxes, representing unknowable realities in human affairs (Farson, 1996). These paradoxes, according to Farson, cannot be controlled or managed. Effective change leaders engage these situations by tapping into the collective wisdom of the "community" inside their districts instead of relying on their own unique perspectives. Farson (1996) suggests that change leaders wrestling with paradoxes find their strength as leaders "not in control, but in their passion, sensitivity, tenacity, patience, courage, firmness, enthusiasm and wonder" (p. 35).

RESPONDING QUICKLY TO THE UNEXPECTED CONSEQUENCES OF CHANGE

The organization design of most school systems is bureaucratic and hierarchical. In turbulent times this mechanistic design (Daft, 2001) can create in a school district arthritis-like symptoms that prevent people from reacting quickly to seize unexpected opportunities (discussed later) or to protect the system from startling threats. A more appropriate organization design for today's school systems is what organization theorists call the "organic" design, one that increases a school system's flexibility and speed in responding to opportunities and threats in its external environment.

WORKING TO ANTICIPATE AND PREVENT IATROGENIC EFFECTS

With transformational change, change leaders must be aware of "iatrogenic" effects. These dreadful effects, commonly found in the field of health care, are defined as "physician induced": a patient dying of staphylococcal infection induced by a doctor who did not wash her hands before treatment; or the patient becoming deathly sick with an infection caused by a surgical tool inadvertently left inside the body by a surgeon. In school districts engaged in systemic change, with every "big" change or improvement there may be iatrogenic effects that are exactly the opposite of what you intended. Therefore, it is important for you to apply principles of systems thinking (chapter 1) to anticipate unintended consequences of your planned changes.

SURVIVING ENVIRONMENTAL "TSUNAMI"

Another source of unexpected consequences is found in a school district's external environment. Some external forces roll over a school district like a flooding tsunami. It is very difficult, perhaps impossible, for people in the district to influence the direction of these forces or their consequences (for example, consider the impact of the No Child Left Behind [NCLB] legislation).

The field of organization theory and design tells us that all organizations exist in two classes of environments: the task environment and the general environment. The task environment is the one by which people in an organization are most affected. For school systems, elements of the task environment include their state departments of education, local colleges and universities that prepare educators, local businesses, local community groups, and so on. A school system's general environment includes societal pressures, the economy, and the like. Educators may be able to identify threatening or unhelpful forces in their task environments and then work to exert some influence on these forces in an attempt to anticipate and then manage their impact. However, the general environment is essentially beyond the influence of educators; they are often at the mercy of forces from the general environment that affect their districts.

RECOGNIZING THE DIFFERENCE BETWEEN PROBLEMS AND PREDICAMENTS

Unexpected outcomes come in the form of paradoxes. Some of these will be problems to be solved, but others will be true predicaments. While problems can be solved, predicaments cannot. Farson (1996) tells us that people can only muddle through predicaments. While problem solving requires analytical thinking, muddling through predicaments requires interpretive thinking that puts a larger frame around the puzzling situation so its complexity can be understood. In fact, predicaments worsen if they are treated as problems to be solved. Change leaders moving their districts toward transformational change will need to interpret and work their way through predicaments more than they solve problems.

ACCEPTING THE IMPORTANCE OF EQUIFINALITY

"Equifinality" is a concept from the field of organization development (Cummings & Worley, 2001). In plain English it means there is more than one acceptable way to achieve the same goal. Within the context of systemic school improvement, it means that given a strategic framework to work within, educators can be innovative in how they create improvements within their district. But whatever innovations they imagine, changes must be aligned with the overall strategic direction of the district—that is, they must fit within the strategic framework. The opposite of equifinality is found in situations where senior administrators identify changes to be made, issue directives that must be obeyed as to what must be changed, and then tell people exactly how to make the changes. Giving people freedom to innovate within specified boundaries (the strategic framework) is not an easy thing for control-minded change leaders to do; however, when equifinality is encouraged and supported it gives people the bounded autonomy they need to innovate (complete autonomy would move a system toward anarchy). Autonomy, by the way, is one of six psychological requirements for creating a motivating work environment (Emery & Thorsrud, 1976).

MANAGING HUMAN RELATIONS

Effective human relations in school districts are like glue—they can hold things together. Ineffective human relations are like solvent—they can dissolve the connections between and among people. Whole-system change in school districts requires glue, not solvent, because when change leaders are trying to transform their entire school district they need ways to bind people together in support of their districts' new grand visions and strategic directions.

Effective human relations involve more than communicating better, although good communication is an important element of human relations. Effective human relations also create authentic opportunities for people throughout a district to participate actively and meaningfully in the transformation of their district instead of simply complying with directives to change. Effective human relations require change leaders to identify people who support change, those who object to it, and those who haven't made up their mind. Effective human relations focus not only on people inside a district but also on individuals and groups in the external environment. Finally, effective human relations help change leaders to recognize, honor, and work through resistance to change. Five examples of important human relations that need to be managed are highlighted below:

ENABLING OTHERS TO LEAD AND CONTRIBUTE

There is no question that the superintendent of schools as the senior executive in a school district must lead whole-system change. Her leadership must be unequivocal and visible. However, her leadership alone is insufficient for creating and sustaining whole-system change. A superintendent's leadership is like a tree. To succeed in the transformation of a school system, there must be a forest of leaders throughout a school district. Creating a forest of leaders will require a superintendent to have a change of heart and a change of mind about how to involve faculty and staff in a district's transformation journey.

WORKING WITH ALLIES, OPPONENTS, ADVERSARIES, BEDFELLOWS, AND FENCESITTERS

Peter Block (1991) advises managers about how to use positive political skills to work with five categories of people inside organizations. Block theorizes that managers can use two dimensions when making political decisions about how to interact with people inside those five categories. The first dimension is "level of agreement." The second dimension is "level of trust." Each dimension runs from high to low. The five categories are:

- *Allies*: defined by high trust and high agreement. You trust them, they trust you, and you are in agreement about what needs to be done.
- *Opponents*: defined by high trust but low agreement. You trust them, they trust you, but you disagree about what needs to be done.

- *Adversaries*: defined by low trust and low agreement. You don't trust these people and they don't trust you. Further, you disagree on what needs to be done.
- *Bedfellows*: defined by low trust and high agreement. You don't trust these people and they don't trust you, but they agree with what needs to be done.
- *Fencesitters*: the undecided, the uncommitted, the "I can't make up my mind" people.

Block's "five category" concept dovetails with another important change management principle, that of "critical mass." Critical mass is a physics concept given to us by Kurt Lewin (1951). It serves as metaphor for change leadership. A critical mass is that number of people needed to launch and sustain successful change. The critical mass number seen most often in the literature on change is 25%—that is, change leaders need about 25% of their faculty and staff to be committed to and willing to support the change process (Block might call these people allies and bedfellows). About 50% of the faculty and staff will stand on the sidelines and observe what's happening, not yet ready to make a commitment one way or the other (these people might be called fencesitters in Block's model). Another 25% will actively resist the change. Of that final 25%, some will be "opponents," whose minds and hearts can be changed and who may eventually support the change. The remaining people in that last 25% group are hard-core "adversaries" who will probably never accept or support your change leadership and who may actively work to undermine your leadership.

Identifying the 25% critical mass in support of change, communicating with the 50% fencesitter group, and working to bring opponents into the ally camp constitute one of the significant challenges that change leaders must meet before they launch systemwide change. In the change methodology you will read about in chapter 4, this political work begins during the pre-launch, preparation phase.

WORKING WITH EXTERNAL STAKEHOLDERS

In chapter 4 you will read about the three paths that must be followed if you want to create and sustain whole-system change in your school district. One of those paths is "improve environmental relationships." A school district's external environment has two parts: the general environment (the economy, world events, societal norms and values), which districts have no chance of influencing, and the task environment (those individuals and groups that a school district interacts with directly and therefore can influence). Key players in a district's external task environment include: local community groups, state departments of education, parent groups, competitors (private schools, both nonprofit and for-profit), critics, and suppliers (which include not only suppliers of textbooks, equipment, and so on but also colleges and universities that prepare future teachers and school administrators).

Change leaders need to improve their district's relationship with these and other key players. To do this, first they have to know who the key players are. Second, they must assess the nature of the relationship they have with the key players and develop strategies for working with each one. Third, they determine what the key players need, want, and expect. Fourth, they determine if, when, and how to respond to their needs, wants, and expectations. Fifth, they use effective public relations communications that are timely, accurate, honest, simple, clear, and powerful and that are tailored to each key player.

MANAGING RESISTANCE TO CHANGE

Sometimes people and systems don't change quickly. There are various reasons for this slowness, such as inadequate resources, weak or failed leadership, and lack of motivation. This slowness is usually characterized as resistance to change.

There are at least four reasons for resistance to change. The first reason is that people frequently resist the efforts of other people to impose change on them. The second main reason is related to human psychology and the need for stability or equilibrium in our lives. The third reason is fear—fear of losing prestige, power, relationships, or a job. The fourth reason is related to an organization's reluctance to change. (Each of these reasons for resisting change will be explored in more depth in chapter 7.) One of the most powerful ways to respond to all four sources of resistance is through involvement. This is why principles of participation and collaboration were built into the transformation methodology you will read about in the next chapter.

BUILDING TRUST

One thing's for sure—even if change leaders have the courage, passion, and vision to lead whole-system change, they will get nowhere if their teachers and professional staff don't trust them. Trust is the foundation for respect. Respect is the cornerstone of professional influence. Influence is the essence of leadership. No trust + no respect + no influence = less than effective change leadership. Chapter 5 offers more information about the importance of trust.

MAINTAINING PERSONAL ENERGY AND COMMITMENT

Systemwide change takes time. William Pasmore (1988) suggests it takes anywhere from 18 to 36 months. John Kotter (1996) believes it can take between five to seven years. Common sense suggests a pragmatic estimate of the required time: "Plan for the worst and hope for the best." Therefore, assume it will take your school system five to seven years to complete its transformation journey. If transformation takes that long, another challenge change leaders will confront is creating and deploying strategies for maintaining their personal energy and commitment, as well as the energy and commitment of their colleagues, so all of them can persist toward their transformation goals.

CONCLUSION

School districts are systems. Systems are complex and sometimes mysterious entities that confound people as they attempt to create and sustain change. Leading transformational change predictably raises significant challenges that come in the form of paradoxes and problems. This chapter identified 21 key challenges that leaders may face when trying to transform their school districts.

Clearly, to navigate a river of complex change made dangerous by invisible system dynamics hidden beneath the surface and marked by the rapids formed by resistance to change, a map (your district's strategic framework) and a compass (a special methodology designed to create transformational change in school systems) will certainly be important. Yet even with a map and compass, you still need people to move the vessel (your district) along the river and through the rapids. Helping people choose to make the journey (rather than being directed to do so) will require you to use your power and political skills in sophisticated and ethical ways.

If you use power and political skills unethically, people will not make the journey effectively, or maybe not at all. They will despise you and distrust your motives. Their resistance to your leadership will increase, and some of them will figure out creative ways to scuttle the vessel and end its journey to the future.

NOTES

1. You can visit the website for their transformation journey at www.indiana.edu/~syschang/decatur/index.html.

2. For more in-depth discussion of this challenge, please see Duffy, F. M. (2003).

REFERENCES

Baldrige National Quality Program (2003). Education Criteria for Performance Excellence. Retrieved on September 4, 2003, from www.quality.nist.gov/PDF_files/2003_Education_Criteria.pdf.

Beckhard, R. (1983). Strategies for large system change. In W. L. French, C. H. Bell, Jr., & R. A. Zawacki (Eds.), *Organization development: Theory, practice, and research* (pp. 234–242). Plano, TX: Business Publications.

Block, P. (1991). *The empowered manager: Positive political skills at work.* San Francisco: Jossey-Bass.

Bronfenbrenner, U. (1979). *The ecology of human development: Experiments by nature and design.* Cambridge, MA: Harvard University Press.

Bronfenbrenner, U. (1977). Toward an experimental ecology of human development. *American Psychologist, 32*(7), 513–531.

Burke, W. W. (2002). *Organization change: Theory and practice*. Thousand Oaks, CA: Sage.

Collins, J. (2001). *Good to great: Why some companies make the leap . . . and others don't*. New York: HarperBusiness.

Cummings, T. G., & Worley, C. G. (2001). *Organization development and change* (7th ed.). Cincinnati, OH: South-Western College.

Daft, R. L. (2001). *Organization theory and design* (7th ed.). Cincinnati, OH: South-Western College.

Duffy, F. M. (2004). *Moving upward together: Creating strategic alignment to sustain systemic school improvement*. Lanham, MD: Rowman & Littlefield Education.

Duffy, F. M. (2003). *Courage, passion, and vision: A superintendent's guide to leading systemic school improvement*. Lanham, MD: Rowman & Littlefield Education and the American Association of School Administrators.

Duffy, F. M. (2003, Winter). I think, therefore I am resistant to change. *Journal of Staff Development, 24*(1), 30–36.

Emery, M., & Purser, R.E. (1995). *The search conference: A powerful method for planning organizational change and community action*. San Francisco: Jossey-Bass.

Emery, F. E., & Thorsrud, E. (1976). *Democracy at work: The report of the Norwegian democracy program*. Leiden, Netherlands: Martinus Nijhoff.

Farson, R. (1996). *Management of the absurd*. New York: Simon & Schuster.

Kegan, R., & Lahey, L. L. (2002). *How the way we talk can change the way we work*. San Francisco: Jossey-Bass.

Kotter, J. P. (1996). *Leading change*. Boston: Harvard Business School Press.

Lewin, K. (1951). *Field theory in social science*. New York: Harper & Row.

Pasmore, W. A. (1988). *Designing effective organizations: The socio-technical systems perspective*. New York: John Wiley & Sons.

4

THE DESTINATION OF THREE PATHS: IMPROVED STUDENT, FACULTY AND STAFF, AND SYSTEM LEARNING

This chapter provides trail markers for three paths that must be navigated simultaneously to achieve whole-system change. Next, an explanation of why these paths are nonlinear is provided. You will also find a "map" and "compass" to navigate the winding paths. The map includes specific conditions that must exist in a school system before educators can engage that system in transformational change. Another feature on the map is a set of eight principles to help change leaders in school systems navigate whole-system change to create unparalleled opportunities to improve student, faculty and staff, and whole-system learning. The compass is a special methodology designed to help you create and sustain whole-system change. The methodology is called Step-Up-to-Excellence.

Every time Step-Up-to-Excellence is presented to an audience, at least one person calls out "yes, but"—statements questioning whether the methodology is practical, doable, or valid. Two "yes, buts" that are frequently heard and responses to them are explored in this chapter.

THREE PATHS TO IMPROVEMENT

Over the past 30 years we have learned a lot about how to improve entire systems. One of the core principles of whole-system change is that

three sets of key organizational variables must be improved simultaneously. These three sets of variables are characterized as "change paths"
in the methodology presented below.

Path 1: Improve a District's Relationship With Its External Environment

A school district is an open system. An open system is one that interacts with its environment by exchanging a valued product or service in
return for needed resources. If educators want their districts to become
high-performing school systems, they need to have a positive and supporting relationship with stakeholders in their districts' external environment. But they can't wait until they transform their districts to start
working on these relationships; they need positive and supporting relationships as they begin making important changes. So they have to improve their district's environmental relationships at the same time they
start improving their work processes and social architecture.

Path 2: Improve a District's Core and Supporting Work Processes

"Core" work is the most important work of any organization. In school
districts, the core work is a sequenced instructional program (e.g., often
a pre-K-to-12 instructional program) conjoined with classroom teaching
and learning (Duffy, 2002, 2003). Core work is maintained and enriched
by "supporting" work. In school districts, supporting work roles include
administrators, supervisors, education specialists, librarians, cafeteria
workers, janitors, bus drivers, and others. Supporting work is important
to the success of a school district, but it is not the most important work.
Classroom teaching and learning is the most important work, and it
must be elevated to that status if a school system wants to increase its
overall effectiveness.

When trying to improve a school system, the core and supporting
work processes must be improved. Further, the entire work process
(e.g., pre-K to 12th grade) must be examined and improved, not just
parts of it (e.g., not just the middle school program, or not just the language arts curriculum, or not just the high school program). One of the

reasons the entire work process must be improved is found in the systems improvement principle, "Upstream errors flow downstream." This principle reflects the fact that mistakes made early in a work process flow downstream, are compounded, and create more problems later on in the process. For example, consider a comment made by a high school principal when he first heard a description of this principle. He said, "Yes, I understand. And, I see that happening in our district. Our middle school program is being 'dumbed-down' and those children are entering our high school program unprepared for our more rigorous curriculum. And, there is nothing we can do about it." Upstream errors flow downstream. In chapter 1, Ackoff (1981) offers other principles that require you to improve your entire school system instead of pieces of it.

Improving student learning is an important goal of improving the core and supporting work processes of a school district. But focusing only on improving student learning is a piecemeal approach to improvement. A teacher's knowledge and literacy is probably one of the more important factors influencing student learning. Taking steps to improve teacher learning must be part of any school district's improvement efforts to improve student learning.

Improving student and teacher learning is an important goal of improving work in a school district. But this is still a piecemeal approach to improving a school district. A school district is a knowledge-creating organization, and it is, or should be, a learning organization. Professional knowledge must be created and embedded in a school district's operational structures, and organizational learning must occur if a school district wants to develop and maintain the capacity to provide children with a quality education. So school system learning (i.e., organizational learning) must also be part of a district's improvement strategy to improve its core work.

Path 3: Improve a District's Internal "Social Architecture"

Improving work processes to improve learning for students, teachers and staff, and the whole school system is an important goal but it is still a piecemeal approach to change. It is possible for a school district to have a fabulous curriculum with extraordinarily effective instructional methods but still have an internal social "architecture" (which includes organization culture, organization design, communication patterns, power and political dynamics, reward systems, and so on) that is demotivating, dissatisfying, and demoralizing for teachers and staff. Demotivated, dissatisfied, and demoralized teachers cannot and will not use a fabulous curriculum in remarkable ways. So, in addition to improving how the work of a district is done, improvement efforts must focus simultaneously on improving a district's internal social architecture and on redesigning the core and supporting work processes. Why? Because it is important to ensure that the new social architecture and the new work processes complement each other. The best way to ensure this complementarity is to make simultaneous improvements to both elements of a school system.

Hopefully, this three-path metaphor makes sense, because the principle of simultaneous improvement is absolutely essential for effective organization improvement (e.g., see Emery, 1977; Pasmore, 1988; Trist, Higgin, Murray, & Pollack, 1963). In the literature on systems improvement this principle is called "joint optimization" (Cummings & Worley, 2001, p. 353).

A MAP AND COMPASS TO NAVIGATE THE THREE PATHS

To navigate whole-system change you need a map and compass. The map provided here has certain features that will help you navigate the three winding paths described above. The first feature is a set of conditions that need to exist in a school district before educators in that district can begin whole-system change. The second feature is a set of eight principles to guide your district's transformation journey. The compass for your journey is the special methodology called Step-Up-to-Excellence. Before examining the map and compass, let's orient ourselves to the change topography.

The Change Topography

One of the traditional approaches to managing change was developed by Kurt Lewin (1951). It is illustrated in figure 4.1. What Lewin said is that to change a system, people first envision a desired future. Then,

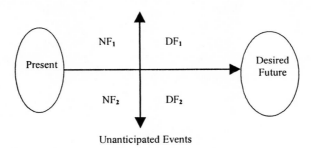

NF$_1$ = near future, planned
DF$_1$ = distant future, planned
NF$_2$ = near future, unplanned
DF$_2$ = distant future, unplanned

Figure 4.1. The Traditional Change Path

they assess the current situation and compare the present to the future looking for gaps between what is and what's desired. Next, they develop a transition plan composed of long-range goals and short-term objectives that will move their system straight ahead, toward its desired future. Along the way there would be some unanticipated events that emerge, but it is assumed that the "pressure" of anticipatory intentions (goals, objectives, strategic plans) will keep those unexpected events under control and thereby keep the system on a relatively straight change path toward the future. The problem with this approach is that it doesn't work in contemporary organizations.

Instead of the "straight-ahead-to-the-future" assumption represented in figure 4.1, the complexities of contemporary society and the pressures for rapid change, combined with an increasing number of unanticipated events and unintended consequences during change, create a winding change path. This winding change path is illustrated in figure 4.2.

If change leaders in school systems assume that the strategic path from the present to the future is relatively straight when the actual path is winding, people engaged in systemic change will soon be off the true path and lost. To see how they would go off the true path (the winding path) trace your finger along the assumed straight path in figure 4.3. Wherever the straight path leaves the winding path, people become lost. When lost, people will revert to their old ways, thereby enacting the

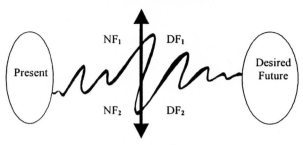

NF₁ = near future, planned
DF₁ = distant future, planned
NF₂ = near future, unplanned
DF₂ = distant future, unplanned

Figure 4.2.   The Nonlinear Change Path in Complex Organizations

French folk wisdom, "The more things change, the more they stay the same."

To move an entire school system along a change path like the one described above, change leaders in school districts need a whole-system transformation methodology that provides a map, compass, and landmarks to find and navigate the three nonlinear paths to higher student, teacher and staff, and whole-system learning. This kind of methodology will work only if certain conditions exist within school systems and if the

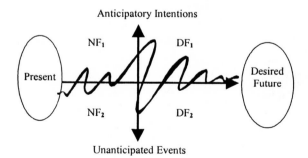

NF₁ = near future, planned
DF₁ = distant future, planned
NF₂ = near future, unplanned
DF₂ = distant future, unplanned

Figure 4.3.   The Assumed Straight Change Path

methodology is based on key principles for navigating whole-system change (Duffy, 2004b).

The Change Map

Conditions for Effective Whole-System Change   No methodology created to support a school district's effort to engage in whole-system change is likely to work in low-performing districts, because these districts do not possess the conditions necessary to engage in whole-system change. The conditions for effective whole-system change are:

- Senior leaders who act on the basis of personal courage, passion, and vision—not on the basis of fear, self-survival, or self-interest
- Leaders and followers who are willing and able to break or circumvent rules to create powerful innovations—not those who are rule bound
- Senior leaders who conceive of their districts as whole systems—not as a confederation of individual schools and programs
- Leaders and followers who have a clear view of the opportunities that systemic transformation offers them—not a view of "we can't do this because . . ."
- Leaders and followers who possess the professional intellect, change-minded attitudes, and change navigation skills to move their districts toward higher levels of performance—not people without an inkling about the requirements of navigating systemic change
- Human, technical, and financial resources to sustain a large-scale improvement process over five to seven years (large-scale change can take this long)—not resources "stolen" from successful programs to pay for systemic change.

If the above conditions begin to emerge within a low-performing district prior to engaging in systemic change, whole-system change methodologies may have a chance of producing desirable improvements in those districts. Therefore, instead of depriving low-performing districts of opportunities to engage in whole-system change, change leaders should first focus on developing the conditions listed above as part of their efforts to prepare their district for whole-system change.

EIGHT PRINCIPLES FOR NAVIGATING
WHOLE-SYSTEM CHANGE

There are eight principles that should be considered when creating a framework for any methodology to transform entire school systems (Duffy, 2004a). These principles are summarized below.

Principle #1: A school district's external environment is complex and unstable. The environments school districts find themselves in are increasingly complex and unstable. This complexity and instability is being driven by the triple engines of standards, assessments, and accountability (Duffy, 2002). In complex and unstable environments, school districts need to be able plan for the future while also being able to respond quickly to unanticipated events.

Principle #2: The capacity to anticipate the future and respond quickly to unanticipated events is partially a function of an organization's internal social "architecture." A school district's social architecture includes its culture, communication patterns, power and political dynamics, the reward system, policies and procedures, and organization design. Social architecture has a significant influence on educators' capacity and willingness to plan for the future and to respond to unexpected events. A new social architecture for school systems that would increase capacity and willingness would:

- Favor skill-based work, professional knowledge, and networked relationships
- Be anchored to a network of teams with their collective knowledge, talent, and resources
- Support and encourage flux (discussed below under principle #7) rather than linear, sequential change
- Create broad and easy opportunities for participation and communication
- Connect people to each other and to resources in ways that help a school district as much as possible to take charge of its own destiny (as opposed to being externally forced to improve).

Principle #3: Biological metaphors most accurately describe how social networks function. The biological metaphor that seems to work best for organizations with a networked internal social architecture is "ecosystem." In nature, some ecosystems offer scarce opportunities for life (polar ice caps), while others offer overflowing opportunities (equatorial jungles). If we think of a school system as an ecosystem, it too can offer scarce or abundant opportunities for success. Scarcity or abundance of opportunities in school districts depends on a district's collective vision for its current and future capacities and competencies. This collective vision guides people's thoughts, feelings, and actions. If most people in a district choose to think, feel, and act as if their district can never improve, they won't improve. If most people in a district choose to think, feel, and act like they do have the creative potential to move their district toward breathtakingly higher levels of performance, they can and will make that journey toward higher levels of performance. The power of choice, either individually or collectively, has been repeatedly proven to have an extraordinary effect on human performance. As Jean Paul Sartre (1934) once said, "We are our choices."

Principle #4: Creating a web of accountabilities using networked teams doesn't mean that authority and control are surrendered to the networked "mob." In all school districts, the voice of leadership must always be present and heard even if significant steps are taken to redesign leadership positions so incumbents can practice effective transformational leadership instead of being managers of the status quo. Without the voice of leadership from the top of a school district, people freeze when there are too many change options to be considered. Without some element of leadership at the top, the many at the bottom are often paralyzed by an overabundance of choices. A social architecture that honors and uses formal leadership roles while simultaneously creating and sustaining networked teams will provide powerful moments for creating innovative ideas to improve student, faculty and staff, and whole-system learning.

Principle #5: A networked social architecture stimulates creativity and innovation. Creativity and innovation present breathtaking opportunities for improvement. As opportunities for improving schooling emerge and are taken, still newer opportunities will begin to emerge at a faster rate. This is somewhat like the financial principle of compound interest. Therefore, change leaders need to find ways to help educators seize opportunities, succeed at using them, and then help others build their success on earlier successes. This creates compound organizational learning.

Principle #6: Peak performance is an illusion. In the 21st-century environment of a school district there are multiple performance peaks that evoke images of the Rocky Mountains, with some peaks lower than others. What if the peak a district sits atop is a low compared to others, but educators inside the district don't realize it? Wouldn't the perception of being at peak performance be an illusion?

Another problem for school districts is not too much success but too little perspective. Great success creates a perceptual wall that obstructs the view of opportunities to move toward higher levels of performance. If educators in a district cannot see the next higher performance peak, how can they go there? They cannot go to what they cannot see.

A third problem for school districts is that successful districts become remarkably creative in defending their status quo. They argue against the need to improve because they see themselves already at their peak.[1] But sitting too long on any performance peak when there are higher peaks to climb will not be tolerated by our 21st-century society.

All school districts sit atop a performance peak, no matter what that level of performance might be. The path to the next higher performance peak is not a straight "as the crow flies" line. A clear view of the next higher level of performance is not a straight shot forward and upward. There is only one way to get to the next higher peak—a district has to go downhill before it can go back up. It has to become temporarily less effective, less skilled, and less successful.

The "first down, then up" principle is a plain English way of describing Seyle's (1956) "general adaptation syndrome" theory. This theory suggests that when an organization is stressed (e.g., by the requirements of change), its performance will decline before it ascends to a new level of performance. The problem for school districts is, however, that the more successful a school district is, the less inclined it is to let go of what it does and move down the performance curve toward the edge of chaos (a phrase coined by Roger Lewin, 1992). This capacity to let go has to be built into a school system.

The "first down, then up" journey happens when educators start questioning their success. Not everything they do has to be abandoned completely, but everything they do needs to be questioned thoroughly.

During this questioning, they must be open to stunning opportunities for innovative ideas to improve student, teacher, and whole-system learning. They must also be ready to discard programs and activities that are proven to be ineffective, or effective but clearly not aligned with the district's grand vision and strategic direction. By getting rid of failing or nonaligned programs and activities space is created for new programs and activities.

Principle #7: School district improvement models must move from the concept of change to concept of flux. The field of organization improvement is moving away from the concept of change to the concept of flux (Kelly, 1998). While change focuses on creating new programs, ideas, and so on, flux is about managing creative destruction followed by rebirth. Flux breaks down the status quo and creates a temporary foundation for innovation and the rebirth of a school district. Innovation, in turn, continues to disrupt the status quo, especially if it results in breakthrough improvements into a system (please refer to figures 3.1 and 3.2 in the previous chapter, which illustrate the principle of breakthrough improvement). Because innovation is a core requirement for transforming your district, your quest for innovation must be unending; robust innovation can only be sustained if your school district hovers at the edge of chaos, never falling over the edge.

Innovative systemic flux brings educators and school systems to the edge of chaos. Despite the gut-wrenching prospect of teetering at the edge of chaos, there is a need to sustain innovative flux so school districts can move unwaveringly toward higher performance peaks. By teetering at the edge of chaos, school systems can find stunningly creative solutions to the puzzles they are trying to solve—puzzles like "How do we establish and sustain positive and productive relationships with our community?" "How do we provide children with world-class instruction?" and, "How do we provide our teachers and support staff with a motivating and satisfying work life?"

Sustaining innovation is particularly tricky, because it requires the nerve-wracking condition of a school system being out of balance and at the edge of chaos (i.e., in a state of controlled yet creative disequilibrium). Thus, a school district wanting to sustain innovative thinking and puzzle solving must create for itself a state of controlled disequilibrium in much the same way that people skillfully dancing on ice remain on the verge of tumbling but continually catch themselves and never fall. To be innovative, to move to the next higher peak of performance, a school system cannot anchor itself to its past or current performance peak. Change leaders in school districts must build into their districts the capacity to exploit flux, not outlaw it.

Principle #8: Don't solve problems, seek opportunities. When change leaders seek to find opportunities instead of seeking problems to be solved, this shift in perspective builds and sustains creative and emotional energy for school district renewal and embeds a positive approach to innovation into the internal social architecture of a school system. Lippitt (1980) validated this perspective through research that confirmed that people tend to perform more productively and develop better long-term plans when working on positive goals and visions rather than focusing on solving problems. Focusing on exciting opportunities releases creative energy and keeps people engaged over a longer period of time. Thus, instead of asking "What's wrong?" educators should seek opportunities to improve their school systems by asking and answering four questions: (1) "What future do we want for our system?" (2) "Where are we now?" (3) "What do we need to do in order to create that desirable future?" and (4) "How do we simultaneously navigate three winding change paths leading to that future?"

THE COMPASS TO HELP YOU NAVIGATE THE THREE PATHS: STEP-UP-TO-EXCELLENCE

A whole-system transformation methodology for navigating the three paths toward whole-system transformation was described in detail in earlier publications (Duffy, 2002, 2003, 2004c). Some of you are familiar with the developmental history by which this methodology reached its current form, which is known as Step-Up-to-Excellence. This methodology combines for the first time proven and effective tools for whole-system improvement. Although these tools have been used singly and effectively for more than 40 years, they never have been combined to provide educators with a comprehensive, unified, systematic, and systemic methodology for redesigning their entire school systems. The methodology is illustrated in figure 4.4. Because this methodology has been described in detail in other publications, it is only summarized here.

Step-Up-to-Excellence is an innovative approach to creating and sustaining whole-system change in school districts. It is a five-step process preceded by a "pre-launch preparation" phase. It proceeds as follows:

- Pre-launch preparation
- Step 1: Redesign the entire school district
- Step 2: Align the performance of clusters
- Step 3: Align the performance of individual schools
- Step 4: Align the performance of teams and individuals
  (Steps 2–4 are collectively called "Create Strategic Alignment.")
- Step 5: Evaluate the performance of the entire school district.

Pre-Launch Preparation

One of the most common reasons for failed transformation efforts is the lack of good preparation and planning (Kotter, 1996). What happens

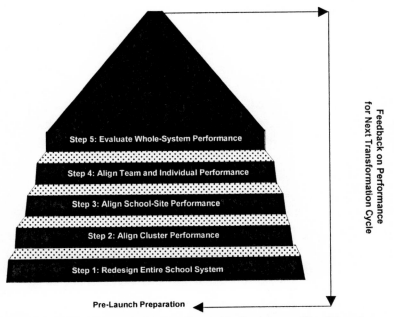

Figure 4.4. The Step-Up-To-Excellence Methodology—Five Steps to Whole-District Improvement

during this preparation phase will significantly influence the success (or failure) of your transformation journey. You have to take the time to do these activities in a carefully considered manner. Quick fixes almost always fail eventually even though they may produce the immediate illusion of improvement.

The early pre-launch preparation activities are conducted by the superintendent of schools and several hand-picked subordinates. He may wish to include one or two trusted school board members in this small planning team. It is also important to know that this small team is temporary and it will not lead the transformation journey. It has one purpose and one purpose only—to prepare the system to engage in systemic change.

At some point in the pre-launch preparation phase, a decision will be made to launch the transformation effort or not to. If a launch decision is made, the remaining activities are transferred to a "strategic leadership team" composed of the superintendent and several others, including teachers and building administrators appointed to the team by their peers (not by the superintendent). This team also appoints and trains a transformation coordinator, who will provide tactical leadership for the transformation.

Near the end of the pre-launch preparation phase, the strategic leadership team will organize and conduct a "community engagement conference," which could bring into a single room thousands of people (the upper limit to audience size is around 2,500 people; however, school systems would probably have groups in the hundreds rather than the thousands), who will then self-organize into smaller discussion groups around topics related to the district's transformation effort. The results of this conference are used later in the pre-launch phase to develop a strategic framework for the district.

After the community engagement conference, educators in the district are involved in the transformation process. One of the key events for involving other educators is the "district engagement conference." The results of this conference create a new strategic framework for a district that includes a new mission, vision, and strategic plan.

There are many more pre-launch preparation activities that need to be completed. A full description is found in Duffy (2003, 2004c).

Step 1: Redesign the Entire School District

During step 1, the entire school district is transformed by making simultaneous improvements in three sets of school district variables: the district's relationship with its external environment, its core and supporting work processes, and its internal social architecture. This is a core principle from the field of organization improvement.

Steps 2–4: Create Strategic Alignment

After redesigning the district as suggested above, steps 2–4 invite change leaders and their colleagues to align the work of individuals with the goals of their teams, the work of teams with the goals of their schools, the work of schools with the goals of their clusters, and the work of clusters with the goals of the district. Collectively, these steps are referred to as "create strategic alignment."

Creating strategic alignment accomplishes three things (Duffy, 2004c). First, it ensures that everyone is working toward the same broad strategic goals and vision for the district. Second, it weaves a web of accountabilities that makes everyone who touches the educational experience of a child accountable for his or her part in shaping that experience. And third, it forms a social architecture that is free of bureaucratic hassles, dysfunctional policies, and obstructionist procedures that limit individual and team effectiveness. You may recall that W. Edwards Deming (1986), among others, says that it is these dysfunctional hassles, policies, and procedures that cause at least 80% of the performance problems that we usually blame on individuals and teams.

Step 5: Evaluate the Performance of the Entire School District

Finally, in step 5, the performance of the entire transformed district is evaluated, including the performance of its clusters, schools, and teams. The purpose of this level of evaluation is to measure the success of everyone's efforts to educate children. Evaluation data are also reported to stakeholders in the environment to show them how effective the district is.

After change leaders and their colleagues work through all five steps of Step-Up-to-Excellence, what do they do next? They focus on sustaining school district improvement by practicing continuous improvement at the district, cluster, school, team, and individual levels of performance. Then, after a predetermined period of stability and incremental improvements, they "step up" again by cycling back to pre-launch preparation. Achieving high performance is a lifelong journey for a school district.

IN ANTICIPATION OF "YES, BUT"

Whenever the Step-Up-to-Excellence is presented to an audience predictably two key objections are voiced. These common objections and responses to them are presented below.

Objection #1: "Yes, This Is an Interesting Idea, But Where Is This Being Used?"

One of the greatest "innovation killers" in the history of mankind is captured in the question, "Where is this being used?" or its corollary, "Who else is doing this?"

Can you imagine Peter Senge (1990) being asked this question when he first proposed his *Fifth Discipline* ideas, or perhaps Morris Cogan (1973) when he first described the principles of *Clinical Supervision*?

New ideas, by definition, are not being used anywhere, but they want to be used. However, being the first at doing anything, especially doing something that requires deep and broad change demands a high degree of courage, passion, and vision. Many change leaders in education do indeed have the requisite courage, passion, and vision to be the first to try innovative ideas for creating and sustaining systemic school improvement. These heroic leaders need a methodology especially designed to create and sustain whole-system change.

The most direct answer to the above objection is that Step-Up-to-Excellence is being used in the in the Metropolitan School District of Decatur Township in Indianapolis, Indiana. The methodology is blended with a methodology created by Dr. Charles Reigeluth called "Guidance

System for Transforming Education" (GSTE). Dr. Reigeluth is also facilitating that systemic change effort.[2] This is the direct answer to the objection, but more needs to be said.

New methodologies to create and sustain districtwide change are not perfect, and they never will be. Educators should not even try to find a perfect methodology. Instead, they need to examine new methods for navigating whole-system change, study how they work, find glitches in the processes, and search for logical flaws in the reasoning behind the methods. Then, assuming that a method is based on sound principles for improving whole systems, educators should think about how they might correct the flaws to make the method work for their districts.

Some people read about whole-system change and exclaim, "Impossible!" Impossible is what some people think can't be done until someone proves them wrong by doing it. Whole-system change not only "is possible" but is being done successfully in school systems throughout the United States—for instance, in the Baldrige Award–winning Chugach Public Schools in Anchorage, Alaska, the Pearl River School District in New York, and other districts engaged in districtwide change and described in a research study by Togneri and Anderson (2003). The districts in that study were:

- Aldine Independent School District, Texas
- Chula Vista Elementary School District, California
- Kent County Public Schools, Maryland
- Minneapolis Public Schools, Minnesota
- Providence Public Schools, Rhode Island.

The improvements these districts experienced were guided by many of the principles described in this chapter. So if educators read about a methodology that seems impossible, they should ask, "If other school districts are using ideas and principles like these, why can't we?"

Some of you will read about whole-system change and say, "Impractical." Not only are the core principles and change tools based on these principles practical, but many of them are proven to work in school districts and other organizations throughout the United States. So if and when you think that trying to improve an entire school system is impractical you should ask, "If other school districts have used these principles effectively, why can't we?"

Some people will read this chapter and proclaim, "Wow, this guy is really far out with his thinking. He is way outside the box." It is my hope that readers will say this. If they do, I have succeeded in offering them some innovative ideas to think about and apply. When they see something that seems "way outside the box," they should ask, "If this idea is outside the box, what box are we in?" and, "Do we want to stay inside this box of ours?"

Objection #2: "Yes, This Is a Nice Idea, But How Do We Pay for This?"

The second biggest innovation killer in the world is found in the question, "How do we pay for this?" Unlike traditional reform efforts, whole-system change cannot be sustained solely through small increases in operating budgets. Because systemic reform touches all aspects of a school district's core operations, it imposes significant resource requirements on a district and demands a rethinking of the way current resources are allocated, as well as some creative thinking about how to use "extra" money that will be needed to jump-start systemic reform.

Financing whole-system change will also require the continuation of both school-based budgeting and centralized budgeting processes. Financing whole-system improvement is not an "either centralized or school-based" endeavor. It requires a "both centralized and school-based budgeting" approach.

Because there seems to be a scarcity of literature on financing whole-system change, educators need innovative, ground-level tactics, methods, and sources to help them find the resources they need to transform their school systems into high-performing organizations of learners. What follows are some insights about how to do this.

Fundamental Principles for Funding Systemic School Improvement The following are some fundamental principles that are important for financing whole-system change.[3] Many of these principles are advocated by school finance experts (e.g., Cascarino, 2000; Clune, 1994a; Keltner, 1998; Odden, 1998). The fundamental principles are:

- Think creatively about securing resources. Instead of saying "We can't do this, because, . . ." say, "We can do this. Let's be creative in figuring out how."
- Create a new mental model for financing school system improvement that helps you think outside the box for developing innovative solutions to your resource allocation challenges.
- Develop a new mental model for financing school system improvement that helps you create innovative solutions to resource allocation challenges (Odden, 1998).
- Fund systemic improvement as you would fund a core program or activity, with real dollars that are a permanent part of your budget.
- Reallocate current operating money to support whole-system improvement (Keltner, 1998).
- Over time, reduce "extra" resources for whole-system improvement to near zero while increasing internal resources to support systemic improvement.
- As needed, combine federal funds in innovative ways to directly support districtwide improvements in teaching and learning (see Cascarino, 2000, p. 1).
- Focus your thinking on financing for adequacy rather than on financing for equity (see Clune, 1994a, 1994b).
- When seeking outside money, make sure that the requirements and goals of the funding agency do not conflict or constrain the vision and strategic direction of your redesign effort.
- Employ superior communication skills so all stakeholders recognize the true purpose of your budget reallocation strategy, how it will work, and what the benefits will be.

CONCLUSION

New change theory is based on the concept of flux. It recognizes that change is nonlinear and requires school districts to function at the edge of chaos, as educators seek controlled disequilibrium to create innovative opportunities for improvement. New change theory tells us that to improve the performance level of a school district the system must move downhill before it can move up to a higher level of performance. New change theory requires school districts to use a networked social architecture, by which innovations are grown from within and used to create whole-system change. New change theory requires a simultaneous ability to anticipate the future and respond quickly to unanticipated events. New change theory requires a methodology specifically designed to enact the concepts and principles that are part of the theory.

Finally, new change theory requires change leadership that is distributed throughout a school district—change leaders who are courageous, passionate, and visionary, and who use their power and political skills in ethical ways. Heroic leaders are priceless, and they are absolutely necessary. Heroic leaders work their magic by helping others to see the invisible, to do the seemingly impossible, and to create new realities heretofore only imagined. Creating world-class school districts that produce stunning opportunities for improving student, faculty and staff, and whole-system learning can only be done under the stewardship of these kinds of leaders.

NOTES

1. Recently, I had a meeting with a team of administrators from a private school to discuss the prospects of engaging that school in whole-system change. When we started talking about how they might move from good to great one of the administrators proclaimed, "We don't need to get better at what we do. We are already the best." Her expression is an example of "good being the enemy of great."

2. You may visit the website for that district's transformation journey at www .indiana.edu/~syschang/decatur/change_ process.html.

3. These principles were developed in collaboration with Jason Cascarino and Chris Henson. Jason is Director of Marketing and New Initiatives for Citizen Schools in Boston. Chris is the Assistant Superintendent for Business and Facility Services for the Metro Nashville Public Schools in Tennessee. Chris is also the former Assistant Director for Finance and Administration for the Franklin Special School District in Tennessee, where he helped develop financial strategies to pay for that school system's transformation.

REFERENCES

Ackoff, R. L. (1981). *Creating the corporate future.* New York: John Wiley & Sons.

Cascarino, J. (2000 November). *District Issues Brief—Many programs, one investment: Combining federal funds to support comprehensive school reform.* Arlington, VA: New American Schools. Retrieved on October 12, 2003, from www.naschools.org/uploadedfiles/ManyPrograms.pdf.

Cogan, M. L. (1973). *Clinical supervision.* Boston: Houghton Mifflin.

Clune, W. (1994a). The shift from equity to adequacy in school finance. *Educational Policy,* 8(4), 376–394.

Clune, W. (1994b). The cost and management of program adequacy: An emerging issue in education policy and finance. *Educational Policy,* 8(4), 365–375.

Cummings, T. G., & Worley, C. G. (2001). *Organization development and change* (7th ed.). Cincinnati: South-Western College.

Deming, W. E. (1986). *Out of the crisis.* Cambridge, MA: Massachusetts Institute of Technology, Center for Advanced Engineering Study.

Duffy, F. M. (2004a summer). The destination of three paths: Improved student, faculty and staff, and system learning. *Forum,* 68(4), 313–324.

Duffy, F. M. (2004b). Navigating whole-system change: Eight principles for moving an organization upward in times of unpredictability. *School Administrator,* 61(1), 22–25.

Duffy, F. M. (2004c). *Moving upward together: Creating strategic alignment to sustain systemic school improvement.* Leading Systemic School Improvement Series, No. 1. Lanham, MD: Rowman & Littlefield Education.

Duffy, F. M. (2003). *Courage, passion, and vision: A superintendent's guide to leading systemic school improvement.* Lanham, MD: Rowman & Littlefield Education and the American Association of School Administrators.

Duffy, F. M. (2002). *Step-Up-to-Excellence: An innovative approach to managing and rewarding performance in school systems.* Lanham, MD: Rowman & Littlefield Education.

Emery, F. E. (1977). *Two basic organization designs in futures we are in.* Leiden, Netherlands: Martinus Nijhoff.

Kelly, K. (1998). *New rules for the new economy: 10 radical strategies for a connected world.* New York: Penguin Books.

Keltner, B. R. (1998). Funding comprehensive school reform. RAND Corporation. Retrieved on January 15, 2004, from www.rand.org/publications/IP/IP175/.

Kotter, J. P. (1996). *Leading change.* Boston: Harvard Business School Press.

Lewin, K. (1951). *Field theory in social science*. New York: Harper & Row.

Lewin, R. (1992). *Complexity, life on the edge of chaos*. New York: Macmillan.

Lippitt, R. (1980). *Choosing the future you prefer*. Washington, DC: Development.

Odden, A. (1998 January). *District Issues Brief: How to rethink school budgets to support school transformation*. Arlington, VA: New American Schools. Retrieved on October 25, 2002, from www.naschools.org/ uploadedfiles/ oddenbud.pdf.

Pasmore, W. A. (1988). *Designing effective organizations: The socio-technical systems perspective*. New York: John Wiley & Sons.

Sartre, J. P. (1934). *Theory and practice of psychotherapy*. New York: Brooks/Cole.

Senge, P. M. (1990). *The fifth discipline: The art and practice of the learning organization*. New York: Doubleday.

Seyle, H. (1956). *The stress of life*. New York: McGraw-Hill.

Togneri, W., & Anderson, S. E. (2003). *Beyond islands of excellence: What districts can do to improve instruction and achievement in all schools—a leadership brief*. Washington, DC: Learning First Alliance.

Trist, E. L., Higgin, G. W., Murray, H., & Pollack, A. B. (1963). *Organizational choice*. London: Tavistock.

II

POWER, POLITICAL BEHAVIOR, AND ETHICS

Part II has three chapters. Chapter 5 presents information about using power and political behavior to lead whole-district transformation. Chapter 6 introduces readers to ethical decision making during times of great change. Finally, chapter 7 provides guidance on using power and political behavior in ethical ways to manage resistance to change.

5

USING POWER AND
POLITICAL BEHAVIOR TO LEAD
WHOLE-SYSTEM TRANSFORMATION

Courageous, passionate, and visionary leaders should use power and political behavior in ethical ways to help their districts move toward desirable futures. Leaders unwilling to lead in this way probably will fail in leading their school systems toward those futures. This chapter focuses on using power and political behavior. The next chapter presents information about the ethical use of power and political skills.

Power exists when a person is able to convince other people to do something. There are four common power strategies to move others to action. These are displayed in figure 5.1. In that figure you see four quadrants created by the intersection of "balance of power" and "level of goal agreement." If the balance of power between individuals or groups is relatively high but there is a low level of goal agreement, the power strategy of choice is *negotiate*. If the balance of power is low and the level of goal agreement is also low, the power strategy is *unilaterally decide*. If the balance of power is high and the level of goal agreement is high, the power strategy is *cooperate*. And when the balance of power is low but the level of goal agreement is high, the power strategy is *influence*. If people fail to act after you use any of these power strategies, you are powerless in your relationship with them.

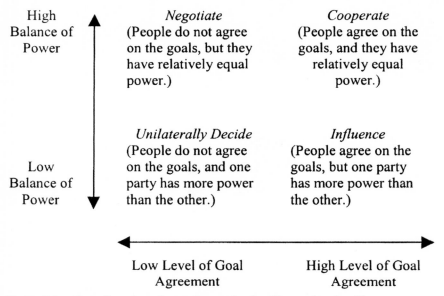

Figure 5.1. Four Common Power Strategies for Change Leadership

Clearly, the *unilaterally decide* strategy is a dangerous one for change leaders, because it can create resentment, anger, and retribution. The *influence* strategy, although it seems like it ought to be a good strategy, can backfire if the person or group with more power uses that power in negative ways to intimidate people. The effectiveness of the *negotiate* and *cooperate* strategies can be increased if they are based on a solid ethical foundation.

Each of the power strategies shown in figure 5.1 requires political behavior. Political behavior aims to shape the power strategy to elicit desirable behavior from others. When political behavior is exercised in the best interest of the other person and for the best interests of a school district, that behavior is exercised in an ethical manner.

Power and political behavior can be used in negative or positive ways. Power and political behavior used in negative ways are often effective in the short term but ineffective in the long term. In the short term, negative power creates compliance, not commitment. Compliance creates immediate action desired by a leader. Commitment, on the other hand, motivates people to do what's best for a school district without being or-dered to do so. Commitment trumps compliance, because commitment creates long-term positive outcomes.

"Empowerment" is a popular buzzword. Leaders are encouraged to empower their followers by sharing power with subordinates. But they are often reluctant to do so, because they believe power sharing is a zero-sum game whereby their power is reduced in quantity by sharing it. This fear is analogous to sharing the money in your wallet. If you share it with others, you have less money. But sharing power is actually more like sharing knowledge. If you share what you know, you are still left with the same amount of information you had before you shared it. Also, sharing your knowledge enhances it, as the recipient shares her knowledge with you. Sharing power works the same way. When you dis-tribute some of your power you still have what you started with, and the quality of your power is enhanced as others use it.

Empowerment, however, is insufficient. People also need to be *en-abled*. Enabling people to use power given to them is often overlooked in the literature on empowerment. Enabling people to use newly re-ceived power means giving them the resources they need to succeed, re-moving obstacles to their success, training them on how to use their new power effectively, and so on.

The use of power and political behavior is particularly important for transforming entire school systems, because transformation is a complex endeavor that must follow simultaneously three meandering paths to-ward the future. Transformation requires substantial change, not the least of which are reshaping organization culture, dissolving the status quo, and restructuring power relationships. Transformation also re-quires political support from people both inside and outside a school district. Without the application of power and the skillful use of political skills, transformation will not happen.

The dysfunctional use of power and political behavior is common. As-tute observations of organization life show us that leaders sometimes use power and political skills in dysfunctional ways. This dysfunctional be-havior frequently manifests itself in two forms: gentle paternalism (we know what's best for you, so we'll decide for you) and mean-spirited au-thoritarianism (just do what we tell you and don't ask questions). When these dysfunctional behaviors emerge during a transformation journey they produce significant emotional and psychological consequences for people working in a district (e.g., reduced commitment to organization goals, lowered job satisfaction, declining motivation, and deteriorating communication).

The negative use of power and political skills has many underlying causes. A few of these causes were discussed in the preface to this book. One of the possible causes discussed in the preface is a function of expectations for leadership behavior in school systems. Leaders are expected to do the difficult or the nearly impossible. Then they are often rewarded for doing the wrong things. For example, principals might be expected to spend time in classrooms observing teachers and giving them feedback on their performance, but central-office administrators reward them instead for submitting their budgets and schedules on time. Superintendents are expected to provide executive level leadership for school district improvement, but school boards sometimes reward them instead for attending to the personal political agendas of school board members.

A second reason for the dysfunctional use of power and political skills is that future school district leaders rarely receive skill training in their professional preparation programs on how to use power and political skills effectively. These topics are frequently discussed in graduate courses on education leadership, but most graduate education develops concepts and principles, not skills. Graduate courses to teach future leaders about the ethical use of power and political skills would be designed more like training workshops (which focus on skill building) rather than lectures or seminars (which focus more on knowledge building). These workshop-like courses would help future leaders develop technical and political competence to be effective in their roles as change leaders.

A third underlying cause of the negative use of power and political skills is that dysfunctional leadership behavior often emerges out of a leader's frustration with trying to engage people to collaborate for change, meeting significant resistance, trying again, failing again, and then giving in either to paternalism or authoritarianism. What this cause also implies is that some people in school districts do not know how to follow. If leaders make an authentic and repeated effort to engage people in collaboration and leaders demonstrate that they are listening to their colleagues, whatever ideas and plans emerge from the collaboration should be supported and nurtured by followers. Often, however, this is not the case. Followers too have negative political agendas that can interfere with a transformation process. Their undermining of the transformation process or their road-blocking behavior can motivate leaders to use power and political behavior negatively (see Libia Gil's essay in part III for a real-life example of this).

A fourth possible reason for the dysfunctional use of power and political skills is the dominant mental model burned into the brains of American leaders. It is a societal mental model that guides leaders to act either as benevolent dictators (paternalism) or despicable autocrats (mean authoritarianism). These two approaches to leadership are so prevalent that there is no other way to explain them except to describe them as societal mental models.

THE POLITICAL FOUNDATIONS OF MANAGEMENT PHILOSOPHIES

Organization Politicians

What images does the term "organization politician" elicit—manipulative, untrustworthy, power hungry, deceitful, winning at all costs, liar, corrupt, egocentric? In organizations, people who are labeled "politicians" are often held in great disdain. A person acting politically runs the risk of being tagged with pejoratives suggested in the opening sentence. Consequently, some managers often go out of their way to avoid appearing political in their work, even to the point of denying the existence of the political foundations of their managerial behavior. Yet it is only through political behavior that managers are able to accomplish things, and it is in the effective use of political skills that managers are transformed into leaders.

Effective Leaders Are Politicians

Whether or not they are willing to admit it, effective leaders are excellent politicians. They recognize that an organization is at least as nonrational as it is rational. They know that leaders who naively assume that rational management behavior is what works best (planning, organizing, staffing, directing, controlling, budgeting, and reporting) are often the losers in the organizational game of power and politics.

Leader-politicians recognize the value of conflict in organizations. Leaders are often trained to be collaborators and peacemakers, both of which aim to eliminate conflict. They are not trained to engage in conflict in productive ways. But conflict, if engaged effectively, forces the issues into the open and displays them in the vivid colors of emotions fueled by passionate beliefs and strongly held values. The true dimensions of an issue become clear as people take positions that define extreme boundaries of that issue. Knowing where people stand and understanding the dimensions of an issue are both important for effective conflict resolution. After the fighting is done and the issues are defined and resolved, the leader-politician also knows that fence mending must occur. Thus, the leader-politician must be both a warrior and a healer and know when to be each.

Leader-politicians use power. Effective change leaders know that power must be used with skill and finesse and based on an ethical foundation. They know that their personal power must be used like a laser, which focuses its beam of projected light particles narrowly and targets it precisely, and is extraordinarily effective.

Despite the fact that effective leaders are also effective politicians, many people in school systems eschew political behavior, denigrate those who demonstrate it, and sometimes punish that behavior when they see it in others. Yet the philosophies that guide the managerial behavior of leaders are nothing less than the extension of a political philosophy into leader behavior. That is to say, when education administrators and supervisors act on their beliefs about how things should be done in their school district, these actions are really nothing less than a political agenda in use. Therefore, leaders who deny they are political and scorn those who are political are, in fact, highly political themselves—an interesting irony.

To illustrate the political foundations of leadership philosophies, a questionnaire is presented below (Marshak & James, date unknown). This questionnaire was designed with a focus on management rather than leadership, but the managerial beliefs and political philosophies identified in the questionnaire also apply to leadership. The questionnaire asks you to express your level of agreement with fourteen management belief statements. Following the belief statements you will find descriptions of fourteen political philosophies that underpin each of the managerial belief statements. First, respond to the management belief statements, then match up your highest-ranked choices with the political philosophies that follow.

Management Philosophy Questionnaire

The following questionnaire was developed by Robert Marshak[1] and Dorothy James (used with permission). It offers fourteen statements of managerial beliefs. In the space provided, express the degree to which you agree with each of the statements. Use a scale of 1 to 5, where 1 = Disagree, 2 = Slightly Disagree, 3 = Neither Disagree Nor Agree, 4 = Slightly Agree, and 5 = Agree.

_____ 1. Everyone in the organization has a special role to play. Some, by nature, are best suited for leadership roles, while others are best suited to be followers. Each person has a place, should know that place, and should stick to it.

_____ 2. Because an organization is structured in response to its particular mission, goals, and environment, there must be a variety of roles to be filled by people in the organization. Further, the organization which takes into consideration the *common* interest of all its people will be the *best* organization.

_____ 3. If a person in the organization is not committed to the purpose and goals of the organization, then that person does not have the right to participate in the decision-making processes of that organization.

_____ 4. The newest custodian has a job to do just as the most senior administrator in the organization has one to do. Given that each person is seeking to do their jobs, everyone in the organization has the right to decide whether or not to comply with management directives that may affect their jobs.

_____ 5. If people in an organization were left to their own devices, there would be warfare of all against all. Therefore, there is a need for strong and central leadership to keep the organization from deteriorating into aggression and anarchy.

_____ 6. An organization should be organized on the principle that people come into the organization relatively equal and independent. As such, no one in the organization should harm the professional life, freedom, or possessions of these people. Further, no one should be dismissed without his or her consent, which is gained through a group process where majority rules.

_____ 7. Organizations are subject to the principle that the whole is greater than the sum of its parts. Thus, each person entering an organization must subsume his or her individual needs and interests to the common good of the organization.

_____ 8. Organizations are really nothing more than contrivances of human ingenuity designed to respond to human needs. As such, organizations have a permanent contract with society—with the past, the present, and the future. Therefore, there must be restraints on people in the organization, on their liberties, and on their rights so that the implied contract with society is protected.

_____ 9. People in organizations are basically narrow minded, self-centered, and present oriented. Thus, the need for management arises, so that the greatest good can be achieved for the greatest number.

_____ 10. In an organization, the individual is more important than the achievement of organizational goals. Individuals are, therefore, ends in themselves. They are not a means to organizational ends, and they are not to be subjected to the will of management.

_____ 11. An organization is best designed and most healthy when the interests of individuals in the organization become one and the same with the common interests of the organization. Through the acquiescence of individual needs to organizational needs, both the individual and the organization find gratification, one in the other. Further, in pursuit of the goal of making individual needs submissive to organizational needs, there is a need for a great and unique leader to emerge—a leader who is not afraid to lead with authority, directness, and control.

_____ 12. As individuals grow professionally, they become more valuable to themselves and to others. Thus, the worth of an organization, in the long run, is a function of the worth of the individuals within it. An organization that prevents or inhibits the development of its people so that they may remain docile instruments of management will find that no great things can be accomplished with undeveloped people. Thus, the professional growth of individuals is critically linked to organizational effectiveness.

_____ 13. A healthy organizational environment cannot exist without providing autonomy to the people in the organization. Paradoxically, the organization can extend autonomy *only* indirectly—that is, autonomy *cannot* be given through rules, regulations, or management directives. In fact, if the organization tries to take direct action to extend autonomy to its people, it may do more harm than good. But the organization can indirectly allow autonomy to develop by removing the barriers to achieving true autonomy for its people.

_____ 14. In organizations, autonomy is a privilege of the strong— those who are not superficial and who regard morality as timidity. A strong person has duties only toward his or her equals. Toward others of a lesser rank a strong person may act as he or she sees fit, for this is a natural and fitting relationship. And this strong person may act with egoism, for this is a characteristic of a distinguished person.

Next, match the above management belief statements that you agreed with (the 4s and 5s) to the political philosophies (below) underpinning them. The identifying number for each of the political philosophies described below corresponds to the identifying number for each management belief statement described above; for example, political philosophy #1 corresponds with management belief statement #1.

Political Philosophies Underpinning Management Philosophies

1. "We have laid down, as a universal principle, that everyone ought to perform the one function in the community for which his nature is best suited him . . . when each order . . . keeps to its own proper business in the commonwealth and does its own work, that is justice and what makes a just society" (Plato, in *The Republic*).

2. "Constitutions are various: there must thus be various kinds of citizens; . . . In one variety of constitution it will be necessary that mechanics and laborers should be citizens; in other varieties it will be impossible. . . . Those constitutions which consider the common interest are *right* constitutions, judged by the standard of absolute justice. . . . One sort of constitution may be intrinsically preferable, but there is nothing to prevent another sort from being more suitable in the given case" (Aristotle, in *The Politics*).

3. "No person has a right to an interest or share in the disposing or determining of the affairs of the Kingdom, and in choosing those that shall determine what laws we shall be ruled by here . . . that has not a permanent fixed interest in this Kingdom" (Lt. Gen. Henry Ireton, in the "Debates on the Putney Project," 1647).

4. "The poorest he that is in England has a life to live as the richest he; and therefore truly, Sir, I think it clear that every man that is to live under a Government ought first by his own consent to put himself under that Government" (Col. Thomas Rainboro, in "Debates on the Putney Project," 1647).

5. "The state of men without civil society (which state we may properly call the state of nature) is nothing else but a mere war of all against all; and in that war all men have equal right into all things; . . . all men as soon as they arrive to understanding of this hateful condition, do desire (even nature itself compelling them) to be freed from this misery. But that this cannot be done except by

compact, they all quit that right they have to all things. . . . [T]he original of all great and lasting societies consisted not in the mutual good will men had towards each other, but in their mutual fear they had of each other. . . . It is most manifest by what hath been said, that in every perfect city . . . there is a supreme power in some one . . . we call absolute" (Thomas Hobbes, in *De Cive*, 1642).

6. "The state of Nature has a law of Nature to govern it, which obliges everyone, and reason, which is that the law, teaches all mankind who will but consult it, that being all equal and independent, no one ought to harm another in his life, health, liberty or possessions. . . . Men being . . . by nature all free, equal, and independent, no one can be put out of his estate and subjected to the political power of another without his own consent, which is done by agreeing with other men, to join and unite into a community for their comfortable, safe, and peaceable living, one amongst another, in a secure enjoyment of their properties, and a greater security against any that are not of it. . . . When any number of men have so consented to make one community or government, they are thereby presently incorporated, and make one body politic, wherein the majority have a right to act and conclude the rest" (John Locke, in *Second Treatise on Civil Government*, 1762).

7. "Each of us puts his person and all his power in common under the supreme direction of the general will, and, in our corporate capacity, we receive each member as an indivisible part of the whole" (Jean Jacques Rousseau, in *The Social Contract*, 1762).

8. "You began ill because you began by despising everything that belonged to you. . . . Government is a contrivance of human wisdom to provide for human *wants*. . . . In this sense the restraints on men, as well as their liberties, are to be reckoned among their rights. . . . Society is a permanent contract . . . a partnership between those who are living . . . those who are dead, and those who are to be born" (Edmund Burke, in *Reflections on the Revolution in France*, 1790).

9. "Men are not able radically to cure either in themselves or others that narrowness of soul which makes them prefer the present to

the remote. . . . Government, therefore, arises from the voluntary convention of men. . . . The chief spring of actuating principle of the human mind is pleasure or pain. . . . [Government must achieve the greatest pleasure for the greatest number]" (David Hume, in *A Treatise of Human Nature,* 1737).

10. "Man and every rational being *exists* as an end in itself, *not merely as means* for arbitrary use by this will or that; but he must in all his actions . . . be regarded *at the same time as an end*" (Immanuel Kant, in *Groundwork of the Metaphysics of Morals,* 1785).

11. "Only the study of world history itself can show that it has proceeded rationally, that it represents the rationally necessary course of the World Spirit . . . a state is then well constituted and internally vigorous when the private interest of its citizens is one with the common interest of the state, and the one finds gratification and realization in the other . . . human actions in history produce additional results, beyond their immediate purpose and attainment, beyond their immediate knowledge and desire . . . world historical individuals [e.g., Caesar, Napoleon] . . . grasp . . . a higher universal, make it their own purpose, and realize this in accordance with the higher law of the spirit . . . so mighty a figure must trample down many an innocent flower, crush to pieces many things in its path" (Georg Wilhelm Freidrich Hegel, in *Reason in History,* 1838).

12. "In proportion to the development of his individuality, each person becomes more valuable to himself, and is therefore capable of being more valuable to others. . . . The worth of a State, in the long run, is the worth of the individuals composing it; . . . a State which dwarfs its men in order that they may be more docile instruments in its hands even for beneficial purposes . . . will find that with small men no great thing can really be accomplished; and that the perfection of machinery to which it has sacrificed everything will in the end avail it nothing, for want of the vital power which, in order that the machine might work more smoothly, it has preferred to banish" (John Stuart Mill, in *Essay on Liberty,* 1859).

13. "The good life is the end of all social activity. It cannot exist without freedom. The State can only further it indirectly, and may, by mistaking its sphere and capacities, do harm. But the State's compulsions are not the only hindrances to liberty, and the good citizen will consider what in social and economic conditions are harming the conditions necessary to the living of the good life, and ask whether the state's compulsion may not be so used in the removal of these harmful conditions as to produce an addition of real liberty" (Thomas Hill Green, in *Lectures on the Principles of Political Obligation*, 1879).

14. "Very few people are capable of being independent; it is a privilege of the strong . . . men are superficial . . . morality is timidity. . . . 'Exploitation' is not a part of a vicious or imperfect or primitive society: it belongs to the *nature* of living things, it is a basic organic function, a consequence of the will to power which is the will to life[;] . . . it is the *basic fact* underlying all history. . . . [O]ne has duties only toward one's equals; toward beings of a lower rank, toward everything foreign to one, one may act as one sees fit. . . . Egoism belongs to the nature of a distinguished soul" (Friedrich Nietzsche, in *Beyond Good and Evil*, 1885).

One lesson learned from the Marskak-James questionnaire is that even those leaders who claim to be apolitical are in fact political. They are political in the sense that the management beliefs they espouse or practice are based on a political philosophy and that when they enact that management belief they are operating from a political agenda.

THE PARADOXICAL BLEND OF POWER, POLITICS, AND ETHICS

Whenever power, politics, and ethics are discussed simultaneously, a paradox is occasionally created. "How," people may think, "can a change leader use power in a political way and be ethical at the same time?" Yet effective change leadership in a school district results from the skillful interplay of power, politics, and ethics. This section presents an argument in support of this belief. Let's explore each element of the power/politics/ethics triad.

Power

Power is woven tightly into the fabric of organizational life (Mintzberg, 1984). It is possible to interpret every decision and every social relationship within an organization using power as a controlling variable. Leaders and followers use power to accomplish goals and, in some cases, to strengthen their own positions (Cornelius & Lane, 1984). Power used within the framework of an organization's structures (job descriptions, policies, procedures, and so forth) is basically nonpolitical in nature. Power used outside of the framework of these structures is basically political and will often present ethical dilemmas. Therefore, a sophisticated understanding of power, knowing how and when to use it, and being able to anticipate its probable effects, significantly influences a leader's success or failure in using power.

Power is derived from interpersonal, structural, and situational sources. Examples of power from each source are provided below:

Interpersonal Power   French and Raven (1959) provide the classic topology of interpersonal power. They describe five kinds of power.

- *Legitimate power:* this is power gained because of one's position in the organizational hierarchy.
- *Reward power:* this type of power is connected to a person's ability to reward others for appropriate behavior.
- *Coercive power:* this is the opposite of reward power—it is the power to punish.
- *Expert power:* a person has expert power when she possesses special expertise that is highly valued.
- *Referent power:* this is power derived from one's personality or behavioral style. It is often referred to as charisma.

Structural Power   Power is frequently prescribed by structure within an organization (Pfeffer, 1981; Tjosvold, 1985). Structure is a control mechanism for governing an organization. Structure creates formal power and authority by assigning certain individuals specific tasks and giving them the right to make certain decisions. Structure also encourages the development of informal power, by affecting information and communication within the organization. Ivancevich and Matteson (1990, pp. 353–354) describe three sources of structural power:

- *Resource power:* access to and control of resources.
- *Decision-making power:* degree to which a person or unit affects the decision-making process in his school district.
- *Information power:* having access to relevant and important information.

Situational Power A number of organizational situations can serve as a source of power. Leaders have situational power when they are given assignments that allow them to:

- Allocate required resources
- Make crucial decisions
- Access important information.

Politics

Politics is also an integral part of organizational life. Individuals and subunits of an organization engage in politically oriented behavior (Velasquez, Moberg, & Cavanaugh, 1983; Yoffie & Bergenstein, 1985). Political behavior at its most positive influences others in ethical ways to join with others to achieve common goals and dreams.

Ethics

The study of ethics is an ancient tradition, rooted in religious, cultural, and philosophical beliefs (Lewis, 1985). A basic understanding of ethics suggests that it focuses on a critical analysis of human behavior to judge its rightness or wrongness in relation to two major criteria: truth and justice. (Chapter 6 presents an in-depth discussion of change leadership ethics.)

Daft and Noe (2001) offer a set of criteria for determining whether power and political behavior are being used ethically. "Yes" answers suggest ethical behavior; "No" answers suggest unethical behavior. These criteria are:

- Is the behavior consistent with the organization's goals?
- Does the behavior preserve the rights of groups affected by it?
- Does the behavior preserve the rights of individuals affected by it?
- Does the behavior meet standards of fairness?
- Would you wish others to behave in the same way, if that behavior affected you? (p. 437)

EFFECTIVE CHANGE LEADERSHIP:
THE SKILLFUL INTERPLAY OF POWER,
POLITICS, AND ETHICS

To make a real difference, change leaders in school districts need to affect decisions and events. This is what power and political behavior are all about, and there is nothing inherently wrong or evil with power and political behavior. Power and politics are neutral dynamics. Problems arise in the way they are practiced, when they are used either for selfish, negative reasons or for the good of the whole. Therefore, the exercise of power and politics must be done in an ethical manner. Macher (1988) reinforces this belief in his discussion of a concept called "ethical influence." Ethical influence (interpreted to mean the ethical use of power and politics) is based on the premise that straightforward, non-manipulative politics is an effective approach to power and self-respect.

Effective change leadership in organizations results from the skillful interplay of power, politics, and ethics. Power and political behavior are like two edges of the blade of a single sword, while ethical behavior is like the conscience of swordsmen using the blade as an instrument of their intentions—whether for evil or for good. Manley-Casimir (1989) indirectly reinforces this interplay when he says (the terms within the brackets are added):

> The school administrator occupies and works in a context with inherent tensions [politics?], which give rise to the need to reconcile competing claims [the use of power and political behavior?], which in some cases in-

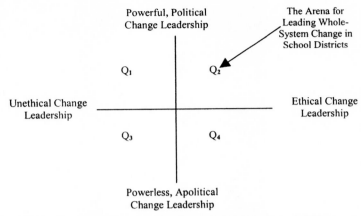

Figure 5.2. Q_2: The Arena for Powerful, Political, and Ethical Change Leadership

volve the voices of conscience [ethics?] and require their recognition and affirmation. . . . Administrative success . . . depends upon the way the administrator handles these tensions in the everyday world of administrative life [the skillful interplay of power, politics, and ethics?]. (p. 3)

A graphic display of the arena for effective leadership formed by the skillful interplay of power, politics, and ethics (Duffy, 1991) is shown in figure 5.2. This figure was constructed using a y axis representing the inseparable forces of power and political behavior and an x axis representing ethical behavior. Both axes represent a continuum, where the poles of the y axis are powerful, political behavior versus powerless, apolitical behavior, and the poles of the x axis are unethical behavior versus ethical behavior. The intersection of the two axes creates four quadrants. Quadrant 1 (Q_1) represents leader behavior that is powerful and political but unethical. Quadrant 2 (Q_2) represents leader behavior that is powerful, political, and ethical. Quadrant 3 (Q_3) captures leader behavior that is powerless and apolitical but unethical. Finally, Quadrant 4 (Q_4) represents leader behavior that is powerless, apolitical, and ethical. Here are a few examples of behaviors within each quadrant.

Q_1 contains powerful, political but unethical behaviors:

- A superintendent attacking a principal who is outspoken in resisting their district's transformation goals.

- A principal punishing people who disagree with her during a meeting.
- An assistant superintendent leaking sensitive information to the media to influence underhandedly a future decision by the superintendent.

Q_2 contains powerful, political, and ethical behaviors:

- A change leader using his position to serve as a mentor to a subordinate, even though there is no formal requirement to do this.
- An assistant superintendent for curriculum and instruction resolving conflict among several internal constituencies by bending some rules so that the district does not suffer.
- A department chair building support for a major change that will benefit multiple stakeholders.

Q_3 contains powerless, apolitical, and unethical behaviors:

- An assistant superintendent for business and administration lying about his involvement in a nonproblematic situation.
- An assistant superintendent whose district pays her way to a professional conference but who never attends any sessions at the conference.

Q_4 contains powerless, apolitical but ethical behaviors:

- A director of pupil personnel services showing up to work as expected but never doing more than his job description requires.
- A department chair showing up for meetings with other chairs but participating minimally in the meetings.
- A principal complying with directives from her superiors without question, even when the directives are in conflict with her personal values.

Effective change leadership occurs in Q_2—powerful, political, and ethical leadership. This conclusion is supported by Bennis and Nanus's (1985) research on effective leaders that identified common traits among "superleaders." The traits were (questions in parentheses were added):

- The capacity to create a compelling picture of the desired state of affairs that inspires performance. (Is this political behavior?)
- The ability to portray the vision clearly and in a way that enlists the support of followers. (Is this political behavior?)
- The ability to persistently move ahead regardless of obstacles. (Is this the use of power?)
- The ability to create a structure that effectively uses others' talents to achieve objectives. (Is this the interplay of power, politics, and ethics?)
- The capacity to monitor followers, learn from mistakes, and consequently improve performance. (Is this, also, the interplay of power, politics, and ethics?)

Courageous, passionate, and visionary change leaders in school districts need to recognize that their effectiveness is the result of the skillful interplay of power, politics, and ethics—that is, they need to be Q_2 leaders. Q_1 leaders cannot become or stay effective if they continuously exercise power and political behavior unethically. In fact, the most dangerous and potentially most destructive leaders are the Q_1s, and they ought to be fired outright. Q_3 leaders should also be removed from their positions, for obvious reasons. Q_4 leaders function in a powerless, apolitical, yet ethical way and do just enough to get by in an aboveboard fashion. They have and wield little influence, yet they somehow remain in their jobs. These people need either to move into Q_2 or be asked to step aside.

It's reasonable to assume that most people who move into leadership positions aspire to become Q_2 leaders. But something happens to them when they actually make the move to a leadership role. Somehow some of them lose their sense of moral direction, their notions of rightness and wrongness, their definitions of truth and justice, and they frequently seek expedient solutions to problems without regard to underlying ethical principles. Before long they change into Q_1s or Q_3s. This presents a leadership development problem for school districts: How can they recruit leaders who are capable of and willing to be Q_2 leaders, and then how do they restructure district reward systems to help leaders stay within the Q_2 arena? The solution to this puzzle is important to the future of leadership for whole-system transformation.

TIPS FOR USING POWER AND POLITICAL BEHAVIOR

Tip 1: Redefine Leader Roles

The voice of change leadership will always be needed in school systems. The need for change leaders, however, doesn't mean that their roles should remain defined as traditional leadership roles. These roles need to be recreated in ways that distribute some of their responsibilities to competent followers throughout their school systems. By distributing selected responsibilities those in formal change leadership positions can free themselves to provide transformational leadership that focuses on communicating, envisioning, building relationships, and moving people ever closer to their districts' transformation goals. Additionally, these roles must be retooled to assure that the change leaders possess both technical and political competence for leading change.

Tip 2: Redefine Follower Roles

It is assumed that people naturally know how to follow leaders. However, human experience in organizations of all kinds tells us that people naturally know how *not* to follow—especially highly educated professionals. We've all experienced this phenomenon either as leaders or as followers working against our leaders. We have seen situations where we pule about the lack of leadership in our organizations. Then, one from among us stands up to assume leadership. Suddenly, the new leader is under attack by arrows of criticism. He or she has to arm wrestle almost everyone to get things done. Then, either from fatigue or having been driven away, the leader steps down. And once again, the "we need good leadership" puling begins. This cycle continues unabated until an extraordinary leader emerges who skillfully uses power and political skills in ethical ways.

Leaders need leadership development. Followers need followership development. School systems should educate all faculty and staff about how to follow. The purpose of this education should not be to create a legion of automatons mindlessly following their leader. Instead, their education should focus on what it means to be a follower, how to follow effectively, how to engage in productive conversations with colleagues, and so on.

Follower roles also need to be redefined by injecting special leadership responsibilities into those roles. Competent followers deserve the chance to provide leadership within their teams, schools, clusters, and throughout their school districts. When these roles are redefined in this way, a person's "plate" full of responsibilities also needs to be balanced so that new leadership responsibilities are not piled on top of existing responsibilities.

Tip 3: Distribute Leadership Responsibilities

Leadership for whole-system transformation must exist at all levels in a school system, but most importantly it must first exist at the school board and superintendent's levels. Effective senior-level change leadership is like a tree. It has roots, a trunk, and a canopy. Its roots are made of unwavering courage. The trunk is a burning passion to educate all children. The canopy is a grand vision of a school district that creates excellent student, faculty and staff, and whole-system learning. Like a healthy tree, this kind of leadership must also be rooted in rich and fertile "soil"; which is a school district's internal social "architecture" enriched by a code of ethics, trust, commitment, and collaboration.

This kind of leadership will not by itself result in a transformed school system. Only when the "tree" becomes a "forest" will the potential for whole-system improvement be tapped. It is only when courage, passion, and vision are replicated throughout a school system like the fractals we read about in the new sciences (see Wheatley, 1992) that motivation to engage in whole-system improvement will spread like a contagion (see Gladwell, 2000).

Tip 4: Create a Chain of Excellence

A school district's effectiveness is connected to its ability to create customer and stakeholder loyalty and support. Loyalty and support are linked to customer and stakeholder satisfaction with schooling in a district. Satisfaction, in turn, is related to a district's ability to deliver on its promises. Delivering on promises depends on teacher and staff loyalty and retention, and so on. This chain of cause-and-effect loops can be envisioned as a chain of excellence. This "chain" provides a powerful framework for weaving and strumming a web of accountabilities within your district, and it is an outcome of creating and sustaining strategic alignment (strategic alignment is created in Steps 2–4 in the *Step-Up-to-Excellence* methodology summarized in chapter 4). In the end, if you want your district to experience sustained high performance by achieving its strategic goals and if you want your district to be among the best in your state, you must create and sustain alignment among your faculty and staff, your district's strategy, its work processes, and its internal social architecture with customer and stakeholder expectations—that is, you need to create a chain of excellence.

Tip 5: Retool Your District's Reward System

A school district should have systematic[2] ways of recognizing and rewarding performance using both intrinsic and extrinsic rewards that reinforce behavior that supports the district's mission, vision, and strategic priorities. In addition, a district needs a performance management program (see Duffy, 2002) that will help administrators, supervisors, and team leaders make fair and objective decisions about individual, team, school, and cluster performance based on observable, measurable, or quantifiable behavior.

Tip 6: Identify Allies, Opponents, Adversaries, Bedfellows, and Fencesitters

Peter Block (1991) describes ways managers can use positive political skills at work. His model for doing that identifies five political categories within which individuals and groups in your school system will fit. These categories are allies, opponents, adversaries, bedfellows, and fencesitters (see chapter 3 for additional information about these categories). It is very important to identify as best you can who in your school system fits into each of these categories. Then you need to develop ethical political strategies for working with people in each group.

Tip 7: Practice Stakeholder Management

Table 5.1 illustrates a matrix you can create to (1) identify key stakeholders in your district's environment, and (2) assess the benefit and harm each may experience if certain changes are implemented. This approach to managing stakeholder relationships is a core process for strategic planning.

Tip 8: Tune Into the Undercurrents in Your School System

Farson (1996) discusses the importance of paying attention to the grumbles and gripes flowing throughout an organization. These expressions of discontent are part of the undercurrent in the ebb and flow of life in an organization. You should pay close attention to the quality, or nature, of this discontent in your school district.

The quality of discontent in your district is important, because transformational change is partially a consequence of deliberately cultivating higher-quality discontent, followed by creating innovative ideas for improvement. Abraham Maslow (in Farson, 1996, p. 93) often advised change agents to listen to what people complain about. In less healthy organizations, people complain about little things—"low-order grumbles," according to Maslow. These gripes are manifestations of deficiency needs. In healthier organizations, people have high-order gripes that focus on more altruistic concerns. In very healthy organizations, people engage in meta-gripes—complaints about their need for self-actualization. Therefore, as you engage in whole-system improvement, repeatedly assess the quality of discontent to see if it is moving toward higher-order complaining. If it is, this could be a good sign that your change effort is succeeding.

Engaging your district in transformational change will not eliminate the grumbling. The improvements you create and sustain won't create contentment. Instead, as your transformation journey succeeds and as you create effective improvements, your people's expectations will rise,

Table 5.1. Stakeholder Management Matrix

Stakeholders	Benefits and Disadvantages of Proposed Change A	Benefits and Disadvantages of Proposed Change B
Critics (e.g., individuals and groups)		
Competitors (e.g., private schools and home "schoolers")		
Suppliers (providers of money; supplies; equipment; and new employees, including teacher education programs in local universities)		
Customers (those who purchase your services through their tax dollars [i.e., parents of school-aged children], businesses that employ graduates, colleges, and universities enrolling graduates)		
Other Stakeholders (community groups, state departments of education, the federal department of education, etc.)		

Note: For each stakeholder, identify the benefits and disadvantages of all significant changes that are being proposed for your school system.

and they will want more higher-order improvements. Rising expectations are a powerful generator of human energy in support of change.

Tip 9: Raise Expectations

The theory of rising expectations (de Tocqueville, 1887) explains human motivation to engage in big change (e.g., consider the French Revolution, which ignited when the French people began to *expect* that their lots in life might change). When people have rising expectations, when they see that a new future is really possible, that higher level of expectations creates discontent with the status quo and motivates people to seek change. In the language of systems theory, rising expectations creates disequilibrium. This kind of discontent can be the engine of great change.

Tip 10: Create Short-Term Success

People working in your district must see what is possible—must recognize what can be achieved by engaging in transformation and when it can be achieved. You do this by creating short-term successes that demonstrate that your transformation journey is producing results. These early successes will also help to raise expectations (see Tip 9) for what is yet to come, which will add even more positive energy to your transformation journey.

Tip 11: Honor Resistance to Change

A useful metaphor for understanding forces for and against change in a school district is planning for a community parade. Imagine that you are planning a community parade. You need about 25% of the community's population to help you plan and organize the parade. You can expect about 50% of the population to stand curbside and watch the parade go by. And you can count on about 25% of the population actively to resist your efforts.

Within the 25% group resisting your efforts to transform your district you will have two subgroups, adversaries and opponents. According to Peter Block (1991), adversaries are people who disagree with your goals and who do not trust you (and vice versa). Opponents, on the other hand, are people who disagree with you but trust you. While honoring and exploring the resistance offered by your adversaries probably won't change their attitudes toward your change effort, working with your opponents' resistance could pay off by motivating them to change their minds, or by convincing you to modify your change leadership in response to their concerns, which might convert them to allies.

Tip 12: Invest Time in Helping People to Unlearn Dysfunctional Mental Models

People spend a lot of energy complaining about the need to change but then, once you start a change process, reinvest their energy into resisting those changes. Farson (1996) says there is a parallel in psychotherapy. He describes how people seek psychotherapy to get help changing troublesome patterns of behavior but then are frequently very unwilling to abandon these patterns to make necessary changes. People resist changing their views of who they are, what they think they know, and what they think they are capable of doing (i.e., they resist changing their mental models). But transformational change requires this kind of change in individuals, teams, and whole school systems.

Unlearning and learning mental models is a difficult challenge (see chapter 3 for additional information about changing mental models), yet this kind of professional learning is also crucial to the success of any improvement effort in school systems. All mental models are strongly conservative and extraordinarily resistant to change, and they can be expected to obstruct efforts to make and sustain improvements.

Mental models guide the work of educators by unconsciously shaping their attitudes and behavior. In this way, mental models are inconspicuous yet potent. They are inconspicuous because people often are unaware of their mental models and their effects; they are potent because they significantly influence what people pay attention to and therefore shape what people do and how they do it.

Left unchallenged and unexamined, mental models will influence people to see what they have always seen, do what they have always done, be what they have always been, and, therefore, unknowingly produce the same results they have always produced. Left unchallenged and unexamined, mental models allow people and organizations to extend their current mental models into the future, whereby their past and present ways of doing things are cast before them like a beam of light and are called "the future."

Tip 13: Generate Innovative Ideas for Change, Not More of the Same

Creating innovative ideas is not easy. Implementing those ideas is even more challenging. The fundamental problem with innovation is that really new or unusual ideas require significant change to implement. Significant change requires controlled disequilibrium that disrupts the status quo. Since organizations of all kinds are inclined to protect and defend their status quo, they are either consciously or unconsciously managed so as to discourage innovation and change.

Yet genuine transformation requires truly innovative ideas for improving your district's relationship with its external environment, its core and supporting work processes, and its internal social architecture. Innovation that creates breakthrough change (see chapter 3) requires change leaders who are willing to break or bend rules (Duffy, 2004).

Tip 14: Question Everything Your District Does—Everything

In chapter 4, the system change principle of "first down, then up" was introduced. The "first down, then up" journey happens when educators start questioning their success. Not everything you do as a school district has to be abandoned completely, but everything you do needs to be questioned completely. Yet when people are considering change, they often fight to preserve what they have been doing. However, doing more of the same will not move your district upward breakthrough levels of performance (see figure 3.2 in chapter 3). If you focus on doing more of the same, that focus may blind you to stunning opportunities to improve student, faculty and staff, and whole-system learning.

Tip 15: Do Not Use Incremental Change as a Substitute for Transformational Change

Dr. Martin Luther King, Jr., in his famous "I have a dream" speech (August 28, 1963) used a metaphor that captured the nature of incremental change. He called it the "tranquilizing drug of gradualism." Incremental change is a "tranquilizing drug" because it gives people the illusion of making progress. Yet true progress is only achieved by creating breakthrough improvements (see chapter 3). Breakthrough improvement is not achieved through incremental change.

There is a place and a time, however, for incremental change. Its place and time are found after you complete your transformation and your system enters into a period in which you stabilize the changes, reinforce the positive things that happened, tweak promising changes that were not fully successful, and eliminate changes that were totally ineffective. These actions represent a period of continuous improvement. Continuous improvement (aka incremental change) should follow and support transformational change—not precede or supplant it.

Tip 16: Demonstrate Unequivocal Support for the Transformation Journey

Change leaders, especially the superintendent and school board members, must be 100% behind your district's transformation. You must also have solid political support for change both inside and outside your district. If your colleagues see your commitment to change as real, visible, and powerful, they are more likely to commit themselves to the transformation. On the other hand, if they see change leaders as lukewarm supporters of the change or dithering like a mule between two bales of hay, unable to commit to the transformation journey, they will see an opening that invites resistance to change.

There are many reasons why leaders are unable or unwilling to commit to great change. One reason is that school district transformation is difficult. But as President George W. Bush said in his inaugural address on January 20, 2005, "The difficulty of the task is no excuse for avoiding it."

Other reasons for being unable to commit to transformation are eloquently captured in a quote by Dr. Martin Luther King (which appeared in the dedication of this book). Dr. King said (date unknown),

Cowardice asks the question, "Is it safe?"
Expediency asks the question, "Is it politic?"
Vanity asks the question, "Is it popular?"
But, conscience asks the question, "Is it right?"
And there comes a time when one must take a position that is neither safe, nor politic, nor popular, but one must take it because one's conscience tells one that it is right.

School district transformation requires senior leaders who have the courage, passion, and vision to commit unequivocally to that transformation journey because it is the *right thing to do*.

Tip 17: Make a Transformation Methodology a Permanent Part of Your School District

Transformational change is not a onetime event. It is a journey that lasts for the life of your school system. This journey will require periods of significant change followed by periods of stability and incremental improvements. Significant change can be sustained by integrating a permanent change methodology into your district's organization design—a methodology that runs continuously for the life of your school district. There are no quick fixes—there are no short cuts—for transforming a school system. It is a lifelong journey for a school system that continues long after current employees have retired.

Tip 18: Identify Political Trade-Offs for Each Major Improvement Idea

All proposals for change will always require political behavior to implement. One political behavior that will almost always be required is that of negotiating trade-offs to gain support for a proposed change. Your efforts to negotiate trade-offs with adversaries and opponents (see the earlier reference to Peter Block's political model) will be more effective if your negotiation partners perceive you as trustworthy and genuinely interested in responding to their concerns. Negotiation will probably work better with opponents (who trust you even though they disagree with you) than with your adversaries (who don't trust you, disagree with your goals, and will probably fight you every step of your district's transformation journey).

All systems have different levels, so the trade-offs you may need to make can occur at each of these levels. Table 5.2 shows these different system levels and provides examples of opportunities for political trade-offs.

Tip 19: Set Boundaries for the Improvements

One of the core principles of systemic change is that there are many different acceptable routes to a single goal. The term of art for this principle is "equifinality" (Cummings & Worley, 2001). Even though equifinality should be encouraged and rewarded, it must be practiced within predetermined boundaries.

The change methodology highlighted in chapter 4 and described in more detail in other publications (Duffy, 2002, 2003, 2004) starts with a "pre-launch preparation" phase. At the end of the pre-launch preparation phase, you and your colleagues conduct a "district engagement conference." The product of that conference is a new strategic framework to guide your district's transformation. A strategic framework contains your district's mission statement, vision statement, strategic plan, and the boundaries within which changes can be made. These boundaries put a fence around your transformation journey and identify acceptable and unacceptable routes toward your strategic goals. Within these boundaries educators should be encouraged to exercise innovative thinking and risk taking and be rewarded for doing so as long as the innovations are clearly aligned with your district's grand strategy and strategic direction.

Tip 20: Create and Sustain Strategic Alignment

Although you want to promote equifinality and innovation, everything that happens in your district must be aligned with your district's strategic

Table 5.2. Political Trade-Offs at Different Levels of a System

System Levels

The System-Environment Level: The school system linked with its external environment, which includes external organizations and agencies as well as individuals and groups.

Opportunities for Political Trade-Offs
- Managing relationships with external stakeholders
- Assessing stakeholders' dreams, aspirations, and concerns

The Whole System Level: All operations within the school system.

Opportunities for Political Trade-Offs
- Assessing faculty and staff's dreams, aspirations, and concerns
- Participating in strategic planning

The Cluster Level: Clusters of schools and supporting units, with each cluster containing an entire work process (e.g., in a pre-K–12 school district each cluster of schools would contain one high school and all the middle and elementary schools that feed into it).

Opportunities for Political Trade-Offs
- Empowering and enabling educators within clusters to plan for change within their clusters
- Creating opportunities for collaboration for organizational learning.

The Individual School or Supporting Unit Level: Individual school buildings and service departments (e.g., cafeteria and maintenance) within each cluster.

Opportunities for Political Trade-Offs
- Empowering and enabling teams to plan and implement changes within their schools and units.
- Managing conflict

The Team Level: Teams (within buildings and departments and across buildings and departments).

Opportunities for Political Trade-Offs
- Empowering and enabling teams of faculty and staff to work in support of the district, cluster, and school or unit's performance goals.
- Setting goals

The Individual Level: Individual faculty and support staff.

Opportunities for Political Trade-Offs
- Empowering and enabling individual faculty and staff to work in support of the district, cluster, and school or unit's performance goals.
- Managing individual performance

framework. You cannot have individuals and teams doing their "own thing" with total disregard for your district's mission, vision, and strategic goals. Creating and sustaining strategic alignment will require sophisticated political skills and the judicious use of power. Strategic alignment is created in Steps 2–4 of the Step-Up-to-Excellence methodology presented in chapter 4.

Tip 21: Build Trust

One thing's for sure—if you have the courage, passion, and vision to lead whole-system change you will get nowhere if your teachers and professional staff don't trust you. Trust is the foundation for respect. Respect is the cornerstone of professional influence. Influence is the essence of leadership. As noted in chapter 3 in the section about trust, "No trust + no respect + no influence = less than effective change leadership."

Mistrust in senior leaders in organizations of all kinds is as widespread and contagious as the flu in the late fall. Someone gets it, and then it spreads through the whole population like a wildfire. Unlike the flu, however, once mistrust spreads there is almost no chance of recovering from it quickly, if you can at all. That which makes trust even more difficult to understand is that it takes a very long time to build and only a moment to destroy.

Tip 22: Don't Try to Change People First—Instead Change the System First

When you act on the premise that you can and should change people first, you will get nowhere with your transformation goals. Instead, if you give up the misinformed goal of changing individuals as the starting point of your district's transformation journey you can proceed more effectively. Then, as you create changes in your district's core and supporting work processes, its internal social architecture, and in its relationships with the external environment you will see subsequent change in individuals as they adapt to and adopt the changes; in other words, change the system first, then changes in individual behavior will follow.

The principle of "change the system first" is also supported by Beer, Eisenstat, and Spector (1990). They observe that many change efforts fail because the change process used is

> guided by a theory of change that is fundamentally flawed. The common belief is that the place to begin is with the knowledge and attitudes of individuals. Changes in attitudes . . . lead to change in individual behavior . . . and changes in individual behavior, repeated by many people will result in organizational change. . . . This theory gets the change process exactly backward. In fact, individual behavior is powerfully shaped by the organizational roles that people play. The most effective way to change behavior, therefore, is to put people into a new organizational context, which imposes new roles, responsibilities, and relationships on them. (p. 159)

CONCLUSION

One of the greatest challenges facing school systems in the 21st century is their need for effective change leadership for transforming entire school districts into high-performing organizations of learners that create unparalleled opportunities to improve student, faculty and staff, and whole-system learning. If history offers any guidance for the future, one consequence of *not having* this kind of leadership in a school system is that good education innovations that attempt to improve student learning will come and go, largely with mediocre results. When there is success, it will be isolated in "pockets of excellence." Regarding this phenomenon, Michael Fullan (in Duffy, 2002) says,

> What are the "big problems" facing educational reform? They can be summed up in one sentence: School systems are overloaded with fragmented, ad hoc, episodic initiatives—[with] lots of activity and confusion. Put another way, change even when successful in pockets, fails to go to scale. It fails to become systemic. And, of course, it has no chance of becoming sustained. (p. ix)

Even the best current and past education reform programs are limited in their scope of impact because they focus almost exclusively on changing what happens inside single schools and classrooms. This focus is not misguided. Schools and classrooms are where changes need to happen. School-based reform must continue. But it needs to evolve to a different level, because this focus is insufficient for producing widespread, long-lasting districtwide improvements.

Many of us believe that change in school districts is piecemeal and nonsystemic. Jack Dale, Maryland's Superintendent of the Year for 2000, is one of these people. He comments on the problem of incremental, piece-by-piece change. He says piecemeal change occurs as educators respond to demands from a school system's environment. He asks (in Duffy, 2002),

> How have we responded? Typically, we design a new program to meet each emerging need as it is identified and validated. . . . The continual addition of discrete educational programs does not work. . . . Each of the specialty programs developed have, in fact, shifted the responsibility (burden) from the whole system to expecting a specific program to solve the problem. (p. 34)

Another person who comments on the ineffectiveness of piecemeal change is Scott Thompson, assistant executive director of the Panasonic Foundation, a sponsor of districtwide change. In talking about piecemeal change, Thompson (2001) says, "The challenge [of school improvement], however, cannot be met through isolated programs; it requires a systemic response. Tackling it will require fundamental changes in the policies, roles, practices, finances, culture, and structure of the school system" (p. 2).

Focusing school improvement on individual school buildings within a district leaves some teachers and children behind in average- and low-performing schools. Leaving teachers and students behind in average- or low-performing schools is a subtle but powerful form of discrimination. School-aged children and their teachers, families, and communities deserve better. It is morally unconscionable to allow some schools in a district to excel while others celebrate their mediocrity or languish in their desperation. Entire school districts must improve, not just parts of them.

There are two consequences of piecemeal change within school systems. First, piecemeal improvements are not and never will be *widespread*; second, piecemeal improvements are not and cannot be *long-*

lasting. Widespread and long-lasting improvements require districtwide change led by courageous, passionate, and visionary leaders who recognize the inherent limitations of piecemeal change and who recognize that a child's educational experience is the cumulative effect of his or her "education career" in a school district.

Leading whole-system change, although challenging, is not an impossible task for change leaders. It is, however, a leadership task requiring courage, passion, and vision enacted with power and political skills based on an ethical foundation. This chapter offered insights to the nature of power and political skills for leading whole-system change. The next chapter will take you into the world of change leadership ethics.

NOTES

1. Dr. Marshak may be contacted at Bobmarshak@aol.com.
2. Occasionally, people confuse the terms "systematic" and "systemic." Systematic means organized, planned, and structured. Systemic refers to something that affects a whole system.

REFERENCES

Beer, M., Eisenstat, R. A., & Spector, B. (1990 November–December). Why change programs don't produce change. *Harvard Business Review, 68*(6), 158–166.

Bennis, W., & Nanus, B. (1985). *Leaders: The strategies for taking charge.* New York: Harper & Row.

Block, P. (1991). *The empowered manager: Positive political skills at work.* San Francisco: Berrett-Koehler.

Bush, G. W. (2005 January 20). Presidential Inaugural Address. Accessed on January 30, 2005, from www.cnn.com/2005/ALLPOLITICS/01/20/bush.transcript/.

Cornelius, E. T., & Lane, F. B. (1984, February). The power motive and managerial success in a professionally oriented service industry organization. *Journal of Applied Psychology, 6*, 32–39.

Cummings, T. G., & Worley, C. G. (2001). *Organization development & change* (7th ed.). Cincinnati, OH: South-Western College.

Daft, R. L., & Noe, R. A. (2001). *Organizational behavior.* Orlando, FL: Harcourt College.

De Tocqueville, A. (1887). *L'ancien régime et la revolution.* Paris: Lévy.

Duffy, F. M. (2004). *Moving upward together: Creating strategic alignment to sustain systemic school improvement.* Leading Systemic School Improvement Series, No. 1. Lanham, MD: Rowman & Littlefield Education.

Duffy, F. M. (2003). *Courage, passion, and vision: A superintendent's guide to leading systemic school improvement.* Lanham, MD: Rowman & Littlefield Education and the American Association of School Administrators.

Duffy, F. M. (2002). *Step-Up-to-Excellence: An innovative approach to managing and rewarding performance in school systems.* Lanham, MD: Rowman & Littlefield Education.

Duffy, F. M. (1991, Fall). Q2—Power, politics, and ethics: The arena for effective leadership in higher education. *College and University Personnel Association Journal, 42*(3), 1–6.

Farson, R. (1996). *Management of the absurd.* New York: Simon & Schuster.

French, J. R. P., & Raven, B. (1959). The basis of social power. In D. Cartwright (Ed.), *Studies in social power* (pp. 150–167). Ann Arbor: Institute for Social Research, University of Michigan.

Fullan, M., in F. M. Duffy (2002). *Step-Up-to-Excellence: An innovative approach to managing and rewarding performance in school systems.* Lanham, MD: Rowman & Littlefield Education.

Gladwell, M. (2000). *The tipping point: How little things can make a big difference.* Boston: Little Brown.

Ivancevich, J. M., & Matteson, M. T. (1990). *Organizational behavior and management* (2nd ed.). Homewood, IL: Richard D. Irwin.

King, Jr., M. L. (1963, August 28). Retrieved on November 30, 2004, from www.quoteland.com/library/speeches/dream.asp.

King, Jr., M. L. (date unknown). Quote retrieved on January 30, 2005, from www.quotedb.com/quotes/63.

Lewis, P. V. (1985). Defining "business ethics": Like nailing jello to a wall. *Journal of Business Ethics, 4*(5), 377–383.

Macher, K. (1988 September). Empowerment and the bureaucracy. *Training and Development, 42*(9), 41–45.

Manley-Casimir, M. (1989). Conscience, community mores and administrative responsibility: A prologue. *Administrator's Notebook, 33*(4), 3.

Marshak, R., & James, D. (date unknown). *Management philosophy questionnaire.* Unpublished questionnaire.

Mintzberg, H. (1984, October). Power and organizational life cycles. *Academy of Management Review, 9,* 207–224.

Pfeffer, J. (1981). *Power in organizations*. Marshfield, MA: Pitman.

Thompson, S. (2001 November). Taking on the "all means all" challenge. *Strategies for School System Leaders on District-Level Change, 8*(2). Retrieved on September 10, 2003, from www.aasa.org/publications/strategies/Strategies_11-01.pdf.

Tjosvold, D. (1985, Summer). Power and social context in superior-subordinate interaction. *Organizational Behavior and Human Decision Process, 35*(3), 281–293.

Velasquez, M., Moberg, D. J., & Cavanaugh, G. F. (1983, Autumn). Organizational statesmanship and dirty politics: Ethical guidelines for the organizational politician. *Organizational Dynamics, 12,* 65–79.

Wheatley, M. J. (1992). *Leadership and the new science: learning about organization from an orderly universe*. San Francisco: Berrett-Koehler.

Yoffie, D., & Bergenstein, S. (1985). Creating political advantage: The rise of the corporate political entrepreneur. *California Management Review, 28*(5), 124–139.

6

CHANGE LEADERSHIP ETHICS: A MORAL COMPASS FOR NAVIGATING WHOLE-SYSTEM TRANSFORMATION

Using power and political skills in ethical ways is difficult. Adding to the difficulty is the fact that unethical behavior is expedient and occasionally rewarded in the short term, especially when change leaders are expected to create change quickly. This expectation, in turn, can motivate change leaders to find expedient ways to accomplish goals and to make changes. When stressed by expectations for quick and substantial change and when motivated to make expeditious decisions, leaders can land dead center in the dark world of the unethical.

Change leaders need to be high-integrity leaders. Paine (1997) says, "Integrity in its broadest sense refers to the qualities of self-governance, responsibility, moral soundness, adherence to principle, and constancy of purpose" (p. vii). High-integrity leaders *cannot* be sustained in low-integrity organizations. This principle is particularly important for school systems, given their special role in our society. A high-integrity school system is created by developing and embedding a code of ethics within the district's internal social architecture (which includes organization culture, policies, procedures, communication processes, and so on) and rewarding people for enacting the values in that code. A high-integrity school system sits squarely on a foundation of social responsibility and moral values.

Districtwide integrity requires more than ethical thinking by change leaders. In school systems, educators at all levels need change leadership skills, supportive organizational structures, and excellent communication skills to apply principles of ethical decision making. This requires change leaders to develop for ethical decision making a framework that creates appropriate changes in their school district's internal social architecture— changes that help educators develop the attitudes, concepts, and skills needed to make effective ethical decisions and then reward them for doing so.

CHANGE LEADERSHIP PROVIDES A FERTILE CONTEXT FOR ETHICAL DILEMMAS

Ethical issues in change leadership emerge as people argue about and work together to create and sustain whole-system change. As change leaders and their colleagues collaborate for systemic change, the potential for unethical behavior and abuse of power develops quickly. For example, change leaders can let their personal values take precedence over and then obstruct their districts' values and thereby impede their transformation journeys, or they may use their power to abuse their relationships with others in their school districts.

Although ethical guidelines (i.e., a code of ethics, which will be discussed later in the chapter) can help reduce the emergence of ethical issues, these issues can never be totally eliminated. The reason ethical issues cannot be totally eliminated is discussed by White and Rhodeback (1992). These authors suggest that people have idiosyncratic values, goals, needs, and abilities. These variables influence how each person enacts his or her role in an organization and thus creates the conditions for role conflict and ambiguity. The ways people deal with role conflict and ambiguity create ethical dilemmas. Since these idiosyncratic variables constantly influence the enactment of organization roles, the potential for the emergence of unethical behavior is unavoidable.

Other ethical dilemmas are specifically tied to change leadership. The most common ethical dilemmas that materialize during times of great change are misrepresentation, misuse of data, coercion, value and goal conflict, and technical ineptness (Cummings & Worley, 2005). Let's explore each of these common ethical dilemmas, which were interpreted for the challenge of providing change leadership to create and sustain whole-system change in school districts.

Misrepresentation

This ethical dilemma occurs when change leaders claim that change methodologies they are recommending will produce results that are beyond the scope of those methodologies (e.g., claiming that a school-based improvement method can create whole-system change). This claim creates false expectations that, in turn, create ethical dilemmas. Misrepresentation happens most often early in a change process as change leaders try to build support for change in their districts by way of hyperbolic claims.

Misuse of Data

Data are collected during any change effort. These data should be used to make informed decisions about the kinds of changes that are required, the directions of those changes, and the duration of the change process. When these data are used inappropriately ethical issues arise. The inappropriate use of data includes "spinning" the data to support one's point of view, enhance one's personal power, or scapegoat individuals or groups. Leaking sensitive data to news organizations or other groups outside a district for political reasons can also cause ethical problems.

Coercion

Coercion happens when people are ordered to change or face negative consequences.[1] If educators are expected to take responsibility for creating and sustaining change within their classrooms and schools, they should have a "voice" in shaping the future of their district and they should be allowed to participate actively in the change process without feeling coerced. Giving "voice" to participants in a change effort is a leadership challenge that must be handled with great care and sophistication because it is easy for "giving voice" to turn into a charade that can collapse into a pit of fierce resistance to change.

Value and Goal Conflict

This kind of conflict creates an ethical dilemma when educators are not clear about the change goals for their districts or when there is significant disagreement about how to achieve those goals. This conflict is especially important for change leaders when a small but vocal coalition of dissenters within a school system want change to go in a direction that conflicts significantly with the values of the school system as represented in the district's mission and vision statements.

Technical Ineptness

Change leaders need to have a significant amount of technical competence to lead whole-system change. They also need political competence. When change leaders don't have the prerequisite technical and political competence, their ineptness at leading systemic change creates ethical dilemmas that jeopardize the performance of their districts and threatens the morale of their colleagues because incompetence often results in a failed change effort.

Technical and political ineptness also occurs when change leaders propose a change methodology or improvement strategy that they personally like but is inappropriate for the kind of change their school district needs—for example, proposing to create learning communities only at the building level, because they "love" the idea, when their district desires a systemwide approach to developing professional knowledge.

Several frameworks for identifying and resolving ethical issues such as the ones summarized above are discussed later in the chapter.

EXPERIENCING UNETHICAL LEADER BEHAVIOR

Many of you are or have been engaged in some kind of change effort within your school districts. In thinking about that change effort, can you recall instances of leader or follower behavior that could be characterized as unethical? Were facts intentionally misconstrued to make things look better than they really were? Were lies proffered to ration-

alize mistakes? Was money misappropriated to support personal projects instead of supporting projects for the "good of the whole"? Were
leaders' friends "taken care of" and others ignored or punished? Were
the facts "spun" to cover up inferior results or incompetence?

Unethical behaviors like those suggested above undermine the success of large-scale, districtwide change. When these kinds of behaviors
are observed they destroy trust, increase cynicism, and create enemies.
If successful districtwide change is desired, leaders (formal and informal) must use a moral compass to navigate whole-system change. Using
a moral compass means making decisions for the good of the whole system, decisions that are based on ethical principles and values.

The Importance of Ethical Principles and Values

Ethical principles and values are important elements of change leadership and sources of strength for a school district. Ethical principles
and values bring strength to a school district because they are intensely
practical in the sense that they can guide human behavior by providing
moral direction and by defining important limitations on what is and is
not acceptable behavior.

In discussing ethical principles and values, it is tempting to dive
deeply into the history and philosophy of ethics. I have resisted this
temptation here in favor of presenting an examination of the practicali-
ties of ethical decision making for change leadership. Although an overly
philosophical examination of change leadership ethics is to be avoided,
a little philosophical discussion provides a solid foundation upon which
the remainder of the chapter can rest.

The Origins of Ethics

Adler and Cain (1962) tell us that "the word ethics comes from the
Greek word ethos, which originally meant the 'accustomed place' or
'abode' of animals. It was then applied to mankind to mean 'habit,' 'dis-
position,' or 'character'" (p. 40). Aristotle tied the concept of "happiness" to the study of ethics. In Aristotle's view, happiness referred
specifically to the general well-being of mankind (Beckner, 2004, p. 7).

Some of the others in the history of humankind contributing to Western civilization's early conceptualization of ethics include Thomas Aquinas, Thomas Hobbes, Martin Luther, John Locke, Niccolo Machiavelli, Immanuel Kant, David Hume, John Stuart Mill, Jeremy Bentham, and John Dewey. The great religions of the world also have contributed to our understanding of ethics, as have religions of the native peoples of Africa and Australia.

Ethics Defined

Beckner (2004) defines ethics as the "study of ideas, ideas about right and wrong, and these ideas are couched in terms and concepts which require definition and understanding" (p. 25). The terms and concepts that Beckner is referring to are: rights, freedom, responsibility, duty, justice, and equity. Let's briefly examine each one of these terms.

Rights   Ottensmeyer and McCarthy (1996) define rights by saying, "When we say that a person has a moral (or legal) right in a given situation, we mean that it is ethically (or legally) permissible for him or her either to act in a certain way or to insist that he or she be treated in a certain way without obtaining anyone's permission to do so" (p. 15). In our society, some rights apply to all circumstances within which people may find themselves. For instance, our Declaration of Independence proclaims that "life, liberty and the pursuit of happiness" are God-given rights. Rights of this class are considered "absolute."

Not all rights are absolute; some are "prima facie." Prima facie rights are more common, and they include those rights that can be ignored or taken away when justified by circumstances. Ethical problems emerge when these rights are ignored, abridged, or terminated while arguments as to who has the authority to do that remain unresolved. Consider, for example, the longstanding battle between those who are pro-choice and those who are pro-life. Pro-choice advocates argue that women have the "right" to make choices about their reproductive behavior. Pro-life advocates, on the other hand, argue that pro-choice is, in fact, not a right; they argue that no one has the "right" to kill another human life, even if it's in an embryonic state.

Freedom   Freedom and rights are inextricably linked. Americans, in particular, are strong proponents of individual freedom (e.g., the Declaration of Independence speaks of individual freedom and rights, not group rights; the Constitution protects individual rights, not group rights). Freedom cannot and should not encroach on another's freedom or happiness; therefore, there *are* obligatory limits to freedom. In the same way that efforts to limit or terminate prima facie rights leads to ethical problems, deciding what the limits on personal freedom are also creates considerable ethical debates and disagreements. On one extreme, people subscribing to the politics of libertarianism argue for a great deal of freedom unconstrained by government policies, legislation, or moral values. At the other extreme is socialism, which severely constrains individual freedom for the sake of the "the common good."

Responsibility Rights and freedom are not without consequences. Rights and freedom burden people with responsibility and accountability. People must be held accountable for the consequences of the choices they make while exercising their rights and freedom. This requirement is sometimes ignored or rejected by people who are wildly and proudly narcissistic.

Duty Pojman (2002) says that moral people are those who "must perform moral duty solely for its own sake ('duty for duty's sake')" (p. 142)—for example, "One must tell the truth because it is the right thing to do, not just because it will be more likely to keep you out of trouble" (Beckner, 2004, p. 31).

Duties are always framed as imperatives. Immanuel Kant (Carnegie Mellon University, date unknown) tells us there are two kinds of imperatives: "hypothetical" imperatives and "categorical" imperatives. Hypothetical imperatives are often stated in the form, "If you want *this,* then do *this.*" Categorical imperatives are simple "do this" statements. Kant's view of both kinds of imperatives is absolutist—meaning, there are no exceptions to the "rules."

Not all ethics philosophers subscribe to Kant's absolutist worldview. Ross (1930), for example, declares that "we have certain prima facie duties that we must always adhere to unless serious circumstances or reasons tell us to do otherwise. . . . [C]onsequences [do not] make an action right or wrong, but . . . it is necessary to consider consequences when we are making our moral choices" (p. 65). The practical implication of this principle is that sometimes it is necessary to ignore one's duty to do the morally right thing (which is often stated in the leadership literature as "managers do things right" [meaning that they attend to duties] and "leaders do the right things" [they do the right thing, their duty notwithstanding]).

Justice   Durant (1991) explains Plato's definition of justice as, "Each man shall receive the equivalent of what he produces, and shall perform the function for which he is best fit" (p. 33). More recently, philosophers have identified several variations of justice. These are:

- *Procedural justice:* applying rules consistently and fairly
- *Substantive justice:* focusing on the "rightness" of rules and procedures
- *Retributive justice:* punishing wrongdoing
- *Remedial justice:* compensating people for past injustices
- *Distributive justice:* sharing benefits and burdens in a morally correct way.

Equity   While justice focuses on applying rules fairly and in proportion, equity is about the "bending of the rules" to fit the situation (Beckner, 2004, p. 39). The legal principles of equal employment opportunity and affirmative action are examples of applied equity. These principles emerge from a belief that certain members of our society did not have an equal opportunity to succeed in life, and therefore certain rules about access to employment or to higher education need to be "bent" to compensate for this lack of equal opportunity.

Egalitarianism is an extension of the concept of equity. It goes far beyond the basic tenets of equal opportunity or affirmative action. Egalitarianism is fueled by the worldview that there are certain rights held equally by all human beings and not just by a few (e.g., not just by those in leadership positions, not just by those who work hard to succeed, not just by those who by genetic randomness have superior intelligence). Stated more bluntly, egalitarianism suggests, for example, that the fact that you are a leader doesn't in itself give you the right to the "perks" you get; that having worked hard to become wealthy doesn't give you the right to keep all your money, and that therefore, a large percentage of your income will be confiscated through government taxation and redistributed to others; and that the mere fact that you are very intelligent doesn't give you the right to be rewarded for that intelligence by superior educational opportunities. Egalitarianism results in public statements by politicians like, "We're going to take things away from you on behalf of the common good" (Hillary Clinton in Fouhy, 2004).

CHARTING AN ETHICAL COURSE FOR WHOLE-SYSTEM CHANGE

A useful and practical way to examine the ethics of change leadership is to use a compass metaphor. A compass helps us find our direction and lay out a course to follow. The compass illustrated in figure 6.1 facilitates an examination of the legal and ethical issues suggested by the double-headed arrows in the figure—for example, the arrow connecting "legal actions" to "illegal actions" or the one connecting "guided by conscience" to "lack of conscience." Let's explore the change leadership behaviors implied by the double-headed arrows in figure 6.1.

Moving Around the Compass

Legal Versus Illegal Behavior   Federal and state legislators enact laws with which educators must comply. These laws, for example, often focus on financial practices within school districts, school attendance,

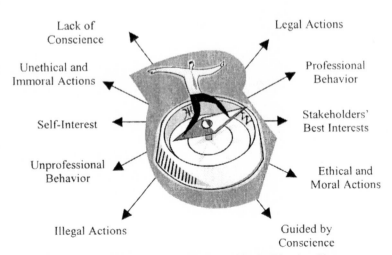

Figure 6.1.   Compass Points for Guiding Whole-District Change

and compensatory education programs. These laws also include human resource management practices, such as equal employment opportunity policies. When change leaders are considering courses of action for improving their school district they need to consider whether their ideas for change are legal or illegal.

Professional Versus Unprofessional Behavior   Almost all fields have standards that guide professional behavior within the fields. These standards should not be confused with codes of ethics, which will be discussed later. Instead, these standards focus on the quality of one's knowledge and the effectiveness of one's skills. They describe what an effective professional should know and what he or she should be able to do.

Stakeholders' Best Interest Versus Self-Interest   Leaders who habitually make decisions to satisfy their self-interest act in violation of the ethical principle of making decisions for the best interest of stakeholders. Stakeholders include not only people outside of a school district (external stakeholders) but also the people working in a district (internal stakeholders). Regarding this principle, Stephan and Pace (2002, p. 142) say, "Most people agree that the best policies are those that produce the greatest good" for a school system.

Ethical and Moral Actions Versus Unethical and Immoral Actions There is a thin distinction between ethics and morality. In fact, the two terms are often considered synonyms. Ackoff (1999), however, sees an important distinction. He believes ethics has the function of promoting cooperation, while morality has the function of reducing conflict. He says, "This makes ethics proscriptive—telling us what *should* be done—and morality, prescriptive—telling us what should *not* be done. Ethics is concerned with 'thou shalt' and morality with 'thou shalt not'" (p. 279).

Ackoff continues his analysis of the difference between ethics and morality by suggesting that "good" and "evil" are ethical concepts and that "right" and "wrong" are moral concepts. He also argues that "good and evil" and "right and wrong" are not dichotomies. Instead, they represent degrees of difference—for example, giving people increased opportunity to participate in decision making is a good thing, but the degree to which this opportunity is increased determines *how* good it is.

Stephan and Pace (2002) also suggest that there is an important difference between ethics and morality on one hand and fashion, etiquette, and artistry on the other. They say, "Fashion, etiquette, and artistry have to do with prevailing customs, styles, and tastes, which we often call fads, rages, or crazes, and are assumed to reflect temporary, transient, and more personal uses of things. Ethics, on the other hand, concern decisions, thinking, and actions that can have serious consequences for the welfare of human beings in general" (p. 143).

Shaw and Barry (1989) offer a deeper understanding of the differences between customs, styles and tastes, and ethics. They suggest that customs, styles, and tastes may be legitimized and validated by authoritative bodies but that ethical standards are not. Instead, ethical standards are validated by the adequacy of the reasons that justify them.

Guided by Conscience Versus Lack of Conscience Decision making for change can benefit from the application of a decision-making strategy from game theory—that is, given a possible decision or course of action, what is the worst that could happen and probably will? The answer(s) to this question can stimulate a change leader's conscience—her personal core values and beliefs—by informing her about whether or not the probable consequences of a decision or course of action are acceptable or unacceptable, legal or illegal, moral or immoral, and ethical or unethical. Leaders who do not tap into their conscience and who ignore the "little voice" inside their heads run the risk of making decisions that hurt themselves, hurt others, and ultimately impair their school systems' transformation journeys.

The Threat of Moral Relativism

There is a longstanding philosophical argument about whether individuals can be held accountable for conforming to moral values. Those who believe individuals cannot and should not be held accountable to moral values practice what is called "moral relativism" (sometimes called "ethical relativism").

Velasquez, Andre, Shanks, and Meyer (2004) discuss the nature of ethical relativism. They say,

> Ethical relativism is the theory that holds that morality is relative to the norms of one's culture. That is, whether an action is right or wrong depends on the moral norms of the society in which it is practiced. The same action may be morally right in one society but be morally wrong in another. For the ethical relativist, there are no universal moral standards—standards that

can be universally applied to all peoples at all times. The only moral standards against which a society's practices can be judged are its own. If ethical relativism is correct, there can be no common framework for resolving moral disputes or for reaching agreement on ethical matters among members of different societies. . . . Most ethicists reject the theory of ethical relativism. (p. 1)

Moral relativism stands on a weak foundation. Consider a moral relativistic perspective on our country's current war on terrorism, extracted from notes posted to a "Listserv" with a focus on organization development and change. The relativists on that Listserv made comments like, "Yes, we think what the terrorists did was wrong. But, they thought they were right. So, where do we get off thinking the United States is morally right in this war and the terrorists are morally wrong?"

Intentional or not, moral relativism often presents itself as a way to avoid being held accountable for unethical or immoral behavior. Franks (2001) supports this conclusion: "The logical result of the relativist thinking that permeates much of postmodern, deconstructionist thought is the elimination of any objective standards of right and wrong, and with it, the concomitant ability to justify punishing anyone for anything" (online, page unknown).

Moral relativism results in moral confusion. Moral confusion threatens the fabric of life in a school district. When there are no standards for ethical and moral behavior in a school district, ethical and moral dilemmas are left unresolved. In the worst case, they are reinforced and left to wreak havoc.

You do not want to suffer from moral confusion when leading systemwide change. You do not want to equivocate in recognizing the difference between right and wrong (moral issues), good and evil (ethical issues), or innocence and guilt. Setting a moral and ethical course for your district's transformation journey is extraordinarily important.

CULTURAL RELATIVISM: THE CONJOINED TWIN OF MORAL RELATIVISM

While moral relativism suggests that there are no absolute standards for judging right and wrong, good and evil, and innocence and guilt, *cul-*

tural relativism subscribes to the philosophy that all cultural beliefs are essentially equally valid and that truth itself is relative, depending on the situation, environment, and individual. Those subscribing to the theory of cultural relativism "hold that all religious, ethical, aesthetic, and political beliefs are completely relative to the individual and his or her cultural identity. Relativism often includes moral relativism (ethics depend on a social construct), situational relativism (right or wrong is based on the particular situation), and cognitive relativism (truth itself has no objective standard)" (All About GOD Ministries, Inc., 2004, page unknown).

If a person from another country comes to the United States and engages in immoral behavior and others try to hold him or her accountable for that behavior, the cultural relativist says, "You can't hold her accountable for that behavior. What's immoral here in the United States is not immoral where she comes from so you can't hold her accountable." If a change leader works to develop a common set of values and beliefs for his school district, the cultural relativist responds by arguing, "Whose values are these? We have a diverse community. How can you possibly create a set of shared values and beliefs with this kind of cultural diversity?"

Cultural relativism is the force behind extreme elements of the multicultural movement in the United States. Some multiculturalists are striving to create a society that venerates cultural differences rather than cultural commonalities. Instead of seeking to bring people together around a core set of societal values, these divisive multiculturalists are working to "balkanize" American society (Schlesinger, 1998). The results of their efforts to divide America have been characterized as a culture war (Vazonyi, 1998). Within the context of this culture war, our legislative system struggles to define objective standards for defining the laws, and our judiciary find themselves occasionally mired in the questionable position of interpreting the laws to conform to the philosophy of cultural and moral relativism. Worse, judges might ignore the wishes of society as expressed in its laws and societal values and impose their own values on society, by "legislating from the bench."

According to the relativists, all points of view are true, with one major and important exception. The point of view that is false according to the relativists is the one that teaches that there *is* truth, or right and wrong, or good or bad. This irony illuminates a major flaw in the relativists' philosophy. If all points of view are true, how can one be false?

In most instances the ultimate goal of moral and cultural relativism seems to be to free people from being held accountable to ethical and moral standards and to block the emergence of shared dreams, values, and visions. Moral and cultural relativism threaten ethical decision making. Moral and cultural relativism seek to eliminate common moral values and prevent the emergence of shared beliefs within communities and school systems. Moral and cultural relativism feed narcissistic behavior. Moral and cultural relativism provide soil for the seeds of anarchy in school districts.

Leading With Moral Certitude

One consequence for school systems of acquiescing to cultural and moral relativism is that change leaders in those districts will lose their moral compass as educators kowtow to the relativists' worldview by refusing to develop and enforce districtwide moral and ethical values. In the absence of commonly held moral and ethical values, change leaders become reluctant to criticize aberrant behavior for fear of being labeled "racist," "homophobic," "sexist," or "intolerant." However, despite the claims of the moral and cultural relativists, it is possible for educators to develop a common set of ethical and moral values to guide human behavior in their school systems. Consider the following quote from Beyer (2004), who supports this conclusion: "As individuals, we exhibit ethical behavior through our social conduct and interactions with others, by adhering to culturally approved ways of acting, and developing character traits acceptable in the culture in which we live. As a group, an ethical culture is developed and exhibited through shared and agreed upon values, beliefs, and norms of behavior" (p. 53).

Beyer's core point is found in the phrase "in the culture in which we live." This phrase suggests that our personal cultural heritage is subsumed by the "culture in which we live." In fact, in most countries of the world, individuals moving to those countries from other parts of the world are expected to conform to the cultural and moral values of their new country. The exception, of course, is the United States, where the divisive politics of extreme multiculturalism argue for the balkanization of America (Schlesinger, 1998) based on cultural and ethnic heritage.

The phrase "in the culture in which we live" can also apply to the culture inside a school district. Therefore, it is reasonable to suggest that people working in school districts ought to examine their organizations' cultures, drive out immoral and unethical norms, and replace those with a common set of moral and ethical values and norms that will guide human behavior "in the culture in which they work." Of course, driving out immoral and unethical norms won't be an easy task, because the moral and cultural relativists will fight you with viciousness and ferocity. This is one challenge where your personal courage, passion, vision, power, and political skills will be significantly tested.

Not only is it possible to develop a set of shared ethical and moral values for a school system, but many believe it is absolutely necessary, For example, Paine (1994) says, "Managers must acknowledge their role in shaping organizational ethics and seize this opportunity to create a climate that can strengthen the relationships and reputations on which their companies' success depends. Executives who ignore ethics run the risk of personal and corporate liability in today's increasingly tough legal environment" (p. 106).

Characteristics of Ethical Leaders

Andrews (1989, pp. 100–101) identifies three qualities that characterize leaders capable of making ethical decisions:

- Competence to recognize ethical issues and to think through the consequences of alternative resolutions
- Self-confidence to seek out different points of view and then to decide what is right at a given time and place, in a particular set of relationships and circumstances
- Tough-mindedness—the willingness to make decisions when all that needs to be known cannot be known and when the questions that press for answers have no established and incontrovertible solutions.

Organization culture in school districts, however, sometimes counter-vails against the above three qualities. The literature on organization psychology is replete with comments about the power of organization norms, reward systems that reinforce the wrong things, and group-think, among other relevant topics. In all cases, when individuals enter a school district for the first time as new employees, they may do so with strong sets of personal moral and ethical values. But almost from the first day those new employees are pressured to conform to district norms and are rewarded for doing so (or punished for not conforming). Therefore, if an individual wants to remain employed in that school dis-trict, he or she will conform. Conforming to a school district's culture that is moral, ethical, and positive is not a bad thing. Conforming to a district's culture where immoral or unethical behavior is tolerated, per-haps even encouraged under the banner of cultural or moral relativism, *is* a bad thing. Within an unethical or immoral culture, the three quali-ties for ethical leadership identified above by Andrews cannot and will not emerge.

FRAMEWORKS FOR ETHICAL CHANGE LEADERSHIP

The Kidder and Born Framework

Kidder and Born (2002) present a framework for making ethical de-cisions. They contend that in the face of ethical dilemmas leaders need to demonstrate moral authority and wise decision making. They suggest a structure for guiding ethical decision making. Their framework sug-gests that ethical decision making should:

- Be rooted in shared core values
- Center on right-versus-right dilemmas rather than on right-versus-wrong temptations
- Provide clear, compelling resolution principles
- Be infused with moral courage.

Let's look at each element of this framework within the context of a school system.

Shared Values   Making decisions within an ethical framework requires change leaders to know what their core values are as well as their community's core values. These values are also often part of a profession's standards—for example, the Statement of Ethics developed by the American Association of School Administrators (date unknown), which holds out such professional values as honesty and integrity.

The challenges change leaders face when trying to help their systems develop core values have already been discussed. One of the significant challenges is from moral and cultural relativists who challenge the validity of developing common values, wrongly claiming that they cannot exist. According to Kidder and Born (2002), when presented with the relativists' question "'Whose values will you teach?' the answer is 'Our values—the ones we can discover by asking our community what values are most important.' The fact is that you don't need to impose values on anyone because you can find the core values already in place" (page unknown).

Ethical Dilemmas   Leaders wrestle with two basic kinds of ethical issues: issues involving right and wrong and issues involving right versus right. The right-versus-wrong issues are usually easy to resolve if you have a clear set of values and performance standards to use as a guide. The more challenging ethical issues are the ones involving right versus right, where two important core values conflict with each other. These present true ethical dilemmas.

Right-versus-right dilemmas, according to Kidder and Born (2002), involve situations where there is a clear moral foundation for each core value but the two are mutually exclusive. Kidder and Born (page unknown) identify four types of right-versus-right dilemmas, a list developed by the Institute for Global Ethics:

- Truth versus loyalty, where issues of personal honesty or integrity come in conflict with responsibility, allegiance, and promise keeping
- Individual versus community, in which the interests of the individual are lined up against those of a larger entity
- Short term versus long term, where the real and important concerns of the present are pitted against foresight and investment for the future

- Justice versus mercy, in which fairness and an equal application of the rules appear to be at odds with the demands of empathy and compassion.

Resolving Two Rights   Resolving the conflict between two core values is quite challenging. Kidder and Born recommend a resolution process, one with three kinds of decision principles: ends-based, rule-based, and care-based.

- *Ends-based thinking:* This kind of thinking focuses on the results of a decision. It is an approach that identifies the consequences of decisions. The option with the most positive consequences is considered the correct course of action.
- *Rule-based thinking:* This approach applies rules to decide which "right" is right. Where ends-based thinking anticipates consequences, this way of thinking doesn't try to identify or predict end results. Instead, people using this approach seek to establish rules that can be applied in all situations, without exception.
- *Care-based thinking:* This is the Golden Rule (that is, "Do unto others as you would have them do unto you") applied to ethical decision making. This approach requires people to put themselves in others' positions to develop an understanding of how a decision might affect those people and then to make a decision that does the least harm.

Moral Courage   The last element of Kidder and Born's ethical framework is moral courage, which, they say, has the following characteristics:

- It differs from physical courage.
- It is not about facing physical challenges that could result in death or injury. Moral courage is what's needed to confront challenges that might harm one's career, reputation, or self-image.
- It is built by practice and repetition.

The Messick and Bazerman Framework

Messick and Bazerman (1996, pp. 9–22) offer practical guidance on how change leaders can practice ethical leadership. They describe three types of theories that leaders need to understand if they want to exercise ethical leadership: theories about the world, theories about other people, and theories about ourselves. Let's take a look at each one.

Theories About the World   Messick and Bazerman state that successful leaders must have an accurate knowledge of the world within which they lead. If they don't have this knowledge, they must know how to acquire it. An example of this kind of knowledge is found in attempting to determine the possible consequences of a new strategy or policy. An inadequate assessment could have consequences that harm a school district.

Theories About Other People   Diversity is a fact of life in all American organizations, especially in many of our public school systems. Stereotypical thinking about the characteristics or behaviors of people from different cultures creates situations within which leaders make unethical decisions based on stereotypes, especially decisions involving promotions, hiring, firing, or training. Knowledge of others must be expanded and used to develop fair and equitable policies and norms for leading change.

Theories About Ourselves   Leaders need confidence, intelligence, and moral courage to make difficult and possibly unpopular decisions. These traits, however, need to be balanced with accurate self-appraisal, modesty, and openness in communicating. Finally, Messick and Bazerman (1996) conclude, "the causes of poor ethical decisions are often the same as causes of poor decisions generally; decisions may be based on inaccurate theories about the world, about other people, or about ourselves" (p. 20). To improve ethical decision making, the authors propose three actions that leaders can take: improve the quality of decision making by making a conscious effort to identify and examine possible consequences of a decision; conduct an ethical audit of possible consequences for each key stakeholder; and be honest in interactions with employees and stakeholders.

The Blanchard and Peale Framework

Blanchard and Peale (1988) provide practical guidance on ethical management. Their recommendations are very popular and are often referred to in the literature. The clarity of their values and the conviction that underlies their recommendations provide change leaders with a powerful framework for ethical leadership. The infrastructure of the Blanchard and Peale framework is referred to as "The Five Ps of Ethical Power," which are: *purpose, pride, patience, persistence,* and *perspective.* Let's briefly examine each one.

Purpose   Purpose within the Blanchard and Peale framework specifically refers to a person's overall objective or intention. In the arena of change leadership in school systems, it refers to the path that change leaders and their colleagues want to follow toward the vision they have for their district. Purpose is often captured in a mission statement and expanded in a vision statement. It becomes the central piece of a district's strategic plan.

Pride   This *P* refers to experiencing a sense of satisfaction that you get from you and your colleagues' work, from the goals that you all achieve, and from the successes that you all help to create. It is exhibited as a strong sense of self-confidence. According to the authors, pride should not be allowed to evolve into self-centered arrogance. It must be balanced with a strong dose of authentic humility.

Patience   Impatience emerges when people lack faith in their purpose and lack the self-confidence they need to keep working toward their goals. Patience is energized by the belief that "no matter what happens, things are going to work out all right because we can handle whatever happens" (p. 57). In the absence of patience, change leaders may succumb to the temptations of the quick fix—the short-term gain—and in so doing sabotage the future they envisioned for their school systems.

Persistence   While patience is important for moving toward goals, persistence is more important. Patience by itself is insufficient. According to Blanchard and Peale, patience linked with persistence is a necessary combination for success.

Persistence is not just about staying the course. It is also about keeping your promises and making sure your behavior matches your words. You have to walk the talk, practice what you preach, do what you say, or, as Argyris and Schön (1978) believe, you have to make sure that your theory of action-in-use matches your espoused theory of action.

Persistence also refers to being an ethical person all the time, not just when it suits you or only when it's convenient. According to Blanchard and Peale, it is particularly "important to act ethically when it is inconvenient or unpopular to do so" (p. 65). When you act ethically in the face of criticism or adversity you demonstrate an unequivocal commitment to ethical principles. Demonstrating commitment in this way is extraordinarily important for change leaders.

Perspective Perspective is the skill of knowing what's important and what's not. In the Blanchard and Peale framework, perspective is the central element—the hub around which the other attributes revolve. Change leaders need the capacity to see the big picture, to discern the whole system, to recognize priorities, and to act accordingly and responsibly.

The Freeman and Gilbert Framework

Freeman and Gilbert (1988, pp. 44–48) offer a set of questions that can help change leaders manage their ethical decision-making process. A short summary of each question reframed to focus on school district improvement follows.

Who is affected? When making decisions, especially decisions about the future of your school system, it is critically important to identify internal and external stakeholders who will be affected both positively and negatively by the decisions that are made.

What are the costs and benefits? While identifying who is affected by the changes you and your colleagues are considering for your district is important, you must also specifically identify what the costs and benefits of those changes might be for those stakeholders. An approach to ethical decision making that is often used when assessing costs and benefits is utilitarianism. The operating principle of utilitarianism is, "Which decision will produce the greatest good for the greatest number of people?" Although this approach creates winners and losers in the decision-making process, ethicists accept this approach as valid if the potential benefits of the decision greatly outweigh the costs.

Who has rights? Rights refer to who is entitled to certain benefits or who is entitled to participate in your decision-making process (Drake & Drake, 1988). The earlier discussion about rights applies here.

What are the decision rules? Over the centuries many philosophers and ethicists have proposed decision rules for resolving ethical dilemmas (for examples, see Behrman, 1988). The diversity of opinions on appropriate and effective decision rules, however, has prevented the emergence of a widely agreed-upon set of rules to use.

However, one set of decision rules that is often used by government agencies and public institutions is based on the principles of distributive justice, which was defined earlier in this chapter. Applied in organizations such as school districts, these principles stipulate that: (1) employees who are similar in relevant respects should be treated similarly, and (2) employees who differ in relevant respects should be treated differently in proportion to the differences between them (Hellriegel, Slocum & Woodman, 1989, p. 403).

Despite the lack of agreement on effective rules for making ethical decisions, the point of this element of the Freeman and Gilbert framework is that you must have a set of decision-making rules for resolving ethical dilemmas. Further, these rules must be communicated broadly to everyone in your district, and they should be part of your district's code of ethics.

CODES OF ETHICS

A code of ethics is a useful tool that serves as a guide for making ethical decisions on a daily basis. It should be written, as a way of clarifying a school system's mission, vision, core values, and operating principles, as well as to reinforce standards of professional conduct. As a point of reference, it should be designed to organize relevant documents, services, and other resources related to ethics within the school system.

A code of ethics, which is sometimes called a code of conduct, serves as an important communication tool that "reflects the covenant that an organization has made to uphold its most important values, dealing with such matters as its commitment to employees, its standards for doing business and its relationship with the community" (Driscoll & Hoffman, 2000, p. 77). A code of ethics is also a tool to encourage discussions of ethics and to improve how educators handle ethical dilemmas they encounter in their daily work. A code of ethics is intended to complement professional standards and districtwide policies and rules, not to replace them.

Even the U.S. military has a Code of Conduct, requiring commanders and individual soldiers, sailors, airmen, and marines to lead and act within specific moral and legal boundaries. Without this code, warriors might act like vicious barbarians. Of course, there are always those individuals who ignore the code of conduct and act in immoral and illegal ways. These individuals are almost always caught and punished.

School districts need codes of conduct too. These codes of conduct serve as a moral compass that guides leaders and followers in the right direction. Without these codes of conduct, leaders and followers might act in unethical and hurtful ways. Of course, even with these codes there will be individuals who will behave unethically. They need to be caught and face the consequences of their choices.

Writing a Code of Ethics

Olson (date unknown, page unknown) offers advice on how to construct a code of ethics. Although the following list is certainly not exhaustive, Olson's questions offer guidance on what should be included:

- Who are the persons or groups of persons affected by your organization or by the members of your organization, and how are they prioritized?
- What are your organization's main areas of action?
- What unethical decisions and actions would your organization like to prevent, and how could they be prevented?
- What type of ethical problems are members of your organization most likely to encounter?
- How can conflicting principles be resolved?

The Ethics Resource Center (date unknown) provides substantial practical advice on how to write a code of ethics. They clearly state that how a code of ethics is constructed will affect people's understanding of the code and their ability to comply with it. Since a code of ethics should be used by everyone in a school system—from building maintenance staff all the way up to the superintendent of schools and school board members—the code should be written in plain language, using simple grammar.

The Ethics Resource Center's recommended guidelines for writing a code of ethics are:

- Be clear about the objectives that the code is intended to accomplish.
- Get support and ideas for the code from all levels of the organization.
- Be aware of the latest developments in the laws and regulations that affect your industry.
- Write as simply and clearly as possible; avoid legal jargon and empty generalities.
- Respond to real-life questions and situations.
- Provide resources for further information and guidance.
- In all its forms, make it user-friendly, because ultimately a code fails if it is not used (online, page unknown).

Form and Content of a Code of Ethics

The Ethics Resource Center suggests that an effective code of ethics have the following sections: a memorable title, a leadership letter, a table of contents, an introduction or prologue, a summary of the organization's core values, provisions and other substantive matters, and information and resources. Let's examine each of these subsections in more detail.

Memorable Title   The title of your code of ethics needs to be memorable so that it attracts and holds people's attention. You need to do some good thinking about what the title should be, because the title you choose will either attract people's attention or make the code relatively invisible.

Leadership Letter   This letter is written by the superintendent of schools and perhaps coauthored by the president of the school board. The letter provides readers with an overview of the purpose of the code of ethics and its contents. It should also be written in a way that unequivocally demonstrates commitment at the top of the school system to developing and supporting an ethical organizational culture. The Ethics Resource Center suggests that the letter cover at least the following topics:

- Why a code? Why now?
- What is the ethical/legal context in which the organization operates?
- What are some of the challenges that management, employees, and members face, and how can this code of ethics be a helpful document for people at all levels?
- What are the major trends facing the industry as a whole that will impact and affect the code and its implementation?
- What kind of example might this set for other organizations, if at all? (page unknown)

Table of Contents A table of contents helps readers see the organization of the code of ethics and provides a quick way to locate specific information.

Introduction or Prologue A well-written introduction provides readers with an advanced organizer (Ausubel, 1960)—a psychological tool for helping people prepare for learning. The Ethics Resource Center suggests that the introduction provide such information as why the code is important, how it will be enforced, and what purpose the code is to serve.

Summary of Core Values A school district's core values should first be expressed in its vision statement. Using the school-district transformation methodology introduced in chapter 4, a new vision statement would be developed near the end of the pre-launch preparation phase.

When stating your district's core values in a code of ethics, it is insufficient simply to list them. You must explain the meaning of those values, tell why they are valued, and provide examples of these values in use. This explanation is necessary if you want everyone to know, understand, and live up to the values.

Code Provisions This subsection of your code of ethics is where you dive deeply into the substance of your code. Provisions typically focus on such topics as standards for professional conduct, performing job responsibilities ethically, and avoiding conflicts of interest.

The depth to which you define these provisions depends on the purpose of your code of ethics. The Ethics Resource Center says that the choice of topics to be included in this subsection will be determined by three factors: "(1) the purposes and objectives of the code, (2) the industry in which the organization operates, and (3) the questions or concerns expressed by the intended users" (page unknown).

Information and Resources   This subsection of your code of ethics identifies other resources that your faculty and staff can use to help them make ethical decisions. These resources can be inside your school district (e.g., printed documents that are available on your district's computer system) or on the Internet.

CONCLUSION

As change leaders in school districts consider which changes to make, which directions in which to take their districts, who to involve in setting these directions, and when to initiate changes, their decisions will affect all parts of their school districts. Further, in addition to the challenges associated with large-scale systemwide change, decisions requiring whole-system action almost always have ethical and legal overtones.

Change leaders in all kinds of organizations often rely more on their personal experience, knowledge, skills, and judgment than on theory or philosophy. Some change leaders in the throes of far-reaching change employ the "ready, fire, aim" (Peters & Waterman, 1988) approach to making decisions, and this often results in decisions with serious ethical flaws. Therefore, within the context of districtwide change, it seems reasonable to suggest that before making "big" decisions change leaders should apply principles of ethical decision while considering alternatives for change, predicting their probable consequences, and identifying ethical issues underlying the alternatives.

Greenfield (1991) recognizes that school leaders face unique ethical demands. These unique demands are clearly a part of a school system's important role in American society. School systems, Greenfield says, are moral institutions, designed to promote social norms, and school district leaders are therefore moral agents, who are often confronted with making forced choices when one moral value conflicts with another.

Moral duty is not only manifested in daily ethical dilemmas that leaders face but embedded in organizational polices, procedures, and structures—that is, embedded in an organization's internal social architecture. This creates an organizational culture within which ethical dilemmas can emerge quickly and unexpectedly, affecting people in varying degrees. Starratt (1991) reinforces this observation, arguing that every social arrangement inescapably benefits some people at the expense of others. Because of this characteristic of the internal social architecture of school systems, it is critically important to develop and use a code of ethics for change leadership.

A code of ethics, however, will not eliminate ethical dilemmas. Kidder (1995) believes that an ethical dilemma is a choice not between right and wrong but between two rights. Dilemmas arise when two or more core values (right versus right) conflict. There is no easy way to resolve ethical dilemmas of this kind; however, the ethical frameworks discussed earlier can help.

Moral leadership is a function of moral leaders. Gardner (1995) says that truly magnificent leaders embody the message they advocate—that is, they walk the talk, practice what they preach, and expect everyone else to do likewise. In enacting these expectations, change leaders will need to use power and political skills in ethical ways. To exercise power and political skills in ethical ways, Block (1993) suggests a perspective of "stewardship," which he characterizes as a leader's willingness to accept accountability for results without always trying to impose control over others.

Sergiovanni (1992) is another who believes that effective schools are those with shared moral values and with ethical standards against which educators' behavior is judged. During times of great change in a school system, establishing these shared values and ethical standards, and then enacting and enforcing them, is very important. Doing this, however, will be challenging in those districts where moral and cultural relativism prevails.

Moral leadership and ethical decision making has been influenced over centuries of philosophical discourse. It is clear from a cursory review of the literature that ethical decision making must become a habit. This kind of decision making is not something you do once in a while when circumstances demand it; indeed, it must be your constant companion on your school district's journey toward higher levels of performance.

NOTE

1. A recent example is found in an online news story from Lansing, Michigan (WRAL Radio, 2005), where it was reported that an insurance company had developed an anti-smoking policy and ordered all employees to quit smoking or face punishment. All employees refusing to comply with the policy were fired.

REFERENCES

Ackoff, R. L. (1999). *Re-creating the corporation: A design of organizations for the 21st century*. New York: Oxford University Press.

Adler, M., & Cain, S. (1962). *Ethics: The study of moral values*. Chicago: Encyclopedia Britannica.

All About GOD Ministries, Inc. (2004 November 26). Cultural relativism: Illogical standard. Retrieved on November 26, 2004, from www.cultural-relativism .com.

American Association of School Administrators (date unknown). AASA's Statement of Ethics for School Administrators. Retrieved on December 5, 2004, from www.aasa.org/about/ethics.htm.

Andrews, K. R. (1989 September–October). Ethics in practice. *Harvard Business Review*, 99–104.

Argyris, C., & Schön, D. (1978). *Organizational learning: A theory of action perspective*. Reading, MA: Addison-Wesley.

Ausubel, D. P. (1960). The use of advance organizers in the learning and retention of meaningful verbal material. *Journal of Educational Psychology, 51*, 267–272.

Beckner, W. (2004). *Ethics for educational leaders*. Boston: Pearson Education.

Behrman, J. M. (1988). *Essays on ethics in business and the professions*. Englewood Cliffs, NJ: Prentice Hall.

Beyer, B. M. (2004). Ethical standards in leadership practice. *NCPEA Education Leadership Review, 5*(2), 53–58.

Blanchard, K., & Peale, N. V. (1988). *The power of ethical management*. New York: William Morrow.

Block, P. (1993). *Stewardship: Choosing service over self-interest*. San Francisco: Berrett-Koehler.

Carnegie Mellon University (date unknown). Kant's ethics. Online guide to ethics and moral philosophy. Retrieved on September 18, 2004, from caae .phil.cmu.edu/Cavalier/80130/part1/sect4/Kant.html.

Cummings, T. G., & Worley, C. G. (2005). *Organization development and change* (8th ed.). Cincinnati, OH: Thompson/South-Western.

Drake, B. H., & Drake, E. (1988 Winter). Ethical and legal aspects of managing corporate culture. *California Management Review, 30*(2), 107–123.

Driscoll, D-M, & Hoffman, W. M. (2000). *Ethics matters: How to implement values-driven management.* Waltham, MA: Bentley College Center for Business Ethics.

Durant, W. (1991). *The story of philosophy: From Plato to the American pragmatists* (2nd ed.). New York: Simon & Schuster.

Ethics Resource Center (date unknown). *Ethics toolkit.* Retrieved on October 31, 2004, from www.ethics.org/values_defined.html.

Fouhy, B. (2004, June 28). San Francisco rolls out the red carpet for the Clintons. Retrieved on August 10, 2004, from www.freerepublic.com/focus/f-news/1162094/posts.

Franks, D. (2001). The dangers of moral relativism. Retrieved on July 3, 2004, from dalefranks.com/relativism.asp.

Freeman, R. E., & Gilbert, D. R., Jr. (1988). *Corporate strategy and the search for ethics.* Englewood Cliffs, NJ: Prentice Hall.

Gardner, H. (1995). *Leading minds: An anatomy of leadership.* New York: Basic Books.

Greenfield, W. D., Jr. (1991 April). *Rationale and methods to articulate ethics and administrator training.* Paper presented at the annual meeting of the American Educational Research Association. (ERIC Document Reproduction Service ED332 379).

Hellriegel, D., Slocum, J. W., Jr., & Woodman, R. W. (1989). *Organizational behavior* (5th ed.). St. Paul, MN: West.

Kidder, R. (1995). *How good people make tough choices.* New York: William Morrow.

Kidder, R. M., & Born, P. L. (2002 February). Moral courage in a world of dilemmas. *The School Administrator Web Edition.* Retrieved on November 2, 2004, from www.aasa.org/publications/sa/2002_02/Kidder.htm.

Messick, D. M., & Bazerman, M. H. (1996 Winter). Ethical leadership and the psychology of decision making. *Sloan Management Review, 37*(2), 9–22.

Olson, A. (date unknown). Authoring a code: Observations on process and organization. Retrieved on November 2, 2004, from ethics.iit.edu/codes/Writing_A_Code.html.

Ottensmeyer, E. J., & McCarthy, G. D. (1996). *Ethics in the workplace.* New York: McGraw-Hill.

Paine, L. S. (1997). *Cases in leadership ethics, and organizational integrity: A strategic perspective.* Boston: Irwin McGraw-Hill.

Paine, L. S. (1994 March–April). Managing for organizational integrity. *Harvard Business Review, 72*(2), 106–117.

Peters, T. J., & Waterman, R. H., Jr. (1988). *In search of excellence.* New York: Warner Books.

Pojman, L. P. (2002). *Ethics: Discovering right and wrong* (4th ed.). Belmont, CA: Wadsworth.

Ross, W. D. (1930). *The right and the good.* Oxford: Clarendon.

Schlesinger, A. M. (1998). *The disuniting of America: Reflections on a multicultural society* (revised edition). New York: W. W. Norton.

Sergiovanni, T. J. (1992). *Moral leadership: Getting to the heart of school leadership.* San Francisco: Jossey-Bass.

Shaw, W., & Barry, V. (1989). *Moral issues in business* (4th ed.). Belmont, CA: Wadsworth.

Starratt, R. J. (1991 May). Building an ethical school: A theory for practice in educational leadership. *Educational Administration Quarterly, 27*(2), 185–202.

Stephan, E. G., & Pace, R. W. (2002). *Powerful leadership: How to unleash the potential in others and simplify your own life.* New York: Financial Times/Prentice Hall.

Vazonyi, B. (1998). *America's 30 year war: Who's winning?* Washington, DC: Regnery.

Velasquez, M., Andre, C., Shanks, T., & Meyer, M. J. (2004). Ethical relativism. Retrieved on December 5, 2004, from www.scu.edu/ethics/practicing/decision/ethicalrelativism.html.

WRAL Radio (2005 January 25). Company fires all employees who smoke. Retrieved on January 25, 2005, from www.wral.com.

White, L., & Rhodeback, M. (1992). Ethical dilemmas in organization development: A cross-cultural analysis. *Journal of Business Ethics, 11*, 665.

7

USING POWER AND POLITICAL SKILLS IN ETHICAL WAYS TO MANAGE RESISTANCE TO CHANGE

Experience teaches us that often when change leaders respond to resistance to change they do so in less than effective ways that are negative and unethical. This chapter is offered because managing resistance to change often results in the unethical use of power and political behavior. You will find herein ideas for using power and political skills in ethical ways to manage predictable human resistance to change—especially resistance to transformational change.

SOME SOURCES OF RESISTANCE TO CHANGE

Defending the Dominant Paradigm

The building-level approach to improving schooling has astounding persistence, despite its clear inability to fulfill its promises. In spite of everything we know about how school districts function as systems and about how systems change, many educators and school reform coalitions tightly embrace the school-based reform model as if it were the only solution to an important puzzle—the puzzle of how to improve schooling throughout an entire school system. This tight embrace is an example of how resistant mental models are to change.

One reason why educators may be reluctant to let go of the building-level approach to improving schooling is that there has been so much hope, energy, and money invested in it; people have staked their entire careers and reputations on that approach. When people stake their careers around an idea, they resolutely defend it against innovative ideas that threaten its existence and therefore, by extension, their career prestige and status. In support of this assertion, Starbuck (1996) observes that professionals are among the most resistant to new ideas and to evidence that contradicts their current mental models. Beyer (1981) explains this resistance by noting that professionals must specialize and that their specialized niches can become dead-ends. Because professionals accrue social status and high consulting fees they have much to lose from significant changes in their fields of expertise. When they protect their expertise they become "blind" to opportunities to change their mental models (Armstrong, 1985). Nagatomo and Hull (1993) also comment on this kind of resistance:

> When the rise of a new theory suggests a change of direction in scholarship, history attests to a common pattern of reaction among the established intellectual community. There is often flat dismissal or at best vehement attack in order to kill and bury the theory, especially if it signals an imminent as well as immanent possibility of shaking the secure and comfortable foundation upon which the existing paradigm of thinking rests. (pp. ix–x)

Another possible reason why educators are reluctant to move away from the school-based mental model for improving schooling is that they are unaware of other ways. In the absence of alternatives, people persist with what they know even if what they know isn't working. Persistence in the face of failure is, we have seen, one of the defining characteristics of mental models.

A third reason why educators may be reluctant to follow a different approach to improving schooling is that they don't want to do what it takes to improve an entire school system. It's easier to focus improvement efforts on a single building, one building at a time. Even if their efforts fail to improve schooling throughout a district, the thought of engaging the entire school system in an improvement process is overwhelming for some people, who back away from the challenge and focus on improving the "pieces" of the system.

A fourth reason for avoiding innovative ideas for changing a school system is fear. For example, a superintendent attending a presentation on whole-system change commented privately during lunch about why he was reluctant to initiate systemic change in his district. He said, "I have a family. I need my salary. I can't afford to take the risk of doing what you described." This statement expressed his fear and demonstrated that he was more worried about keeping his job than concerned about doing his job.

All of the above reasons for resisting innovative approaches to improving school districts, as well as others not mentioned, are examples of mental models. Mental models are extraordinarily resistant to change; therefore, it is important to surface, explore, and unlearn them if you want to transform your school system.

Unwillingness to Modify Mental Models

As we have seen, people construct cognitive representations, mental models, of what they know (e.g., Johnson-Laird, 1983). There are two kinds of mental models: personal and organizational.

Personal mental models are internal paradigms that help professionals know and understand their worlds. An example of a personal mental model for teachers is reflected in a teacher's response to the statement, "Effective classroom teaching is. . . ." Every teacher should have a personal mental model that defines effective classroom teaching. Elements of this mental model might include "communication skills," "classroom management," and "learning styles." A teacher's mental model of effective classroom teaching guides her work. When asked to describe her mental model for effective teaching, a teacher may not be able to provide a detailed description of that model, focusing instead on its general features. The more abstract and vague the mental model is, the less likely it is that the teacher's work will be effective.

An organizational mental model is a collective representation of what an organization stands for and how it accomplishes its goals. An organizational mental model is embodied in its internal social "architecture" and in its relationships with the outside world. An example of an organizational mental model for a school district is: "Our school district is a learning community." Elements of this mental model might include "collective decision making" and "teachers as stakeholders." When asked to describe in words their district's mental model, educators may not be able to provide a complete and accurate description of the details of that model, focusing instead on its general features. As with the personal models, the more abstract and vague the mental model is, the less likely it is that the school district will effectively use that mental model.

What we know prevents us from seeing what we don't know. Unlearning a mental model begins when people can no longer rely on their current knowledge, beliefs, or methods. Current knowledge, beliefs, and methods influence our perceptions, and accordingly blind us to other ways of interpreting events around us (Starbuck, 1996). People will not cast aside their current mental models as long as these models seem to produce reasonable results (Kuhn, 1962). As Petroski (1992) put it, people "tend to hold onto their theories until incontrovertible evidence, usually in the form of failures, convinces them to accept new paradigms" (pp. 180–181). However, people are notorious for sticking with their current beliefs and methods despite very poor, even disastrous, results. Even after abject failure, some people will attribute their failures to some external event or person instead of recognizing the inadequacies of their own personal or organizational mental models.

A school system's social "architecture" blocks unlearning. A school system's internal social "architecture" is that collection of policies, procedures, organizational culture, climate, power and political dynamics, communication patterns, and so on that supports life in a school district. Educators in school districts hold certain beliefs, values, and methods that are collectively built into that architecture. These features help create and justify policies, procedures, decisions, and actions. Further, as people interact, all of these beliefs, values, and methods are woven together to create an organizationwide mental model that reflects what people think their school district stands for and how they think it should function as a district. This organizationwide mental model then takes on a degree of rigidity that makes it very difficult for people to think and act in ways that don't fit the model. People, therefore, often find it difficult to accommodate new and innovative ideas, and they find it challenging to change (which is a key reason people resist innovative, "outside the box" ideas).

Political pressure can stimulate unlearning. Unlearning by people in organizations is also influenced by political pressure. People and groups with power and political influence affect what people think and how they act (Hedberg, 1981). The political influence of school administrators is especially potent, because these managers can either block or support changes proposed by their faculty and staff. Having the political support of these managers is absolutely crucial if teachers and support staff are to unlearn old mental models for teaching, learning, and whole-system change.

Helping People Unlearn Mental Models

Tushman, Newman, and Romanelli (1986) discuss how organizations change. They say that organizations go through long periods of convergent, incremental change that are punctuated by brief periods of "frame-breaking change" (also known as "breakthrough" change—see chapter 3), which results in a major change in an organization's mental model. Starbuck (1996), however, believes that frame-breaking change happens differently. He thinks that breakthrough change happens when people and organizations unlearn their old mental models and then undertake rapid, breathtaking change to enact their new mental models.

Starbuck (1996) suggests that any person, event, or information that raises doubt about current beliefs and methods can become a stimulus for unlearning mental models. He says there are several ways to raise doubt and use it to stimulate unlearning. Each one is summarized below.

It Isn't Good Enough   Dissatisfaction is probably the most common reason for doubting something. Dissatisfaction, however, takes a long time to work. When someone fails or something doesn't work right, people often come up with all kinds of reasons to explain the failures. But none of the reasons focus on mental models. These mental models are quite resistant to change, and it takes many painful failures to become dissatisfied with them.

It's Only an Experiment   If people believe that the new method they are trying or the new idea they are considering is just an "experiment," they are more likely to allow themselves to act outside the box of their mental model. When they are free to step outside their "box," they find opportunities to be surprised. Because these new ways of acting and thinking are just "experiments," the risks associated with failure seem substantially reduced; accordingly, people become more willing and able to consider feedback with an open mind and more likely to evaluate results more objectively. Experimentation allows them to modify their mental models to allow new ways of seeing, understanding, and doing.

Surprises Should Be Question Marks   Unexpected events or results, both positive and negative, can stimulate unlearning. If people are in an experimental mode, the results of their experiments can be surprising. Faced with a surprise result or outcome, people can question what happened and why it happened. Answers to these questions can help people unlearn their old mental models as their answers point to new ways of thinking and doing.

All Dissent and Warning Has Some Validity   When bad news is announced or when warnings about impending failure are given, you should consider this information seriously. Of course, not every person who disagrees with a course of action or a decision should be taken seriously. But, as Starbuck suggests, many competent, well-intentioned people see things going wrong and try to alert others. It is usually a mistake to hastily reject bad news or innovative, outside-the-box ideas.

An organization's internal social architecture tends to block messages and warnings from dissenters. Porter and Roberts (1976) have analyzed why people in hierarchies talk upward and listen upward. Their analysis indicates that people send more messages up the hierarchy than they do down, they pay more attention to information they receive from their supervisors than from their subordinates or peers, and try harder to establish positive working relationships with their supervisors than with their subordinates. The messages that do get passed through to superiors tend to play up good news and minimize or hide bad news (Janis, 1972; Nystrom & Starbuck, 1984). This censoring is problematic for managers and organizations, because bad news is much more likely to motivate people to change than good news (Hedberg, 1981), and managers in many cases aren't getting the "bad" news.

Collaborators Who Disagree Are Both Right   If you have two
qualified people, each with different beliefs about the same issue, both
sets of beliefs nearly always are based in truth. This situation can create
a classic right-versus-right ethical dilemma. The challenge in situations
like this is not to prove one set of beliefs wrong but to try to reconcile
the differences to show that there are commonalities and complemen-
tarities. These efforts to illustrate common and complementary features
can help people unlearn their mental models, as they see that their current mental model can expand to accommodate different ways of thinking and doing.

What Does the "Outsider" Think Strange?   Many people cannot
and do not respect the views of outsiders. It is much easier to listen to
and respect the views of people who work in the trenches with us. After
all, they are familiar with our work. Because outsiders supposedly do not
know us or do not understand our "situation," their observations and
suggestions may appear naive, foolish, impractical, or impossible (as in
"Your idea will never work in this district. You are a professor. You don't
understand what it's like to be a practitioner"). Yet outsiders often see
things without the bias of the insiders. Although outsiders may be less
experienced than the battle-scarred insiders, they are also free of the bi-
ases and the dominant organizational mental models that shape behavior in organizations. Thus, the outsider may see opportunities and possibilities that the insiders cannot see and therefore may be able to offer
breakthrough ideas or methodologies.

The Converse of Every Proposition Is Equally Valid   Starbuck
(1996) tells us that dialectic reasoning suggests multidirectional relationships among variables. For example, a simple bidirectional relationship suggests that if X affects Y, then Y affects X. This bidirectional relationship insists that both the original proposition (X affects Y) and its
converse (Y affects X) are equally valid. Philosopher Georg Hegel
(1969) advocated this form of logical, or "dialectical," reasoning; he
called the original proposition the "thesis," its converse the "antithesis,"
and their union the "synthesis." Dialectic reasoning can be applied to almost all situations, and it helps people break free of the assumptions
that underlie their personal and organizational mental models.

What You Know Is Not Optimal   Starbuck (1996) asserts that no
one should be confident that his current mental models are uniquely

optimal. You can count on the fact that if your beliefs and actions seem valid, others are having experiences that are similarly valid but are very different than yours. If your methods for school district improvement seem excellent, other equally excellent methods also exist. The problem is that once you have a well-formed mental model about what works for you, you don't want to abandon it. You shut yourself off from outside-the-box (the box being your or your district's mental model) thinking and doing. Thus, to break free of the constraints of your current mental models, it is helpful to become skeptical about the effectiveness of your personal and organizational mental models.

The above tips proposed by Starbuck are useful for helping educators become skeptical about their personal and organizational mental models. "It isn't good enough" and "It's only an experiment" are tools they can use to help themselves and their districts identify and consider new ways of thinking about and practicing school-district improvement.

Howard Gardner (2004, pp. 15–19) also offers advice on how to change people's minds—their mental models. He identifies seven factors that when combined have a powerful effect on people's mental models:

- *Reason:* People will sometimes change their minds when given the opportunity to apply principles of rational thinking and decision making.
- *Research:* Some people are inclined to change their minds when they have a chance to research a subject in a systematic manner that helps them verify or invalidate positions.
- *Resonance:* This factor is about intuition—about the vibe that people feel when considering a change of mind. If something "feels" right, changing one's mind is easier to do.
- *Representational redescriptions:* Sometimes the way information is presented to someone is incomprehensible to that person. Changing the way the information is presented (e.g., instead of presenting a list of numbers, present the same information in colorful chart) can help people understand it and thereby create the possibility that it will change their minds.
- *Resources and rewards:* Sometimes incentives motivate people to change their minds about a position or a proposed action.

- *Real-world events:* Given a point of view or a belief, people are known to change their minds when confronted with real-world events that challenge their points of view.
- *Resistances:* The first six factors described above can facilitate mind changing, but Gardner argues that it is unrealistic to think that mind changing will occur without resistance. Therefore, these resistances need to be identified and dealt with if you want to help people change their minds.

Finally, Gardner believes that "mind change is most likely to come about when the first six factors operate in consort and the resistances are relatively weak" (2004, p. 18). He also clearly tells readers that changes of mind occur at different levels and to different degrees; therefore, you should not expect quick results.

Your personal and your district's mental models always bias the information you receive about district, cluster, school, team, and individual performance. This means that either knowingly or unknowingly, the information you gather about performance will tend to support your mental models and that contradictory data will tend to be discounted or ignored. However, it is the contradictory data, the critic's voice, the warnings from afar, and the "outsider's" views that may offer you astounding ways to improve the performance of your district. Thus, when you are surprised by what you see or hear about your district, turn the surprises into question marks, respond to disagreements and warnings as if possibly valid, and act as if outsiders' ideas are as valid as yours.

EIGHT PRINCIPLES FOR USING POWER AND POLITICAL SKILLS TO MANAGE RESISTANCE IN ETHICAL WAYS

Principle #1

Create support by increasing opportunities for authentic participation. The field of organization development tells us clearly that people often accept or even welcome change if they are involved in designing the course of that change (e.g., Emery & Trist, 1973; McGregor, 1960;

Weisbord, 1987). Resistance to change increases significantly when people are forced to make changes that others planned for them. As Weisbord (1987) observes, people will fight tenaciously for the right to design their own work, to produce dignity, meaning, and community within their workplaces.

"District engagement conferences," "cluster engagement conferences," and "organization learning networks" (which are part of the Step-Up-to-Excellence methodology described in chapter 4) are designed to involve educators in meaningful and important ways to create and sustain systemwide change. These conferences and networks are for the people actually doing the work of your district, not just the people higher up in the hierarchy of your school system. When used as described, these tools will dramatically change the internal social architecture of your school system and transform that architecture from a bureaucratic, top-down structure to a democratic one that values top-to-bottom participation and collaboration to create and sustain whole-system change in your district.

Principle #2

Paradoxically, people need both structure and freedom. Bion (1961) described the tendency of people to slip out of "work mode" into predictable and nonproductive behavior during times of change. This slippage occurs when autonomy to make decisions is not balanced properly with structure (i.e., specific knowledge about what needs to be done and personal accountability for doing it).

Bion observed the tendency of groups to slip into nonproductive work behavior. Some of these nonproductive behaviors include looking for leaders to "save" them (i.e., dependency behavior), individuals within groups pairing up and distracting the group from the work at hand (pairing behavior), and fighting about who is right on a given issue or disconnecting from the group (fight/flight behavior). To avoid nonproductive behaviors during times of change, you need to use power and political skills in ethical ways to help individuals and teams maintain high productivity by providing them with the right balance of freedom and structure. This is accomplished by stating expectations clearly and explicitly; by giving people the resources they need to succeed (Abelmann, Elmore, Even, Kenyon, & Marshall, 1999); and giving them bounded autonomy to achieve desired results while simultaneously holding them accountable for those results.

Principle #3

People need to hear about change many times before they actually accept it and make personal transitions. Bridges (1991) and Golarz and Golarz (1995) emphasize the number of times people must hear about change before they actually believe it is going to happen. The length of time before the inevitability of change is accepted depends upon a person's position in the organization and on the perceived value of the change for each person, among other factors. You must communicate both the need for change and the direction of change many times before everyone gets the message.

Principle #4

Motivation to move on must be greater than the need to stay in place. Sometimes people and systems don't change quickly. There are different reasons for this "slowness"—such as inadequate resources, weak change leadership, and lack of motivation. Principle #4 is about lack of motivation to change.

Resistance to change is often caused by a lack of motivation to change. There are at least four main reasons explaining a lack of motivation to change. The first reason is that people resist being ordered to change. The second main reason is related to human psychology and the need for stability or equilibrium in our lives. The third reason is fear— fear of the unknown, fear of losing power, fear of losing relationships, and fear of losing one's job. And the fourth reason is related to an organization's reluctance to change. Let's briefly examine each reason.

People resist being changed. Most people are open to change. Clemson and Clemson (1998) comment on this observation: "The idea that human beings naturally resist change is deeply embedded in our thinking about change. Our . . . assumptions and mental models about change all seem to imply that there is something in our nature that leads us to resist change. . . . Humans do not normally resist change, but many people do resist the efforts of other people to *impose* change on them" (p. 1).

When change is imposed without our involvement, we resist. This is a normal and predictable reaction. Therefore, when preparing to engage in whole-system change, you need to apply principles of participative decision making that involve people so they don't feel like changes are being imposed on them.

Our need for equilibrium in our lives creates resistance. The premise that people normally embrace change is not always true. Resistance also comes from our natural tendency as human beings to desire stability in our lives. How would you feel if you had to change your daily routines, patterns of relationships, and work habits frequently, even if you created the changes yourself? Although some people might at first be excited by all these changes, they probably would grow resistant to the rate and quantity of change. They would probably begin to resist frequent changes because of their psychological need for stability in their lives—some level of predictability—some level of personal control.

People resist change because of fear. Personal anxiety about change, even when you seek it, can also cause resistance, or reluctance to move forward. Cummings and Worley (1997) say, "At a personal level, change can arouse considerable anxiety about letting go of the known and moving to an uncertain future. Individuals may be unsure whether their existing skills and contributions will be valued in the future. They may have significant questions about whether they can learn to function effectively and to achieve benefits in the new situation" (p. 156).

Organization structures create resistance. Sometimes organization structures can stimulate individual resistance to change. At the organization level, resistance to change can come from three sources (Tichy, 1993, pp. 114–118). *Technical* resistance comes from the habit of following common procedures and from the fact that a lot of resources were invested in developing those procedures; people don't want to abandon them. *Political* resistance arises when proposed changes threaten powerful stakeholders, such as top executives, senior staff people, or teacher union leaders. *Cultural* resistance happens when a district's existing cultural norms and assumptions powerfully support the status quo and punish people who challenge it.

One of the most powerful ways to respond to all sources of resistance is through involvement. This is why principles of participation and collaboration were built into the Step-Up-to-Excellence methodology presented in chapter 4. Further, this level of involvement is supported in the literature. For example, Cummings and Worley (1997) say, "One of the oldest and most effective strategies for overcoming resistance is to involve organization members directly in planning and implementing change." Vroom and Yetton (1973) describe how participation leads both to designing high-quality changes and to overcoming resistance to implementing them. Cummings and Molloy (1977) observe that because people have strong needs for involvement, the very act of participation can be motivating, thereby leading to greater effort to make the changes work.

Another way to respond to resistance, according to Clemson and Clemson (1998), is to examine existing policies and procedures to determine which ones are obstacles to innovation. These authors state, "System dynamics studies frequently discover that major problems that everyone thought were external are actually the unintended consequences of internal policies" (p. 5).

Principle #5

People differ in their response to and willingness to embrace innovation. Rogers (2003) describes four different roles people play during change. Each role is accompanied by specific behaviors. These behaviors are summarized below.

The Innovators seek out change and innovation. They are generally on the front line of innovation. Professionally, they tend to hang around with other innovators rather than with their non-innovator colleagues and often move on when their current system stays the same too long.

The Early Adapters are willing to embrace and support change if they see some solid, practical advantage to doing so. They are the forecasters of future trends within a system, and they are key people to include early in any change process. They often ask challenging questions with the intention of testing the feasibility of an idea, rather than shooting it down. Once they see the value of a project they can become valuable supporters and allies.

The Middle Adapters go along with change if they see it is inevitable or if they perceive it to be to their advantage. They watch the early adapters and take their cues from them. These people will constitute the majority of your faculty and staff. If efforts are made to involve these people as soon as possible in your district's transformation, they will often become enthusiastic supporters of change.

The Late Adapters change if they have to, but only then. In school systems, they are the faculty members who often complain, "Nobody told me about this!" months after impending changes are announced. They often conspire to resist change by talking against it with colleagues and trying to generate resistance. They are best managed by trying to involve them in the transformation process and by connecting them with the early and middle adapters. It is important not to overreact to the apparent cynicism of the late adapters. Overreaction, especially if negative, can make them martyrs in the eyes of their colleagues.

Principle #6

How people view innovation and change depends upon where they are situated in the system. Oshry (1995) describes how people at four different levels of a system view the same situations in very different ways. The four levels are: the "tops," the "middles," the "bottoms," and "customers." The different perceptions at these levels influence the behavior of people at those levels as they act out their respective roles.

The tops (senior leaders) see themselves as well meaning but poorly understood and inadequately informed members of their organization. When under pressure they tend to stake out claims for "territory." They need to be supported in their efforts to integrate all of the system's pieces into a coherent, interconnected whole. One key ability for the tops to learn (one that is a requirement of the Step-Up-to-Excellence methodology) is the ability to lead through collaboration.

The middles see themselves as literally caught between people at top and those lower down in the hierarchy. When under pressure they tend to become alienated and isolated. They need support from their colleagues, and they need to know that the tops and bottoms are working toward a common purpose as well. A key learning for middles (a central focus of Step-Up-to-Excellence) is how to strengthen their effectiveness by becoming integrators of everything and of everyone above and below them.

The bottoms of your school system (teachers and support staff) perceive themselves as vulnerable to pressures from forces outside of their control. When under stress they tend to coalesce into alliances of opposition and to perceive themselves as victims. During times of change and innovation, they need to be supported by recognizing their individuality and by creating opportunities for them to collaborate regularly. This gives them the opportunity to participate authentically in the transformation of your school district.

The customers (parents of school-aged children) sometimes feel unsupported and ignored. When this happens they feel that they are being treated as problems rather than resources. They may also feel ignored or discounted as stakeholders in your school system's success. During times of change, selected customers need to be involved from the start in fashioning a vision for the future of your district by being given meaningful opportunities to participate actively in your strategic planning process. In the Step-Up-to-Excellence methodology presented in chapter 4, carefully selected customers (and other stakeholders) are involved in your district's transformation journey through a "community engagement conference."

The more bureaucratic, hierarchical, and threatened a school system becomes, the more these four roles are played out in excruciatingly dysfunctional ways. This is especially true during any attempt to transform an entire school system. This dysfunctional behavior must be replaced with increased authentic opportunities for collaboration and participation. Individuals and groups at all four levels must be acknowledged and rewarded for collaboration toward common transformation goals.

Principle #7

Identify and give voice to people who have a passion for and a commitment to a positive future for your district. Senge (1990) says, "There are two fundamental sources of energy that can motivate organizations: fear and aspirations. Fear underlies negative visions. Aspiration drives positive visions. Fear can produce extraordinary results in short periods, but aspiration endures as a continuing source of learning and growth"

(p. 225). Therefore, a cornerstone of support for innovation and change is empowering and enabling people who have the passion, commitment, and willingness to lead—people who drink from the wellspring of hope, positive dreams, and collaboration, not those who partake of the poisoned spring of fear, cynicism, and unilateralism.

Principle #8

Connect with support and leadership wherever you find it. Innovation in a school system is necessarily a shared responsibility among people from inside and outside of a school system. People working inside your school system and those in your community have a stake in the future of your district. When attempting to build support for innovation, start with the stakeholders who are ready to work with you *now,* while at the same time striving to expand ownership of the transformation process to those who are not yet committed to your transformation journey.

People working within your school district also have a vested interest in how the school system is structured and what happens to their jobs. When communicating with these people, you need to stress the advantages of transformation for them and point out how the changes might benefit them.

Your school system's "customers" (parents and taxpayers) all have a vested interest in the quality, efficiency, and effectiveness of your school district. With these stakeholders, you need to stress the value of whole-system transformation as a process for improving the educational services they will receive from your school system.

CONCLUSION

You need to develop and nurture a spirit of shared leadership and mutual responsibility for transformational change by getting as many people as possible from inside and outside the school system to support and participate in the transformation. The spirit of shared leadership and mutual responsibility will have a positive effect on reducing resistance to change; people who help shape change tend to support it, not resist it. Developing political support for your transformation journey and then reducing resistance to it is an absolute prerequisite to launching your transformation process.

REFERENCES

Abelmann, C., Elmore, R., Even, J., Kenyon, S., & Marshall, J. (1999). When accountability knocks, will anyone answer? Retrieved on May 24, 2004, from www.cpre.org/Publications/rr42.pdf.

Armstrong, J. S. (1985). *Long-range forecasting: From crystal ball to computer* (2nd. ed.). New York: Wiley-Interscience.

Beyer, J. M. (1981). Ideologies, values, and decision making in organizations. In P. C. Nystrom & W. H. Starbuck (Eds.), *Handbook of organizational design* (pp.166–202). New York: Oxford University Press.

Bion, A. (1961). *Experiences in groups and other papers*. London: Tavistock.

Bridges, W. (1991). *Managing transitions: Making the most of change*. Reading, MA: Addison-Wesley.

Clemson, B., & Clemson, M. (1998). The deep barriers to change and how to overcome them. Retrieved on March 15, 2004, from www.odu.edu/~bac/p .DeepBarriers.html.

Cummings, T., & Molloy, E. (1977). *Improving productivity and the quality of work life*. New York: Praeger.

Cummings, T. G., & Worley, C. G. (1997). *Organization development & change* (6th ed.). Cincinnati, OH: South-Western College.

Duffy, F. M. (2003, Winter). I think, therefore I am resistant to change. *Journal of Staff Development, 24*(1), 30–36.

Emery F. E., & Trist E. L. (1973). *Towards a social ecology: Contextual appreciation of the future in the present*. London: Plenum.

Gardner, H. (2004). *Changing minds: The art and science of changing our own and other people's minds*. Boston: Harvard Business School Press.

Golarz, R. J., & Golarz, M. J. (1995). *The power of participation: Improving schools in a democratic society*. Champaign, IL: Research.

Hedberg, B. (1981). How organizations learn and unlearn. In P. C. Nystrom & W. H. Starbuck (Eds.), *Handbook of organizational design, Volume 1: Adapting Organizations to their Environments* (pp. 3–27). New York: Oxford University Press.

Hegel, G. (1969). *Science of logic* (A. V. Miller, Trans.). London: Allen and Unwin. (Original published in 1812.)

Janis, I. L. (1982). *Victims of groupthink* (2nd ed.). Boston: Houghton Mifflin.

Janis, I. L. (1972). *Victims of group-think*. Boston: Houghton Mifflin.

Johnson-Laird, P. N. (1983). *Mental models: Towards a cognitive science of language, inference and consciousness*. Cambridge: Cambridge University Press.

Kuhn, T. S. (1962). *The structure of scientific revolutions*. Chicago: University of Chicago Press.

McGregor, D. (1960). *The human side of enterprise*. New York: McGraw-Hill.

Nagatomo, S., & Hull, M. S. (1993). Translator's introduction. In Y. Yasuo, *The body, self-cultivation, and ki-energy* (pp. ix–xxxvi). Albany: State University of New York Press.

Nystrom, P. C., & Starbuck, W. H. (1984). To avoid organizational crises, unlearn. *Organizational Dynamics, 12*(4), 53–65.

Oshry, B. (1995). *Seeing systems: unlocking the mysteries of organizational life*. San Francisco: Berrett-Koehler.

Petroski, H. (1992). *To engineer is human*. New York: Vintage.

Porter, L. W., & Roberts, K. H. (1976). Communication in organizations. In M. D. Dunnette (Ed.), *Handbook of industrial and organizational psychology* (pp. 1553–1589). Chicago: Rand McNally.

Rogers, E. M. (2003). *Diffusion of innovation* (5th ed.). New York: Free Press.

Senge, P. M. (1990). *The fifth discipline: The art and practice of the learning organization*. New York: Doubleday.

Starbuck, W. H. (1996). Unlearning ineffective or obsolete technologies. *International Journal of Technology Management, 1*, 725–737.

Tichy, N. (1993 December 13). Revolutionize your company. *Fortune*, 114–118.

Tushman, M. L., Newman, W. H., & Romanelli, E. (1986). Convergence and upheaval: Managing the unsteady pace of organizational evolution. *California Management Review, 29*(1), 29–44.

Vroom, V., & Yetton, P. (1973). *Leadership and decision making*. Pittsburgh: University of Pittsburgh Press.

Weisbord, M. R. (1987). *Productive workplaces*. San Francisco: Jossey-Bass.

III

THE VOICES OF REASON: ESSAYS ON POWER, POLITICS, AND ETHICS

Part III is a collection of seven essays written by practitioners and systems thinkers. These people are extraordinarily successful and influential people who have contributed much to how we think about leadership for change. Each essay also offers valuable insights to the nature and consequences of using power and political skills to lead change. Some of these insights are unique, and others cut across all seven essays.

Essay 1 is written by Dr. Russell L. Ackoff and Dr. Sheldon Rovin. Dr. Ackoff is one of the world's most famous thinkers and writers focusing on systemic change in organizations. Dr. Rovin is emeritus professor of health care systems at the Wharton School of Business and past director of Health care Executive Management Programs at the Wharton Executive Education and the Leonard Davis Institute of Health Economics.

Ackoff and Rovin's essay, titled "On the Ethical Use of Power and Political Behavior to Lead Systemic Change," begins with the authors' definitions of power, politics, and ethics. They also help us understand what they mean by leadership and the term "system." One of their key conclusions is that the problems confronting education are connected and interacting; therefore, Ackoff and Rovin argue, solutions to these problems must also be connected and interacting. This connectivity is at the heart of systems thinking to improve organizations. Offering some interesting and informative theoretical information about improving systems, the writers conclude with real-life examples of organizations transformed using the theory they espouse.

Richard Farson is famous for his work as a practitioner, writer, and speaker. His most famous book is the *Management of the Absurd*. His essay, "Decisions, Dilemmas, and Dangers," shares some of his insights on the nature of change in school systems. He writes about the decisions, dilemmas, and dangers that change leaders face. In particular, he examines several paradoxes that education leaders frequently encounter—paradoxes that require the ethical use of power and political behavior to cope with them.

Interestingly, Farson argues that big changes are easier to make than small changes and that big changes often produce more effective outcomes. He argues that gradual or incremental change often encounters more resistance than big change and that the outcomes of gradualism are less effective.

Dr. Michael E. Hickey, the longtime superintendent of Howard County Public Schools, Maryland, and now a professor at Towson University in Maryland, presents his views on change leadership in the third essay, "Parents, Power, and the Politics of School Reform." Hickey argues that one of the necessary and important relationships needed to lead whole-system change is the one between educators and parents, one that focuses particularly on organized groups of parents—for example, the Parent Teachers Association.

Although he believes that the relationship between educators and parents is necessary and important, his experience as a successful school superintendent leads him to observe that often these relationships focus more on process than on substance. Given this observation, he believes that a new era of meaningful, substantive collaboration among parents, other community stakeholders, and educators is needed. He suggests that this substantive collaboration will dramatically increase the likelihood of school system improvement and improve educators' ability to sustain those improvements. He concludes by warning against framing the kind of collaboration he advocates as simply another variety of school public relations—which it is not and should not be.

Dr. Libia S. Gil, the former superintendent of the Chula Vista School District, California, and now the Chief Academic Officer for New

American Schools, Inc., shares her personal experience with leading change using power and political skills in the fourth essay, "Disrupting the Status Quo: A Case for Empowerment."

As superintendent of the Chula Vista School District, Gil learned some valuable lessons about using power and political behavior to lead change. Her essay offers valuable insights about what she learned—not only about the change process but about herself as a change leader. Her experience helped her to realize that school-based improvement by itself is an insufficient change strategy and that system-wide change must also happen. Of particular importance for readers is her description of the resistance she encountered from the leaders of the teachers' union. This resistance included not only the predictable gripes and whines but also picketing and rallies, with the ubiquitous media in attendance, and with all of these actions being informed by a publication of the National Education Association—the teachers' union in her district—titled *Controlling the Collective Bargaining Process.*

Art Kleiner, who along with Peter Senge and others coauthored the *Fifth Discipline Fieldbook*, offers a unique perspective on the consequences of misused power and political skills in the fifth essay, titled "Schools and the 'Hidden Curriculum.'" In his essay, Kleiner introduces an interesting consequence of using power and political behavior in school systems—that is, what students learn from observing and experiencing how others use their power and political behavior. He calls this learning the "hidden curriculum" (see Dr. Hickey's essay for another element of the hidden curriculum).

What students learn about using power and political behavior, according to Kleiner, comes from their experience with "core groups." Core groups are those groups found in all organizations that possess significant power to influence people (see Ackoff and Rovin's essay, which makes a distinction between "power-over" and "power-to"). As students observe these core groups in action and as they experience their power, students learn political skills to manipulate the "system" in their schools; Kleiner offers examples of this kind of manipulation. Kleiner concludes that since core groups are so powerful and so common, school districts and schools should take explicit steps to provide all students with structured and formalized access to core groups in their districts.

The sixth essay, "The Power of an Idea: New American Schools and Comprehensive School Reform," was written by Dr. David T. Kearns (chairman emeritus of the New American Schools Corporation; former Senior University Fellow at the Harvard Graduate School of Education; former deputy secretary of the U.S. Department of Education; and former chairman and chief executive officer of Xerox Corporation), John L. Anderson (currently the vice chairman of New American Schools, having served as president for seven years; a former education consultant to corporations, state-based coalitions, and state governments; and a former executive with IBM), and Nelson Smith (vice president for policy and governance at New American Schools; former executive director of the District of Columbia Public Charter School Board; and former Vice President for Education and Workforce Development at the New York City Partnership).

Kearns, Anderson, and Smith offer a valuable history of the development of the New American Schools, Inc. (NAS). This history provides an example of using power and political behavior at the national level to influence change in schools and school districts. An important element of this historical tour is a brief side trip into the history of the governance of education in America.

The writers explain that although NAS originally focused on influencing change inside individual school buildings, it learned that systemwide change is a necessary foundation for effective school-based improvement. This learning has led NAS to move toward scaling up its efforts to improve education from the level of individual school buildings to promoting and supporting systemwide change.

The seventh and final essay is by Dr. William J. A. Marshall, chairman of the Department of Administration and Supervision at Gallaudet University in Washington, D.C. Dr. Marshall's essay is titled "Lessons in Power Sharing and Leadership Shaping within the Forums of Campus Governance: A Concerto in C Minor."

Marshall's essay is written within the context of shared governance in higher education. However, his observations, hypotheses, and conclusions are relevant to change leadership pre-K–12 school systems. By substituting leadership roles commonly found in public school districts for the higher education roles that Marshall writes about, readers will easily see the relevance of the lessons he offers for power sharing and leadership shaping in school systems. For example, Marshall identifies three key players for shared governance in higher education: the board of directors, university administrators, and faculty. In school districts, the key players are similar: the school board, district administrators, and teachers (often represented by a teachers' union).

In addition to an intriguing set of leadership principles and hypotheses about why certain leadership behaviors manifest themselves, Marshall also offers fascinating explanations of how human psychology influences the leadership behaviors he identifies. These psychological interpretations provide readers with useful ways to explain otherwise unexplainable leadership behavior.

ON THE ETHICAL USE OF POWER AND POLITICAL BEHAVIOR TO LEAD SYSTEMIC CHANGE

Russell L. Ackoff and Sheldon Rovin

BASIC CONCEPTS

Ethics

Our concept of ethics derives from the only desire that is universal, applicable to all who have lived, now live, or will live. One cannot want anything without wanting the ability to obtain it—that is, without also wanting the relevant competence. Therefore, "omnicompetence," the ability to obtain anything one needs and legitimately desires, is necessarily a meta-ideal and the ultimate good of mankind. Its attainment would ensure attainment of all other ideals.

By a "legitimate" desire we mean one that when fulfilled does not reduce the competence of anyone else. This does, however, permit one to reduce the ability of another to harm or incapacitate another.

The pursuit of omnicompetence requires knowledge of what the desires are of those affected by one's choices. Such knowledge can be ensured only by having those affected participate directly or indirectly (through representatives they select) in making all decisions that affect them. Children, the mentally impaired, and those not yet born (all of whom may be affected by decisions made now) cannot participate either directly or indirectly in such decision making. This means they must be represented by advocates selected by others who are also affected by these decisions. Therefore, a decision is (ethically) good if it increases the competence of those it affects; it is bad if it decreases their competence. Of course, it may do neither.

Development is the process in which competence is increased. It is not reflected nearly so much in what one has as in what one can do with whatever one has. Robinson Crusoe is a better model of development than J. Pierpont Morgan. Development, then, of oneself or others is good; to obstruct it is bad.

Development is a matter of learning; growth is a matter of earning. Quality of life is a good index of development, whereas standard of living is an index of growth. One can develop without growing and grow without developing. However, the more one has and the more developed one is, the higher the quality of life that can be realized.

It is through education that development can take place. But to the extent that the educational system is doing the wrong things, it retards rather than promotes development. However, education can also be a function of experience, trial and error, and not necessarily be part of a "formal" system. Again, to the extent that experience enables learning, it facilitates development. There is a difference between having ten years of experience and having one year of experience ten times.

Importantly, development applies to systems as well as to individuals, and it is related to the use and misuse of power.

Power

Power is the ability to produce change in persons, objects, events, and the environment. There are two kinds of power that affect people: *power-over* and *power-to*. Power-over is the ability to get what one wants by the exercise of authority, the ability to reward or punish others for compliance or noncompliance with one's will. It is exemplified by "command and control." Power-to is the ability to induce others to do voluntarily what one wants them to do, to influence rather than control them. We have learned through extended experience that the effectiveness of power-over decreases and the effectiveness of power-to increases as the formal and informal educational level of those affected increases.

For example, consider the most educated workforce in our society, university professors. They have been characterized as being as difficult to lead as a bunch of cats. Most professors do not believe that anyone who has authority over them knows as well as they do how to do what they themselves are paid to do; however, the converse is true, say, for primitive peoples. An architect may have to exercise authority and supervise unskilled and inexperienced laborers when constructing a building, but if he tries to tell competent experienced carpenters or electricians how to do their jobs he will be laughed off the building site.

The objective of one who exercises power-over is to compel others to do as well as he/she knows how; the objective of those who exercise power-to is to induce others to do as well as they know how.

Political Behavior

By political behavior we mean the exercise of power. The use of power-over is autocratic, whereas the use of power-to is democratic. A society or organization is democratic to the extent that the following three conditions are satisfied:

1. Everyone affected by a decision can participate directly or indirectly (through representatives they select) in the making of that decision.
2. Everyone in a position of authority over others is subject to the authority wielded collectively by those others. (Authority is circular, not linear. This includes representatives; they can be recalled or not be reelected by those who selected them.)
3. Everyone can do whatever they want to do, providing it affects no one else; if it affects others, their approval is required before action can be taken.

Leadership

Unfortunately, the word "leader" is used loosely to cover anyone in a position of authority. This is not the way we use it here. For us there are important differences between administrators, managers, and leaders.

- Administrators are ones who direct (autocratically) or guide (democratically) others in the pursuit of ends by the use of means of which both are selected by a third party.
- Managers are ones who direct (autocratically) or guide (democratically) others in the pursuit of ends by the use of means of which both they, the managers, select.
- Leaders are ones who direct (autocratically) or guide (democratically) others in the pursuit of ends by the use of means in the selection of both of which they have participated or have approved.

Leadership is a talent; it cannot be taught. It can be enhanced but not taught, because it is basically an art. For example, most people can be taught to draw, but no one can be taught to be an artist. However, the abilities of those who have artistic talents can be increased by better tools, techniques, methods, and practices.

Now, gathering a few of the concepts discussed above, we can say that leadership is good to the extent that it increases the development (the competence) of those (individuals or systems) it affects.

Systems

A system is a whole that is defined by its function in a larger system (or systems) of which it is a part; for example, an automobile is a device for carrying people and their belongings from one place to another, under their own control and in privacy. Every system contains at least two essential parts, without which it cannot perform its defining function; for example, the motor is an essential part of an automobile, whereas the cigarette lighter isn't. The essential parts of a system satisfy three conditions:

1. Everyone can affect the properties or behavior of the system of which it is a part.
2. The way an essential part affects the system of which it is a part depends on the state or activities of at least one other essential part; for example, the effect the motor has on an automobile depends on what the fuel pump and generator do. In other words, no essential part of a system has an independent effect on the whole.

3. Each subsystem of essential parts of a system, like the parts individually, can affect the behavior or properties of the system as a whole, but never independently of other subsystems.

Therefore, the defining property of a system is a product of the interaction of its parts; it is not the sum of the independent actions of its parts. No part of a system taken separately can carry out its defining function; for example, no part of an automobile can move people about. It follows, then, that when a system is taken apart it loses its defining function and its parts lose theirs, as is the case with a disassembled automobile, which cannot move people from one place to another, and of a motor removed from a car—which can move nothing, not even itself.

It also follows that when the performance of one or more parts taken separately is improved, the performance of the whole may not be; in fact, a system may be destroyed by improving the performance of one or more of its parts. For example, reducing inventories of finished goods of a producing company (which may be good for manufacturing) may reduce sales enough to put the company out of business.

Analytic and Synthetic Thinking

Analysis consists of efforts to understand how a system works by understanding what each of its parts taken separately do and aggregating such understanding into an understanding of the whole. Synthetic thinking consists of efforts to identify the role or function of a system in one or more larger systems of which it is a part.

Analysis of a system can reveal how it works, thereby providing knowledge or know how. It enables us to "fix" a system that is not working or working well. Analysis is exemplified by scientific research. But analysis (which involves taking a system apart and therefore causes the system to lose its defining properties) can explain neither why a system works as it does nor its properties or behavior; for example, no amount of analysis of automobiles can explain why the British drive on the other (wrong!) side of the street. Synthetic thinking is required to do this. Synthetic thinking is exemplified by design—the process of creating something new by putting things together.

Knowledge of how a system works enables us to make it work more efficiently—that is, do what it does right. However, it does not enable us to do the right thing—that is, to be effective. Understanding is required to do this. Understanding is achieved by asking and trying to answer questions that start with "why."

System Versus Network

The distinction between a system and a network is critical. A network has no essential parts. If a link in a network is removed, the points it connects can be "connected" by using intermediate points. For example, if direct communication between Philadelphia and New York is terminated, one can communicate from either to Trenton and also from Trenton to the other. On the other hand, if the motor of an automobile is removed it will not run or perform its defining function.

Change

There are two kinds of change of a system: *reformations* and *transformations*. Reformations consist of changes that leave the functions and structure of a system unchanged—that is, changes in the behavior of the system that leave the system intact. Transformations, on the other hand, produce a change in the system's structure or functioning.

When a system is reformed, it remains the same system but behaves differently. When a system is transformed, it is no longer the same system and no longer behaves as it did before transformation. For example, Franklin D. Roosevelt reformed the United States of America. He made sweeping changes within the existing system. Mahatma Gandhi, on the other hand, led the transformation of India from being part of a colonial monarchy to an independent democracy.

PUTTING IT ALL TOGETHER

The problems confronting education are not separable; they are a set of interacting problems, and, therefore, their solutions necessarily interact. The set of interacting problems constitute what we call a "mess."

As a system, the mess cannot be addressed effectively by addressing its component problems separately. The mess must be addressed as a whole.

The current mess in education derives from its efforts to do the wrong things "righter." The "righter" it does the wrong things, the "wronger" it becomes. Here are a few of the more fundamental wrongs imbedded in current educational activities.

The Focus Is on Teaching, Not Learning

Being taught is more likely than not to obstruct learning. Most of the things we use in living we did not learn by having them taught to us but by doing. Moreover, as everyone who has taught knows, it is the teacher who learns most in a classroom. Therefore, it is the students who should be doing the teaching, if there is any, and the so-called teachers should act as facilitators and motivators of self-organized learning activities of students. The right objective of education is not learning prescribed subjects by being taught them but learning how to learn and being motivated to do so continuously throughout one's life. A principal aim of education, therefore, should be to help students know how to think when confronted with unexpected and heretofore unencountered circumstances and events.

Educators Do Not Know What Students Are Going to Need When They Leave School

Most of what people use in their work or lives after schooling they learn after schooling, at work. It is through mentoring, apprenticeships, experience, and trial and error that the most important things are learned. Moreover, most graduates do not practice in the area in which they were educated; movement between subject areas becomes increasingly common and frequent, despite the fact that most information is transmitted from the perspective of one discipline rather than across disciplines. Finally, many, if not most, innovations in professional and academic fields come from ones who have not been educated in those fields. Thinking outside a box is almost impossible for those inside a box.

Today's School Systems Are Modeled After Factories

Incoming students are treated like raw material coming onto a production line that converts them into a finished product. Each step in the process is planned and scheduled, including work breaks and meals. Few concessions are made to the animated state of the material thus processed; it is lined up alphabetically, marched in step, silenced unless spoken to, seated in rows, periodically inspected and examined, and so on. The material worked on varies widely in quality, but the treatment is uniform. Some students learn best by reading, others by listening, others by observation, and others by experience. When it comes to learning processes, however, one size does not in fact fit all.

The system tries to minimize the number of production (learning) processes and kinds of products it turns out, because the greater the variety, the greater the cost. The educational process is considered to be successful if the final product can be sold at a high price. The system even puts brand names and model numbers on its products. (For example, one of the authors was given a brand name and model number by his high school, "Simon Gratz, 15-36," and later by the University of Pennsylvania, "FA 40, B. Arch.")

Educators have reduced education to a large number of discrete and disconnected parts. They have dissected education into schools, curricula, grades, subjects, courses, lectures, lessons, and exercises. A system of quantification and qualification has been developed to reflect this reductionist concept of education: examination grades, course grades and credits, grade point averages, diplomas, and degrees. Formal education is not treated as a whole, systemically, nor is it appropriately conceptualized as part of a process most of which takes place out of school.

Unlike the young of earlier generations, today's students come armed with concerns about the world and concepts of relevance, which are largely ignored in school. They are overinstructed in what they can better do alone (for example, taking things and concepts apart), and they are underinstructed in what is difficult to do alone (for example, putting what they have learned together into an understanding of the world and their role in it). They are given answers to questions they do not ask and denied answers to those they would like to ask but are prohibited from asking. They are taught to provide expected (hence uncreative) answers to questions asked of them. This suppresses the creativity that provides unexpected answers to unexpected questions.

Educators make little or no effort to relate the bits and pieces of information and knowledge they dispense. Subjects are kept apart, despite the fact that experience is not divisible into disciplines, as schools are. Disciplinary adjectives in front of the word "problem" provide no information about the problem; they provide insight to the point of view of the viewer. Courses in school systems seldom refer to interactions between subject matters, despite the fact that no subject matter is independent of all others. The most important aspect of any subject or discipline is how it relates (interacts) with other subjects and disciplines. School systems disintegrate, rather than integrate, learning.

The mechanistic input/output orientation of current education treats students as though they were machines with the combined properties of tape recorders, cameras, and computers. Students are evaluated relative to their ability to reproduce what they have been told or shown. Typically, examinations measure memorization, not thinking or capacity to learn. Such examinations as are commonly used serve the teachers' purposes, not those of the students. If they did, the examinations would be given again a while after they have been marked to see if the student has learned by correcting previously noted errors. To be fair, however, these simple-minded examinations often are not something that teachers want to use. In many localities teachers are forced to give such exams by administrative boards or legislative bodies, including the federal government.

Cheating is a consequence of the nature of examinations, not the nature of students. Otherwise why would teachers also cheat? Teachers cheat where they too are evaluated by performance on examinations—not their own performance but of those they teach. In the real world those who can effectively use whatever resources they can garner to solve problems are valued highly. Out of school, people seldom work in the uncompromising isolation in which examinations in school tend to place students.

SO WHAT?

We have tried to show (much too briefly) that current school systems require transformation into systems that enable people to learn how to learn rapidly and effectively and to be motivated to do so throughout their lives. Such a transformation requires leadership. The leaders required must provide two inputs to the transformation process. The first is articulation of a vision of what the system ought to be. This vision should be the product of a design effort in which all the relevant stakeholders can participate directly or indirectly. The "idealized" design should be prepared on the assumption that the existing system disappeared last night and that the designers must design a system with which they would replace the existing system if they were able to have whatever system they wanted now.

If a school system's stakeholders do not know what they would do if they could do whatever they wanted, how can they know what to do when they are not so unconstrained? And if they do not know what they would do now if they could do whatever they wanted, how can they meaningfully set goals for five and ten years out?

The outcome of such a design is idealized in the sense that the resulting system is ideal seeking, not ideal. It should be subject to continual improvement with further experience and changing environments. The only certainty is that whatever one thinks he or she wants five or ten years from now will not be wanted then.

Such a vision should be inspiring, a work of art. It should facilitate making short-run sacrifices for the sake of longer-run gains. It should provide the holy grail of a crusade to transform the educational practice now in place.

The second input is that once a vision is prepared and accepted by consensus, plans for working toward its realization should be prepared, also participatively. Here too the leader should articulate the strategy and tactics involved in approximating the realization of the vision produced by the idealized design.

The comparison of such a vision with the current state of school systems reveals the gaps that should be reduced or closed if possible. Such a comparison reveals that the principal obstructions between where a school system currently is and where it would ideally like to be lie in the minds of those who control the system. With this realization comes a revision of what those in control consider to be feasible changes. An inspiring vision makes transforming changes possible.

Because the design process requires the suspension of all constraints, it unleashes creativity. Self-imposed constraints are the principal obstruction to creativity. There are no experts on "what ought to be." Therefore, all stakeholders can participate in the design process and do so on an equal footing. Because people own what they create, stakeholders who participate in the design develop a sense of ownership, and this, in turn, removes a principal obstruction to implementation of a new organization design.

SOME EXAMPLES OF TRANSFORMATION

Although most school districts as whole systems have not gone through any such transformation as has been described here, there are examples of individual educational enterprises that have been transformed under the kind of democratic leadership also described here. At the preschool level an example is the Reggio Emilia approach to early-childhood education; initiated by Loris Malaguzzi (Edwards, Gandini, & Forman, 1995); at the primary- and secondary-school levels, Daniel Greenberg (1994) led such a transformation in creating the Sudbury Valley School.

At the university level, the Social Systems Sciences (S3) Program developed in The Wharton School of the University of Pennsylvania (Gharajedaghi & Ackoff, 1985) broke all the major restrictive traditions imposed on higher education. To avoid turning out graduates from a common mold, the S3 Program established no prerequisites for entry, only exit requirements. The variety of incoming students provided opportunities for their learning from each other. To increase this variety further, students designed their own programs without being constrained by required courses. They were told the minimum they were expected to know and understand by the end of their program, but they could make use of anything offered anywhere in or out of the university to acquire this minimum. They had to defend their programs before a faculty committee, which could require some modification of it. Students were free to modify their program at any time, but again with defense.

In the S3 Program, the principal educational instrument was learning and research cells. These were collectives of five to ten students, assisted by one or more faculty members, which attempted to synthesize what the students and faculty members were learning on their own and from each other. In addition, they tried to synthesize what they had learned and attempted to identify and penetrate the unknown.

Students in learning cells were responsible for educating each other. They were evaluated by other cell members not as learners but as teachers. Obviously, they could not teach what they did not know.

Continuous and close interactions between students and faculty, especially through apprenticeship relationships on research projects, removed the need for examinations. Research cells were organized around work done on sponsored projects carried out in the department's research center. Students were expected to work on such projects for at least four semesters. In this way, students worked with faculty members in an apprenticeship relationship on problems confronting paying clients. This also required learning how to work with personnel from sponsoring organizations, particularly managers. The principal objective of each project was education of the sponsoring organization's personnel as well as students and faculty of the program. The objective was not to solve a problem for the organization but to enable the organization to solve the problem for itself.

The income generated by research enabled the program to support itself, to fund fundamental research, and to provide students with financial support. It generated a surplus each year that went into the school's general fund. This financial independence gave the program a freedom of action that it would not otherwise have had.

Faculty members did not receive extra compensation for working on research projects, but their salaries were increased by a third if they worked during the summers and through a one-month vacation with pay. Further, the program was managed by a Committee of the Whole, in which each student and faculty member had one vote. The students were in a majority, but block voting never occurred. Little time was spent in meetings, and administrative tasks were minimized.

The S3 Program was initiated in January 1973 and became the largest doctoral program in the university. The program had about 150 degree candidates from 20 countries. Its graduates had the largest number of job offers of any group of graduates from the school and were offered the highest average initial salaries. Its graduates were employed in a wide variety of institutions in a number of different countries. They are now about equally divided between government agencies, international bodies, corporations, and academic and research institutions.

Because the S3 Program was the most successful in the school but violated most of the rules and regulations governing other programs offered in the college, it posed a continuing threat to the faculty of these other programs. It was a constant reminder that improvements could be made by transformational changes. A new dean, who could not tolerate a variety greater than one, systematically disassembled the program, starting in 1986, when its initiator and leader reached compulsory retirement age. A university, or other system, can tolerate any amount of failure if the rules are followed; where they are not followed, success is the largest threat to its stability and assurance of its ineffectiveness.

CONCLUSION

Faculties of educational institutions of all kinds are among the most highly educated workforces in the United States. Therefore, they cannot be lead effectively by the exercise of authority even under normal conditions, let alone through a transformational change. A transforming change in an educational institution can be brought about only by leaders who influence (power-to) rather than command (power-over). Such a systemic change must be lead ethically, empowering all those affected by it. This in turn requires their participation, along with a leader, in formulating a vision of a desirable transformed system and a strategy for pursuing its realization. Participative democracy is a political requirement for making a transforming systemic change.

REFERENCES

Edwards, C., Gandini, L., & Forman, G. (1995). *The hundred languages of children*. Norwood, NJ: Ablex.

Gharajedaghi, J., & Ackoff, R. L. (1985). Towards systemic education of systems scientists. *Systems Research*, 2(1), 21–27.

Greenberg, D. (1994). *Worlds in creation*. Framingham, MA: Sudbury Valley School Press.

9

DECISIONS, DILEMMAS, AND DANGERS[1]

Richard Farson

The image of the leader as a decision maker has enthralled and seduced leaders and followers alike for at least a century. Autobiographies of the most revered executives, Chrysler's Lee Iacocca and GE's Jack Welch, for example, chronicle their great decisions. Reading them, one cannot help but develop a picture of successful executives as tough loners, people who reach decisions privately, make them quickly, communicate them firmly, and hold to them tenaciously—usually with the odds against them and at considerable risk to their own reputations.

Leadership as it is practiced by most of us is, of course, nothing like that. Interviewing CEOs, one learns that they make only a few really important decisions in a year, and then only after prodigious research and consultation and soul searching. More than half the time they are not even involved with the internal operations of their organizations but are dealing with industrywide issues, community relations, or government business. Most of the time they are simply talking to people—in meetings, interviews, on the telephone, in the hallways. To the extent that they address internal issues, they are putting out fires, holding the organization together. They question, advise, encourage, urge, commiserate, smooth, inspire, and listen. Still, even though it is not what leaders mainly do, the ability to make decisions continues to be equated with strength of leadership.

One of the most common complaints subordinates have of their bosses, therefore, is that they cannot make decisions. It can be a devastating criticism. Most likely, however, the complaint is based on deeper issues. Often the subordinates don't know what is expected of them, don't feel that their talents are being fully utilized, haven't supplied their bosses with necessary information or recommendations, or are unsure of the amount of influence they can have on the management process. But those are more difficult conclusions for the employees to reach, and they would require the complainers to regard themselves as at least partially responsible for whatever difficulties they are experiencing. So they resort to the complaint that the boss can't make decisions.

PROBLEMS VERSUS PREDICAMENTS

Part of the difficulty comes from associating decision making with problem solving. Managers are led to believe that the job of leadership is one of confronting and solving problems. But leaders at the top seldom face problems. As people make their way up the management ladder, they deal less and less with problems and more and more with what the late philosopher Abraham Kaplan called "predicaments"—permanent, inescapable, complicated, paradoxical dilemmas. Problems can be solved, but predicaments can only be coped with.

A problem has specific causes, pathological roots: something went wrong, something that can be identified and fixed. Problems can be analyzed and solved, one by one. Predicaments, on the other hand, have no clear causes or are caused by factors that we could never consider doing away with. They are complex in the extreme.

Crime, for example, is often cited as a problem. But we search in vain for causes, such as poor parenting, pornography, or too much violence on television. When actually studied, none of these quite pan out. Even appalling social conditions of racism and poverty cannot explain crime. Some societies with racism and poverty far worse than ours have virtually no crime. Absurdly, crime is more likely to come from aspects of our society that we would never want to change. It comes more from affluence, freedom, materialism, private property, mobility, urbanization— even from our attempts to control it, such as policing and penology. That is why crime cannot be solved. It is not a problem in the first place. It is a predicament. We cope.

Problems require analytic thinking. Predicaments, however, require interpretive thinking. To deal with predicaments, leaders must be able to put a larger frame around a situation, see it in the sweep of history, understand it in context. They must be especially alert to deeper paradoxical influences and, therefore, the possible unintended consequences of any decisions that flow from that interpretation.

Top leadership is best characterized as the management of predicaments. Practically every issue faced by school administrators has within it a fundamental dilemma, where one side is as desirable or undesirable as the other. The leader has to manage in that context, knowing that for the most part issues cannot be permanently resolved and that choices made are to some degree arbitrary, because the opposite course holds just as much promise.

PARADOXES IN LEADERSHIP

When Albert Camus said "The absurd is the essential concept and the first truth," he was not alone in identifying paradoxes, or seeming absurdities, as basic to all human affairs. Plenty of CEOs will testify to the centrality of that concept. The absurd always plays a part in any decision process. That is why top leaders are not much interested in the idea that they can predict the future or decisively control events. Organization theorist Charles Handy explains that the term "management" did not originally mean control. Top leaders understand that, and they practice management according to its earlier meanings. To them, the term means what it seems to mean when we say, "Oh, we'll manage." They equate management with coping, which is what leaders do most of the time.

I know how rewarding educational leadership can sometimes be, but I still often wonder how administrators get out of bed every morning and go off to such demanding, frustrating, even dangerous work. I so admire them, and I wish that we could eliminate some of the more maddening aspects that are created by the absurd conditions they face. Perhaps an understanding of those paradoxes will free their energies for

more productive efforts. To that end, let's examine some of the paradoxes they face, the predicaments that underlie the choices they must
make, the absurdities that turn what we often wish could be problem
solving into what it usually must be, coping.

*Teaching is a great profession, but it is one of the few dominated by
its clientele.* It matters not how well trained or experienced a K–12
teacher, principal, or superintendent may be, the client has ultimate
power. Educators may know a great deal about the findings of educational research, the particular needs of their students, the new methods
of instruction, but pressures from the community determine the course
of events. And no matter how wise, dedicated, passionate, or highly motivated they may be, they are all subordinate to (at times even tyrannized
by) the people they are trying to serve. The pressures come not so much
from the students, of course, as from their parents, boards of education,
state legislatures, and other forces in the community that shape the discussions and inevitably compromise professional judgment. We pride
ourselves on the ultimate democratic control of our educational system,
and we would not want it otherwise. Yet the defeat of professional interests by lay control is doubtless greater in education than in any other
field.

Even though teachers and administrators fully recognize that these
pressures often represent only fashionable trends that are unsubstanti-
ated in research and practice, they usually have to bow to those trends,
because of the power of governing school boards and state legislatures.
Physicians, lawyers, scientists, and professors (professions that are also
at least partially supported by public funds) would regard such tight
control over their practice as unprofessional, even unethical, and they
have systems in place to resist such pressures. Indeed, it is a principal
function of professional societies to strengthen their members in such
battles. Education is especially vulnerable, because it involves children,
because everyone has had a prolonged experience in the educational
system, and because parents and others understandably believe they
know what is best for children.

Administrators are pressured to forego education in the arts for an
emphasis on math and science even though they and their teachers
know the central importance of arts education. They now must mandate
homework at every grade level, including kindergarten, even though

they know that homework may be completely unrelated to achievement and excessively burdensome, not just to teachers but to students and parents. They must forbid their teachers to touch children, even though they know that a hug from a teacher could be beneficial and represent no danger. The pressures are undeniable and must be balanced against professional experience to render judgments that recognize, and can embrace, both sides of the dilemmas. The administrator copes.

Education is highly valued, carefully planned, theoretically sound, but incredibly ineffective. Even after devoting 13 years in full-time study, the average graduate is barely literate, could pass few of the tests he or she passed in school, and will not have read a book in the past year. Recently the *New York Times* printed a multiple-choice history and general-information test that was given to Ivy League college seniors. The test was comparable to one that might be administered in about the seventh grade. The median percentage score for these seniors was 53.

We should quickly note that some students spurt ahead, some teaching is brilliant, and some schools manage to get most of their graduates into good colleges. But what happens to make a professionally planned curriculum fail to deliver for most students?

Here again we are faced with paradoxes. We take pride that here in the United States education is a requirement and that almost all children go to school. Yet the consequences of compulsory education (an oxymoron?) make teaching exceedingly difficult. Inquiry and learning take second place to the requirements of discipline and control. The demands for learning what social critic Ivan Illich called the "hidden curriculum" take over (sitting still, raising one's hand, taking turns, standing in line, obeying adult authority, not raising questions in certain subject areas, etc.). These behaviors are taught by the form or ritual of education and are unforgettably learned by all. But while they are usually meant to facilitate learning the subject matter, they are often so demanding that they militate against it. Half of new teachers, who had planned to devote their lives to this profession, become so discouraged by the emphasis on classroom control that they drop out after a few years. The administrator copes.

Today, most teachers are not themselves learners. It is well known that the success of the women's movement in opening the job market depleted professions previously regarded as women's territory, such as teaching. We now miss not only some great women teachers but also thousands of bright young women who might have chosen teaching as a career. In years past, these women teachers represented the cream of the crop. They were well educated, thoughtful, and intelligent pursuers of knowledge—studying and reading on their own.

I remember frequent boyhood visits to my two great aunts, who had both retired from teaching in Chicago; one had even been a superintendent. They were among the most intellectually inquisitive people I have ever encountered. One was a poet and essayist, the other an avid naturalist and birdwatcher. Their home library was filled with great literature and with books on science and politics. Their conversation was all about current affairs. Students who were lucky enough to have been assigned to them embarked on a fascinating journey of inquiry, a journey that their teachers were motivated to take with them.

Many teachers today are not even prepared in the subjects they are assigned to teach, let alone ardent inquirers into other fields. It would seem that teachers, of all people, should be interested in the life of the mind. Sad to say, the education schools in most universities now attract the least qualified and least intellectually oriented students of any schools on campus. Modern education is thus devoid of the most important ingredient—teachers who are themselves eager learners. As a consequence, administrators must make decisions in a situation where the recruitment of intellectually inquiring minds is out of the question, for reasons having little or nothing to do with the administration of any specific school district. It's a predicament. The administrator copes.

Standards can be counterproductive to education. America is now on a binge of concern about standards and accountability, much to the consternation of educators who understand that learning does not flower under such conditions. Indeed, the negative consequences of imposing standards go far beyond oppressing the innovative teacher. As we have become painfully aware, it can lead to teaching to the test and to outright cheating, even by teachers and administrators.

The accountability model is championed most forcefully by superintendents who have been recruited from nonacademic fields, such as business and government. They have succeeded in convincing their boards that students, parents, and community should be regarded as "customers" and that education should be treated more like an enterprise that is market driven. While there can be no argument against caring about the views and concerns of those that education serves, the concept of being driven by the demands of the market is a dangerous one. Indeed, what makes education a profession instead of a business is precisely its rejection of that model. Professions must be goal driven. We can perhaps see the danger more clearly if we imagine medicine or law being market driven. Nothing corrupts a profession more rapidly than a decision to travel down that path.

The obsession with standards shared by politicians, legislators, school boards, and some administrators is based on their inability to distinguish between training and education. Training involves learning skills and techniques, and all who receive such training become similar in those respects. But education is completely different. Education involves the continuing effort to marry a student's individual experience with history, ideas, and new frontiers. The result is that each student becomes a unique product. Training makes people alike, while education makes them different from each other. We need both, but it is important that they not be confused. Test standards apply in one case but not the other.

Aren't reading, writing, and arithmetic the kind of skills that can be trained and measured and are therefore suited to standards? Well, yes and no. If we equate reading with the technique of identifying words, then yes, of course. But why hasn't the average high school graduate read a book in the last year? They "learned to read," didn't they? Yes, most did learn the technique. But more importantly, they learned *not* to read. In the process of learning the skill, they lost interest in the pleasures and importance of reading.

The same is true for writing, arithmetic, and most other skill-oriented subjects. The system that emphasizes training and meeting standards produces the opposite of its intent. Teachers want to graduate students who are even more alive to learning than they were when they first entered the system. But for too many students, our skill training in such areas as arithmetic and writing has a chilling effect on their ultimate abilities and interests in those areas. Consequently, graduates on average are exceedingly poor in all skill categories, requiring colleges to offer extensive remedial education in those areas.

I believe the lesson that educators seem to learn from that fact, however, is the wrong one. Because the colleges have to offer remedial education, the assumption is that not enough emphasis was placed earlier on basic skills, on meeting standards, on accountability. Unfortunately, colleges don't encounter high school graduates who are just poor at reading, writing, or arithmetic: they don't *enjoy* reading, writing, or arithmetic. That is a far more serious issue, one for which there is no remedial program. But the administrator's hands may be tied, because the existing curriculum is mandated. The administrator copes.

Success and failure are interdependent and often indistinguishable. Perhaps the most fundamental problem with testing, standards, and accountability is that they are based on a success/failure model of learning. Everywhere, leaders are becoming aware that if they are to foster innovation, learning, and improved performance, they need to treat success and failure similarly. What? Treat them the same? But haven't we always rewarded success and ignored or punished failure? Isn't that the basis for almost all our thinking about management, teaching, parenthood—everything connected with human performance? Unfortunately, yes. But there is no evidence in favor of such a belief, and a lot of evidence to undermine it.

A century ago, Ambrose Bierce defined accountability as "the mother of caution." The fact is that if we want more innovation, which is the great need of our society and of our school systems, we need to encourage more risk taking and more failure, a lot more. That has been the posture of all of the great innovators, from Edison, Kettering, and the Wright Brothers down through the top leaders of Silicon Valley. Instead of rewards and punishment, these leaders become *engaged* with the person, involved in the project, regarding *any* well-intended outcome as just another step on the way to further achievement. Great teachers, and great administrators, do the same, and they always have.

This means, of course, that the emphasis in education on extrinsic rewards is misplaced. All the prizes, gold stars, awards, and bumper stickers need to be replaced with genuine engagement. Even praise, that most cherished technique of so many parents and teachers, is counterproductive. As Alfie Kohn points out in his book *Punished by Rewards*, children who are praised gradually do no more than is necessary to receive the praise. Praise is a "dissatisfier." Like salaries, it fails to motivate, but if it's expected and not given, it demotivates. In an atmosphere where it is the main currency, it must be given. The challenge is to change the currency from praise to listening, involvement, understanding—to engagement. True rewards are intrinsic to the work. Children who discover how to spell a long word, write their names, tell time, or understand Shakespeare do not need to be rewarded. The reward is in the learning itself.

Administrators, then, are again caught in a predicament—knowing the importance of individual development, innovation, and intrinsic rewards but forced to accommodate the overwhelming and misguided demand for evaluating achievement by outdated concepts of success and failure. Once again, professional judgment is balanced against societal pressures. The administrator copes.

Even when teaching is highly competent, students learn more from each other than they do from their teachers. One of the great ironies of education is that some of the best resources for learning cannot be fully exploited. For example, at all levels of education, through graduate school, students are more likely to learn from their peers than from those whose professional roles are to teach them. That happens without any structured effort to exploit that learning resource; designed into the school day, it can be even more potent.

Students are not the only resources. Retirees, parents, representatives from local businesses and institutions, even ex-convicts, former drug addicts, and others not normally considered desirable resources can be helpful. There are many in the community who might be called upon, let alone the army of professionally interested people who may not hold proper credentials for teaching. Many schools capitalize on these resources. They make an effort to involve members of the community, bring in parents, hire teachers' aides, and employ many forms of peer teaching.

Still, there are barriers to the full utilization of such resources. Paradoxically, those whom one would think would appreciate the potential unburdening of the teaching load on others—the teachers themselves—can be the greatest barrier. Through their professional organizations, they have managed to resist that kind of help, because they perceive it as a threat to their standing and employment. In the name of protecting the public through professionalizing education, they have managed to convince legislators and others of the importance of restricting teaching only to those holding credentials. The administrator copes.

Collaboration, not protectionism, is the wave of the future. Professional protectionism was a 20th-century concept. Because it is demonstrably outdated, it is rapidly giving way to the 21st-century concept of collaboration as the central idea promoting innovation, productivity, and social value. Licensing, registration, certification, accreditation, and all other such protective measures are being rethought. In many fields they are less and less necessary. Fewer than 50% of graduating architects plan to seek licenses. Only 26% of physicians now belong to the American Medical Association.

In most fields—business and industry, for example—if you are doing what you were trained to do, you are obsolete. Not in education, however—it's a paradox. Education is extremely vulnerable to pressures for adopting superficial changes, dictated by parents and legislators, and yet, through its protectionist strategies, it has successfully resisted almost all educational reformers armed with new designs, new technologies, and new ideas that represent fundamental changes. The result is that schools today resemble in almost every way the schools of decades ago, if not centuries ago. As one educational reformer remarked, "Trying to change education is like kicking a mountain of mashed potatoes. It's easy enough to make a small dent, but soon the dent disappears, and the mountain remains." The administrator copes.

Teachers do not need protection, they need elevation. Quite apart from the imminent crisis of teacher shortages, there is such a mammoth educational job to do that teachers should not be protected in place but elevated to the status of *metaprofessionals.* If we are to meet the future challenges, ranging from reducing class size to the overwhelming demands of worldwide education (and with global communication technologies, we can now address those issues), we need to have experienced and well-educated teachers orchestrating the work of other teachers. Teachers must become the architects of education, teaching teachers, designing and coordinating the work of others who, with supervision, can be important resources for learning. Home schooling, already proving to be effective, could be made even better with more professional help from metaprofessional teachers. *Collaboration,* not protection, must be the byword.

One might argue that education is so confined because it is publicly supported by taxpayers. But private education suffers from the same ills.

Moreover, schools operated by private-sector corporations greatly resemble those that are operated by the traditional systems. There is no question that lay control of the school system has contributed to the conditions that make decisions so difficult, but it is not the only cause and may not be the main one. The issue may be more systemic, more influenced by education's own culture and traditions, and more determined by the posture of the administrators.

A DIFFERENT POSTURE FOR MAKING DECISIONS

As decision makers, then, what must administrators keep in mind? What should be their posture? First, as questions come up, administrators need to remember that they are probably dealing with predicaments, not problems. Making the distinction is crucial, because treating predicaments as if they are problems can make situations worse—as it has, to return to our earlier example, in the area of crime.

Second, they might adopt a decision strategy along the lines of what has been called "simultaneous management." For the administrator, that means going in two directions at once, often in opposite directions. Because the future is completely unpredictable and technology changes so rapidly, among the better managers today project planning is often accomplished by creating two teams with the same goal but employing different strategies. Although one team is going to "fail," each team informs the other along the way, and the overall effort is enhanced. The essence of paradoxical management is the ability to embrace the coexistence of opposites.

Third, while it is practiced systematically almost nowhere, is difficult to accomplish, and often exposes administrators to complaints and abuse, they are still well advised to seek the involvement in decision making of the people who must carry out the decision. The paradox energizing the method is that the people who present the difficulties are usually in the best position to handle them. Participative management, based on that fact, has been the core philosophy of almost every leadership training program for more than half a century. Following that practice is not as easy as it sounds, but for those with patience and genuine interest, it remains a valuable leadership posture.

Finally, it is useful to remember that big changes are often easier to make than small ones. Gradualism has never worked. Big changes are hard to resist, for the same reason that big budget items get relatively less attention than small ones. It is simply easier to mobilize resistance to small issues, because we are more used to dealing at that level. Moreover, big changes are sometimes welcomed as long overdue.

Students of leadership tend to agree that the qualities associated with effective leaders are vision, courage, optimism, perspective, humility, and compassion. To affect the stubborn issues that now limit progress in education, to risk the attempt to influence those areas, they will be asking the people they work with to undergo wrenching changes. The personal quality administrators may need most, therefore, is courage.

BEYOND COPING

In the late sixties I wrote a widely reprinted article about the future of education, "The Education of Jeremy Farson." My wife was pregnant with Jeremy at the time, and I calculated that he would graduate with the class of 1984. Because that date had a special place in literature, I wrote about the kind of education that Jeremy might have. My article was not in the least Orwellian, however, because at the time many of us social scientists, and educators too, were excited, optimistic, and confident about the possibilities for a positive transformation of education. My article was full of promise for what our new understandings and new technologies could bring—a fulfilling education that would release the potential of each individual student.

I certainly don't need to explain here that Jeremy's education turned out to be nothing like my predictions. Although I was one of many who worked hard at educational reform in the following years, education was not transformed. Indeed, the education Jeremy received was probably not as good as my own had been. Too many untoward developments, some of which I've mentioned above, and others that administrators know better than I, kept setting us back.

Nevertheless, although what I have said so far in this essay may not show it, I remain optimistic about the possibilities for significant progress in education. My hope is not based just on the recent political attention and funding that education has received. It's based more on the remarkable achievements that have been made in other areas in the last decade or so. For example, great steps forward have been made in understanding the various kinds of intelligence, in creating architectural designs to facilitate learning, and perhaps most important, in developing the advanced communication technology that has led to the Internet.

I know, I know—schools have managed to resist being changed by any technology so far. The "magic lantern" slide projectors, film, radio, television, video, and computers all held the promise, but little changed. The Internet, however, is importantly different from all those previous technologies. For the first time, networking is possible, even on a global basis, leading to the potential redesign of our basic social systems. The implications for educational progress are endless, and not the least of them is the prospect of forming school administrators into a powerfully bonded community—collaborating, studying, planning, and making decisions together, in ways never before imagined. The prospects are encouraging indeed.

The phrase "Education remains our best hope for the future" need not be empty.

NOTE

1. An earlier version of this article appeared as Farson, R. (2002 February). Decisions, dilemmas and dangers. *School Administrator,* 59(2), 6–10, 12–13. Used with permission of the author.

⑩

PARENTS, POWER, AND THE POLITICS OF SCHOOL REFORM

Michael E. Hickey

The relationship between parents and the schools that educate their children is as old as public education itself—which is exactly the problem. Throughout the first century of public education in America, parents for the most part revered the schools and those who worked in them. Educators were viewed as highly educated and highly skilled "experts" to whom parents willingly entrusted their children, confident that they would receive "a good education," even though the parents weren't very clear about exactly what that might look like.

The education system in America was perhaps the most renowned element of this infant democracy, committed as it was to educating every child who came through the door, while presumably providing as well the key to a successful life and career. An educated populace was, after all, driving this upstart society to new economic and social heights that were the envy of every other nation in the world.

The pattern of the relationship between parents and their children's schools that became ingrained in the fabric of our culture over more than 100 years was simple and unilateral: parents entrusted their children to the schools, the school people taught them the 3 Rs (and maybe a little more), and when the schools were finished, the child had been educated. While the model was clearly one based on mass-production principles, it was relatively successful for most children in those days. When it wasn't, however, it was clearly the child's fault. The teacher had taught; the child hadn't learned. Therefore the *child* had failed. Accountability rested with the child—and the parents understood that.

Thus the ingrained relationship between schools and their communities was one of compliance. Parents, except on special occasions, went as far as the schoolhouse door but no farther—unless, of course, they were summoned to meet with the principal to be informed of some educational or behavioral misdeed perpetrated by their child, in which case they were temporarily a partner in the educational process, the one expected to discipline their child to whatever degree the misdeed warranted.

Parents also came to school when invited to attend special events, which were largely social or entertainment occasions, such as musical programs or plays, activities that were on the periphery of education at best but that left everyone with a good feeling. Ah, parent involvement at its very best! In short, a parent's role in his or her children's education was whatever the school determined it would be. Compliance and passivity— the hallmarks of "parent involvement" in *public* education.

THE PARADIGM BEGINS TO SHIFT

Two events began the change process for parents' role in their children's education:

- The advent of the Elementary and Secondary Education Act, Title 1, and its requirements for more formal structures and processes for parental involvement, particularly the Parent Advisory Committee (PAC).
- A growing sense of collective political action, growing out of the decade of the 1960s and manifesting itself in school governance circles perhaps first in the Ocean Hill–Brownsville decentralization struggles in New York City and subsequently in other large, urban systems.

As parents and communities began to find a new voice in the schoolhouse, the schools began to take notice and respond, albeit slowly and reluctantly. Ingrained habits, so long a part of school culture, were hard to change. If school leaders were paternalistic, the parent organizations, particularly the PTA, were maternalistic, and "stay-at-home moms"—largely white and middle class—were the staple of their active volunteer corps. The PTA political voice, which throughout its history resoundingly supported schools against all comers, regardless of the issue, now began to assert its independence from the school system in subtle ways, even as it focused its priorities on continued support for public education in general. The PTA expanded its political reach and growing clout beyond local school board election candidates to place its potentially powerful voting block in support of—*or in opposition to*—aspiring candidates for other local and state offices, depending on their stated or perceived positions on key educational issues, particularly funding and governance.

As schools and school systems began to respond to parent demands for a more meaningful role in their children's education, their first efforts were well intended but ineffective and inadequate, hindered as they were by decades of paternalism. Their early *structural* changes included a vast array of advisory committees on an equally vast array of topics, site-based management teams with parent representatives, and, more recently, School Improvement Teams, with parent representation. Each of these efforts, however, had a fatal flaw: the structure and processes had changed, but the participants, or at least their roles, remained the same. The same activist parents stepped forward into the new roles, and the agendas got a little more exciting, but the schools—with the best of intentions but a limited understanding of the big picture—still controlled, or tried to control, the process and the outcomes—albeit, perhaps, unknowingly.

Process became the controlling factor. The elephant labored and delivered a mouse. Schools went through the motions, but the effort yielded little by way of substantive change. Parent representatives' primary concerns all too often were for their own children (perhaps understandably), and the result was a fragmented, at times self-serving, perspective that lost sight of the forest for the sake of a (family) tree. Parent involvement became an agenda of single-issue interests that so dissipated its focus as to render it less than effective.

This lesson was not lost on schools. While "parent involvement" became a mantra that all administrators knew well, in practice it was largely form over substance, and its potential went unrealized. Even today, "community engagement" has become a prominent buzzword in public education, but like most buzzwords its meaning has become so eroded that it is observed more in the breach than in the practice. Ironically, school leaders believe they are doing a great job in engaging both parents and community in the process of education, and indeed, efforts have improved in both frequency and substance in comparison to 10 or 15 years ago. But from the parents' perspective, most of these efforts are superficial, even if well intended, bounded as they are by a culture and practice that seem to permeate every aspect of public education.

A vivid, data-based description of the extent to which a gulf exists between the views of parents and school administrators can be found in the *20th Annual MetLife Survey of the American Teacher, 2003: An Examination of School Leadership* (Harris Interactive, Inc., 2003). Among its findings, the following highlight the disconnect that exists between the leadership of public schools and the members of the public who constitute their primary audience, the parents of the children they serve.

In describing the relationship between parents and their children's principal, 50% said it was "supportive," "mutually respectful," and "friendly." Only 31% described it as "collaborative," while 27% characterized it as "uncomfortable," "distrustful," or said "there is no relationship," and 21% *did not even know the name of their child's principal* (pp. 47–48).

From the principals' perspective, 89% said they "meet frequently" with parents, but ironically, only half (53%) of the parents believed this to be true. Seventy percent of the parents said the principal's communication with them was limited to written materials sent home with their child (a delivery system that works reasonable well at the elementary level, considerably less well at the middle school level, and is essentially nonexistent at the high school level). Eleven percent of parents said their communication with the principal occurred at various community gatherings, while 7% said there was no communication at all (p. 50). Perhaps most telling of the findings was that 93% of the principals indicated they were satisfied with their relationship with parents, while only 64% of the parents indicated their satisfaction with the relationship between them and their children's principal (p. 62).

Thus, if true, these research findings help explain the wide gulf that exists between the public and their schools. Additionally, although the study did not disaggregate data on the basis of demographic factors, other studies have shown it is highly likely that parent dissatisfaction with communication with schools and principals is disproportionately distributed among so-called hard-to-reach populations, such as the poor, minorities, and families whose language is other than English, the very groups whose connection to the schools needs to be strengthened rather than diminished. Clearly, these findings underscore vividly parents' frustration over the disconnection that exists between them and their children's schools—a fact that is neither fully recognized nor appreciated by school leaders.

GROWING FORCES FOR CHANGE

The momentum for serious change in the role and relationship of parents in their children's schools and the education that happens (or doesn't) there is fueled by a growing body of research that largely supports three primary findings identified by (Henderson and Mapp, 2002, pp. 7–8):

1. Parent involvement (no matter what their income or background) in their children's education produces demonstrable improvement in student performance, class and school completion, attendance, social skills and behavior, and graduation rates.
2. Educators at all levels feel strongly that parent involvement (however defined) in their children's education is important and is a strong factor in the student's success.
3. Parents (again, regardless of income, ethnicity/race, or background) feel strongly that participation in their children's education is both a right and an obligation of parenthood and that, given the *appropriate* opportunity, they *do* participate.

Reinforcing and extending these findings, Henderson (2003) presents research that indicates that:

- Families of all backgrounds are involved at home.
- Programs and special efforts to engage families make a difference.
- Higher-performing schools effectively involve families and community. (p. 23)

Given the above issues, it is both ironic and shameful that in spite of strong acceptance of the value and importance of parental involvement, both parents and educators express strong dissatisfaction with the current state of such involvement and that the educational establishment seems to have placed the issue so clearly on the back burner.

The short-sightedness of this view is underscored by a concept called the "91% Factor," a phenomenon articulated by several observers, most recently columnist George Will of the *Washington Post*. Simply stated, the 91% Factor means that if a child enters school as a kindergartener and never misses a day of school until he/she graduates 13 years later, the school system will have had control over that child's learning experiences for 9% of the child's life up to that point in time. The other 91% (hence the 91% Factor) of the child's life is outside the control and the purview of the school system, presumably mostly in the hands of the family and the community (Will, 2002, p. B07).

While some may consider the 91% Factor an "interesting" side issue, its critical importance is underscored when one considers that the child's learning process does not take place solely within the confines of the school. Powerful learning forces also exist in the external environment, forces that the late Lawrence Cremin (1961), former president of Teachers College, Columbia University, dubbed the "other curricula." These other curricula include the *family*, whether traditional or nontraditional, supportive or dysfunctional; the *peer group*, the power of which one has only to observe briefly at the local shopping mall; the *community itself*, and the value it places on its children; the *media*, one of the most powerful and influential sectors, with its potential for teaching both positive and negative "lessons"; and finally, *the business community* and the values it espouses relating to the family roles of its employees and its philosophy about commercial enticement of the increasingly targeted market of children and youth.

These "other curricula" are the stuff of children's learning in the world external to the school, but they do not remain outside the school walls. They enter the classroom each day with the students, and their potential for impact is both positive and negative. Thus it behooves the leaders of the schools to understand that these other curricula do exist, that they do intrude into the learning environment of the school and classroom, and to take steps to buttress their positive impacts while eliminating, reducing, or at least neutralizing their negative impact. Such an effort doesn't stand a chance of success without a serious and ongoing commitment to the engagement of both parents and community as full and equal partners in the educational process. The African proverb "It takes a whole village to raise the child," which was so prominent in educational circles a few years ago but seems to have faded from common parlance today, is nevertheless still true. Parent and community engagement on a coequal basis is without a doubt in education's best interest—and in an educator's self-interest.

NO CHILD LEFT BEHIND: THE POWER BEHIND THE PRINCIPLE

For all the reasons presented up to this point, it would seem that the importance of parent and community engagement in both *principle* and *practice* would be self-evident. But as has also been shown in previous pages, such is not the case, at least not to the extent required or desired by the parents themselves. That situation is changing—dramatically, rapidly, and substantively—largely because of the impact of the federal initiative that was the vehicle for reauthorization of the Elementary and Secondary Education Act (ESEA) in 2002, otherwise known as No Child Left Behind (NCLB).

One of the fundamental underpinnings of NCLB is the requirement for expanded and substantive engagement of parents and community in meaningful partnerships with educators in all aspects of the educational process. More specifically, it requires opportunities for parents to be involved in the *planning* and *evaluation* of their child's educational program, it holds educators accountable for the delivery of results, and it requires the communication of information to parents about not only their child's but also the school's performance, in a clear, jargon-free form and a format that is meaningful to the parents—thus in a language they will clearly understand.

Federal laws and regulations requiring parent involvement and engagement have been on the books for more than 40 years, going at least back to the initial passage of the ESEA, but like so many other federal fiats they have largely been ignored with impunity, or in some cases honored with good intentions but inconsequential impact. The paradigm shift that NCLB represents for the inclusion of parents and community in fundamental, substantive ways in key elements of teaching and learning is best reflected in a selected listing compiled by the National PTA's Office of Governmental Relations in January 2002, at the time of the law's passage. It lists 54 specific provisions of the act that relate to parent and community involvement; many of them represent significant changes in both the substance and process of parent engagement—changes that, even now, two years after the law's enactment, are not yet appearing on the radar screens of school leaders as they struggle prodigiously to implement what they view as the more direct impacts of the law, those pertaining to student performance and accountability and to teacher qualifications.

But these changes have not escaped the notice of many parents and community organizations; indeed, the U.S. Department of Education has given a high profile to the changed role for parents and others in the educational process in its dissemination of resources and information about NCLB. An abundance of resources can be found on the Internet, with virtually any education-related organization's website containing a link to details and resources aimed at parent involvement. Parent organizations, as well as community action groups, are mobilizing rapidly, with new energy and resources, to ensure that parent and community engagement quickly becomes a "front burner" item for their school leaders. Thus, the potential for conflict is framed, and lines are being drawn. The situation was clearly summarized in a recent online article by Ben Feller (2004, p.1), of the Associated Press:

> No education law has made more promises to parents. Its goal of getting all students to grade level in reading and math is itself built on this prom-

ise: Parents will get vase, timely, understandable information about schools, and use it to make the best choices for their kids.

Yet as the second full school year under the law winds down, many in education say the parental provisions are potentially powerful, but too enormous to deal with or too easy to sidestep while other aspects of the law demand attention.

As a result, many parents who stand to gain do not know what they are missing.

As parent advocates and community action organizations begin to mobilize their efforts to ensure that what Feller reports does not prevail, the tone of their publications and resources is decidedly strong and assertive—and in some cases aggressive. One prominent group, Parent Leadership Associates, offers resources including titles such as: *No Child Left Behind: What's In It for Parents; Closing the Achievement Gaps: Collecting and Analyzing Your School's Data; 8 Tips on Using Your School's* [NCLB-required] *Report Card; Six Key Leverage Points for Parents;* and *10 Tips for Parents Who Choose to Stay Put* (as opposed to accepting the NCLB provision allowing them to transfer their child from a failing school to a higher-performing one). Reflecting on these titles will be reminiscent of a handbook for urban guerillas or community organizers in the decade of the 1960s, although, thankfully, absent any tactics of violence or disruption (at least for now).

In a very real sense, lines are being drawn, strategies prepared, and resources deployed to force the paradigm change from the long-standing culture and process of parent/community engagement in the work of the public's schools to the new era of meaningful, substantive collaboration that has been long sought but seldom realized. It's a change that is long overdue, but to realize its full potential it must be embraced by educators without hesitation or condition. It is time educators realized that the only real solution to the challenges of truly leaving no child behind lies outside the reach of educators alone or of parents alone. The "91% Factor" should make the choice abundantly clear: the mission of public education cannot be achieved in the 9% segment of the child's life that "belongs" to the educational system. Educators must seek out effective opportunities to collaborate with the critical elements and groups that constitute the 91% Factor so that the processes of teaching and learning can be extended to enhance the quality of learning that is desired—and deserved—by *every* child. It is in everyone's—the educators, the parents, and particularly the child's—self-interest. But even more, it is in everyone's best interest.

Eva Gold and Elaine Simon (2004, pp. 28, 30) identify in a recent article in *Education Week* the need for a true sense of "public accountability" that results from true collaboration between and among equal partners in the educational enterprise. They suggest four primary strategies which create that public accountability:

1. Creating public conversations
2. Monitoring practices, programs, and policies
3. Increasing participation in the political arena
4. Building joint ownership and a relational culture.

They go on to summarize clearly the potential that is at stake: "Accountability that is public contributes to school improvement by connecting schools and their communities, by broadening the range of actors who take responsibility for school improvement, and by using a public deliberative process to engage many different stakeholders and maintain the pressure for school improvement" (p. 30).

THE POWER OF TRUE ENGAGEMENT

While it is understandable that most educational leaders are currently so preoccupied with the student performance, accountability, and teacher quality aspects of No Child Left Behind that the parent involvement requirements aren't yet on their radar screen, it would be a fatal mistake to continue pursuit of these school improvement and reform initiatives unilaterally. Authentic engagement can and will dramatically increase the likelihood and sustainability of their success. Validated practices are emerging from studies of highly performing schools, and these must become the strategies of authentic engagement. These include:

• Vigorous outreach activities, especially in culturally diverse settings, to involve representatives from all cultural groups in the community.

- Special efforts to involve the parents of economically disadvantaged, racial/ethnic minority, and language minority students, often underrepresented among parents involved in the schools.
- Work with cultural minority parents and community members to help children cope with differences in norms between the home and the school.
- Communicate repeatedly to parents that their involvement can greatly enhance their children's school performance regardless of their own level of education.
- Communicate to parents that children of all ages benefit from parent involvement.
- Offer parents involvement options to choose from, based on their schedule and interest (Shannon & Blysma, 2003, p. 42).

In brief, school leaders must engage with parents and community members in the process of constituency building, the purposes of which are to:

1. Build understanding and a sense of shared interests.
2. Create political will and hold themselves and the institutions in which they are stakeholders accountable.
3. Change the roles, the relationships, and the power dynamics (*Vital Voices*, 2003, p. 2).

To accomplish this calls for a new depth of understanding among the participants, coupled with a pervasive belief that school reform that ensures that no child will ever be left behind truly does require the whole *village*.

But a word of caution is in order. Parent and community *engagement* is much more than "public relations," if only because educators' understanding of that term has become so meaningless. The real issue is this: NCLB has given parents power nearly equal to that of school officials in making educational decisions about children. This is not about the science fair or the school musical. It is about fundamental educational processes—planning and evaluating their children's educational programs. Knowledgeable parents now have the tools to wage "guerilla warfare" against school leaders if the latter are not responsive. That would serve neither side well, and ultimately the children would suffer. Thus, it behooves schools and their leaders to put aside the superficial public relations tools and processes that they thought served them well in the past (but really didn't) and recognize that parents need—and deserve—to be engaged as truly equal partners.

REFERENCES

Academy for Educational Development and Chapin Hall Center for Children (2003). Vital voices: Building constituencies for public school reform. Report to the Ford Foundation. Arlington, VA: Authors.

Cremin, L. A. (1961). *The transformation of the school: Progressivism in American education, 1876–1957.* New York: Vintage Books.

Feller, B. (2004 March 1). No parent left behind? Law's promises are enormous and elusive. New York: Associated Press.

Gold, E., & Simon, E. (2004 January 14). Public accountability. *Education Week, 23*(18).

Henderson, A. T., & Mapp, K. L. (2002). *A new wave of evidence: The impact of school, family, and community connection on student achievement.* Austin, TX: National Center for Family & Community Connections with Schools.

Henderson, A. T. (2003). *No Child Left Behind: What's in it for parents?* Arlington, VA: Parent Leadership Associates.

Harris Interactive, Inc. (2003). *20th Annual MetLife Survey of the American Teacher, 2003: An Examination of School Leadership.* New York: Author.

National PTA, Office of Governmental Relations (2002 January). Select parent involvement provisions in the No Child Left Behind Act, P.L. 107-110, Reauthorization of the Elementary and Secondary Education Act. Washington, DC: Author.

Parent Leadership Associates (2003). *Closing the achievement gaps: Collecting and analyzing your school's data.* Arlington, VA.

Parent Leadership Associates (date unknown). 8 tips on using your school's report card. Retrieved on September 5, 2003, from www.plassociates.org/eight.html.

Parent Leadership Associates (date unknown). 10 tips for parents who choose to stay put. Retrieved on September 5, 2003, from www.plassociates.org/publications.html#ten.

Shannon, G. S., & Blysma, P. (2003 January). *Nine characteristics of high-performing schools*. Olympia, WA: Office of Superintendent of Public Instruction.

Will, G. (2002, January 6). Broken families and school performance. Washington, DC: *The Washington Post*.

11

DISRUPTING THE STATUS QUO: A CASE FOR EMPOWERMENT

Libia S. Gil

Superintendents who aspire to lead their school systems toward desirable futures will inevitably confront countervailing forces bent on stopping the changes. When confronted with these forces, leaders must use power and political skills in ethical ways in response to the oppositional forces. In this essay, I will share with you a personal story of my use of power and political skills to make significant changes in my former school district.

BACKGROUND

In the fall of 1993, I became the new superintendent of the Chula Vista Elementary School District (CVESD), located in South San Diego County, California. It is one of the most diverse and fastest-growing cities in the country, situated on 100 square miles crossing three municipal jurisdictions.

The rich diversity of students (current enrollment now exceeds 26,000 students) is strengthened by the proximity of the Mexican border, and it is no surprise that Spanish is the dominant language, next to English, in the school district.

Although CVESD enjoyed a positive reputation under the leadership of a dedicated board of education that was focused on meeting student needs, the commitment to higher expectations and outcomes for every student demanded changes for the school district. The Chula Vista Elementary School District was positioned to address the challenges needed to serve the unique needs of individual students.

During this period in our district, "restructuring" was the common label used for implementing decentralized services and for creating a system for "SBDM"—"Site Based-Decision Making" or "School Based-Decision Making." A basic premise we acted on was the belief that those who are closest to students, (teachers, parents, and school leaders) are in the best position to make decisions for meeting student needs, if given appropriate data and resources. Understanding the relationship between school flexibility and greater accountability for student learning was another rationale for moving toward school-level autonomy. This was the platform for launching new initiatives to improve student achievement.

A FUNDAMENTAL ISSUE THAT WE NEEDED TO ADDRESS

Preliminary research and experiences from other districts led to our belief that school autonomy is only significant if there is authority for decision making on basic components of school operations, including staffing, curriculum, and budget. Concurrently, we recognized the significant impact and need for central-office reorganization of roles and responsibilities to serve student needs.

The compilation of the results of initial interviews and an external curriculum management audit showed that educators in our schools believed that they worked to serve the central office. The continuous need to respond to multiple central directives reinforced this perception, and few individuals questioned this traditional practice.

I took immediate action to shift expectations from a "control and compliance" central office role to one of "service and support." The message was clearly conveyed by renaming the central office complex and all major divisions as service and support centers. The understanding was established that the central office can only exist to serve the schools and that its services and functions were judged by the value they added to schools. This reversal of roles produced an array of supportive actions to increase flexibility for schools in all areas of responsibilities.

The top concern that quickly surfaced for all schools was their inability to select their own teaching staff, because of the entrenched practice of seniority-driven transfers. In all cases, the most senior teacher could choose a vacant position without the concurrence of the school, thereby eliminating transfer opportunities for less senior teachers. The board of education recognized the need to address this fundamental issue and viewed it as a building block for successful transition to a School Based-Decision Making model for operation.

Our Change Strategy

Our change strategy was simply to propose a new teacher transfer and selection process through the collective bargaining procedure. With great enthusiasm we introduced a proposal to create a teacher-dominated selection committee at each school site, with the principal having a vote. The goal was to establish greater voice and ownership for teachers in selecting appropriate peers, to increase teamwork for student learning. The expectation was that the teachers' union leadership would embrace the opportunity to strengthen teacher involvement in significant decision making.

How Our Change Strategy Was Received

The teachers' union leadership introduced their position by warning me that the elephant in the room (i.e., seniority-based teacher transfers) was untouchable. I was graphically warned that if I pursued the issue it would be perceived as a line drawn in the sand and a declaration of war. I was puzzled by the message, but I felt confident that I could appeal to their mission to empower teachers.

The initial response from the union leadership was a resounding "No!" Their surprising rationale was that "teachers are not capable of evaluating other teachers." In a spontaneous and blunt reply I stated that I disagreed with that statement, given the professionalism and skills of teachers. Also, I found it to be a demeaning view of their membership: "Obviously," I quipped, "I have more confidence in your membership than you do."

In the next round of negotiations, I continued with the proposal for greater flexibility in staffing selection and again the response was "No!" This time their stated opposition included the rationale that I was asking teachers to perform administrative tasks for which they were not compensated.

Several rounds of negotiations evolved into months of effort with no closure. Several compromise proposals were introduced, which included those of the five most senior teachers. Each was rejected.

During one episode with a union representative, I was asked: "Dr. Gil, do you believe in human rights?" I responded, "Yes." The next question was, "Would you advocate for human rights?" I responded, "Of course." That brought an emphatic statement: "Seniority is a basic human right." We concluded the interaction when I stated that we would have to agree to disagree on the definition of human rights.

Our Change Ordeal

I did not predict or anticipate the level of organized antagonism and resistance during the protracted negotiation sessions. There was picketing and rallying, with media present, at every public board meeting. The boardroom would be packed with agitated speakers who spared neither words nor emotions to vilify the board and me. I was stunned to learn that the issue of providing greater flexibility for teacher selection was suddenly transformed to "Autocratic Superintendent Stripping Seniority Rights from Teachers!" The staff and community were bombarded with communications and publications to build momentum for resisting change in the teacher selection process. The organized oppositional strategies ranged from organized hate-mail campaigns to a "vote-of-no-confidence" to a call for a strike against the school district.

A REASSESSMENT OF WHAT HAPPENED

The experience described above was challenging and difficult. In addition to the almost daily public confrontations, I had to confront the school board and myself with tough strategic questions, such as: What is the purpose of what we are attempting, and why are we doing it? Is this the right strategy to address student needs? What are short-term and long-term goals? Are they connected?

The tactical questions were equally difficult: Is this the right time— being a first year superintendent in a new community with little time for relationship building? Is there an appropriate sequence for the change process? What about the level of communications? Should we, like the union, inundate the staff and community to provide "our side of the story"? Should we respond to false propaganda to correct inaccuracies or take the high road, ignoring them and not taking a defensive position?

There were some serious (as well as light) moments when we discussed initiating our own pickets and rallying against the union rigidity. After a series of planning sessions, we created picket signs with messages like "Focus on Students" and large circle posters with a slash against "Business as Usual" plastered them on boardroom walls. We rejected a suggestion for a poster saying "Seniority Is for Aged Beef," since there was no certainty that the intended humor would be so received.

A Self-Assessment of My Leadership Role

During the prolonged months of ongoing negotiation sessions and board discussions, I had to address painful questions: Why was this happening? What did all this mean and did it make a difference for students? How was teacher dissatisfaction impacting teaching and learning, parents, and students? What were the wrongs and rights of this situation? Was it just a power and control issue?

On a personal level, I asked questions such as: Can I be a change agent and an effective leader? Is my professional credibility destroyed? Do I have the necessary skills and leadership attributes? Am I the right person with the right strengths for the job? I worked hard to maintain a disciplined focus and to separate my personal emotions, which encompassed denial, hurt, self-doubt, fear of failure, and anger, from the professional responsibility to represent the superintendent's role and the school district in a positive and dignified manner.

Setting Myself Up as a Target

After the initial vote of no confidence, the district's Administrators Association leadership proposed a public "vote of confidence" to counter

the negativity generated by union. The principals' gesture was reinforcing and boosted my confidence; however, I recognized a potential ethical issue if the principals' public stance in support of me deepened divisions between administrators and teachers. Therefore, given the volatile
and hostile bargaining environment, we worked cautiously to minimize
negative school-level impact and maximize protection of positive relationships between principals and their staff.

Although it would have been a tremendous relief, a strong message
from a unified group, at that moment I realized that an essential part of
my ethical responsibility was to make myself the target of the opposition; there was no need for principals to share that role. In addition, I
internalized the significance of enduring short-term pain for long-term
gains, clearly understanding that eliminating the seniority-driven
teacher selection process was disrupting the status quo and laying the
foundation for ultimately redesigning a new structure and culture to address student learning needs.

Our Change Process

The processes of impasse, mediation, and fact-finding were conducted through formal hearings and highly regulated legal proceedings.
Planning, preparing documents, and testifying were time consuming
and drained attention from the teaching and learning mission of the
school district.

We conducted special meetings regularly with principals to provide
them with a knowledge base and to keep communication current by
sharing school-site strategies emanating both from the union and the administration. Our approach was to maintain professional and positive relationships with all staff members by providing factual information regarding the issues and the collective-bargaining processes. In pursuit of
contingency planning, we invited an external facilitator from the Administrators' Association to conduct strike preparation workshops.

Part of the pressure tactics used by union leadership included the
acceleration of a propaganda war decrying the elimination of hard-
fought seniority rights. State teacher union leaders coalesced with
neighboring district teacher union leaders to participate in protest

marches and rallies around our district's central office facilities. Board members and I continued to receive hate mail and many hang-up phone calls.

A major revelation occurred when a colleague sent me a document titled "Controlling the Collective Bargaining Process by NEA," offering a matrix of NEA strategies targeting specific audiences for specific purposes. For example, strategy number one was "Misinform your membership" to create support. Other strategies included "accuse the superintendent of being autocratic" to destroy "his" credibility. Each subsequent strategy led to another set of recommended threat and opposition tactics, culminating with a call for a strike. I was taken aback with the recognition of how closely the local union was following each tactic, but it was also reassuring and amusing to learn that the leadership attack was not as personal as I had perceived.

At an evening board meeting several months into the "war," the union leadership unfurled a banner so "No Vote of Confidence in the Superintendent" [sic], pasted with writing paper purportedly containing signatures of all the teachers in the district. The next day I was inundated with phone calls by teachers who apologized and admitted that they had signed blank pieces of paper to support the bargaining team at the request of their union representatives. At no time had they been informed that it was going to be used to attack me. These calls followed many notes and communications that rank-and-file teachers were growing weary of the hostile strategies of their leaders and that fewer and fewer participated in rallies and picketing at the board sessions.

The Final Outcome

After many months of anxious anticipation, a fact finders' report dismissed the union's challenges and supported the direction of the district's proposal. The report was duplicated and disseminated widely to all school sites and the media. It clearly defined the issue as flexibility for teacher selection and not elimination of seniority rights. The right of the district to change practices was affirmed when the school board took formal action to implement the original proposal over the objections of the union. The rank-and-file teachers recognized that they had been misled and betrayed by their union leadership. All schools now form a representative committee facilitated by the principal to interview and select only those teachers who meet posted required and desirable attributes for a vacancy at a school site.

CONCLUSION

The short story I have told here was in reality a lengthy and exhausting journey to challenge traditional practices in our school district; however, the end result created a powerful status quo–breaking precedent. Given historical practices in our district to avoid conflict with the teachers' union leadership and given the prior belief that the union controlled the administration, our successful change effort signaled a dramatic shift in power dynamics and leadership commitment to move forward toward a desirable future for the district.

Further, a solid foundation was set, giving school-based leaders responsibility for building a new organization culture that recognized the school district's right to move in a direction that empowers teachers to select their own peers in the effort to meet needs of students at their schools. Ultimately, a unified vision for the future of the district was crafted with the involvement and support of the board of education, the superintendent, administrators, staff, and community members. Today, nine years later, the change processes we instituted back then continues to thrive, and there is no turning back to the past.

REFERENCES

Gil, L., (2001). School success requires front-line support. *TransFormation*, 6.

Gil, L. (2000). Comprehensive school change: Perspective of a superintendent. *Benchmarks*, *1*(3) 1–3.

Gil, L., & Doyle, D. (2002). One school district's efforts to address the changing face of America's school children. *State Education Standard*, 20–24.

Johnston, G., Gross, G., Townsend, R., Lynch, P., Novotney, P., Roberts, B., Garcy, L., & Gil, L. (2002). *Eight at the top*. Lanham, MD: Rowman & Littlefield Education.

Kuo, V. (1996). The Chula Vista Elementary School District Education Service and Support Center: A case study for the district design project. *National Center for Accelerated Schools Project*, 1–17.

Thompson, S. (2001). Chula Vista, CA: A system of student-centered schools. *Strategies*, 8(2), 8–11.

12

SCHOOLS AND THE "HIDDEN CURRICULUM"

Art Kleiner

Public schools, in the United States at least, have a reputation in some circles for being intransigent, monopolistic enterprises with top-heavy governance structures and incompetent leaders. And that's why, it is said, Johnny can't read. But anyone who knows public schools well knows that this picture is dead wrong.

In reality, the culture of most schools is defined by their highly politicized "core group" environments. Core groups are a phenomenon of every company, agency, institution, and enterprise. In each of these organizations, and in school systems as well (since school systems are organizations), there is some core group of key people—the "people who really matter"—who unconsciously set the tone and direction of the system. When decision makers act, for a variety of reasons they push the organization in a variety of directions; in aggregate, however, the net effort of all these decisions is to promote the perceived needs and priorities of its core group. It's sometimes hard to see this, because the nature and makeup of that core group varies from workplace to workplace, and so do the mission statements and other espoused purposes that get voiced to the rest of the world. But everything that the organization might do—meeting customer needs, creating wealth, delivering products or services, fulfilling promises, developing the talents of employees, fostering innovation, establishing a

secure workplace, making a better world, and, oh yes, returning investment to shareholders—comes second (or maybe "eighth"). What comes
first, in every organization, is keeping the core group satisfied.

School districts are complex core-group environments. The typical
public school system core group is divided among politicians (who set
standards from afar), active parents, school board members and local
politicians (each with his or her own ideologies or priorities), energetic
superintendents (who typically stay less than three years), long-standing
tenured faculty (who have good reason to be skeptical of the energetic
superintendent's ideas), local realtors (whose lobbying is a tremendous
force in many suburban districts), and a few critical administrators (like
the person who sets the school bus schedules and therefore ensures that
teenagers will have to disrupt their hormone-induced sleep cycles to get
up at 7:00 AM for school).

No wonder Johnny can't read. The biggest single factor in most school
systems in improving student performance is not class size or school
budget size but the quality of teachers. A high-quality teaching staff (as
measured by credentials and experience) can even overcome such "ingrained" factors as parents who don't speak English or lower economic
status. But when idealistic teachers feel treated as pawns by the feuding
core groups and disregarded as professionals, they leave. The well-
known teacher shortage in the United States would not exist except for
the fact that almost 50% of the teachers hired for public schools leave
their jobs within the first five years—not for lack of salaries but because
attention is not paid to them.

In such an environment, it's reasonable to ask: What are students
learning? Arguably one of the subjects they learn best isn't on the offi-
cial curriculum. They learn first from their teachers, and then from their
own social structure, how to compromise with a core-group environment. They learn that people are basically powerless against authority,
that legitimacy comes from sources over which there is no control, that
conformity is desired, and that core groups are both unforgiving and arbitrary. In many schools, they learn this lesson more harshly than they
would learn it from any other institution, because it represents the overall unintentional impact of an unusually harsh and fragmented core
group. They carry that lesson on into adolescence, when they set up
core-group structures of their own.

I learned this vividly when I met a trio of high school students in a rural town in Ohio. Nathan, Rick, and Nolan told me how they had decided during a sleepover one night to map the social networks of their school. They fit all the members of their senior and junior classes into a circle of cliques: Preps, Freaks, Hicks, and "Gangstas." (In this rural Midwestern school, even the "Gangstas" were white; they were the kids who listened to hip-hop music.) Nathan, Rick, and Nolan called this social milieu "The Great Game of High School"; they said they spent six and a half out of the seven hours of every school day "trying to find a girlfriend or boyfriend, flirting, dispelling rumors about yourself, starting rumors about other people, and all the other things you do to survive." The pressure to fit in, they said was overwhelming: "You don't join a group because of the way you look. You look the way you look because of the group you join. Resistance is not necessarily futile, but there are consequences." For example, those who do not join in will not have a conventional love life.

The trio said that after mapping the school's groups, they had showed some of the classmates the diagram. Everyone had agreed with the basic concept—yes, the student body could be laid out in a giant concentric circles. Everyone agreed that the "Preps" were the unofficial core group of the school, unconsciously favored with money for school clubs, permission for trips, attention from teachers, and (most important) preferential treatment from the guidance counselors who recommended students for college. Or, as Nathan, Rick, and Nolan put it,

> To a degree that very few parents, teachers, or administrators admit, the game determines your success at school. Parents, teachers and administrators may claim that every student has the same opportunities, is accorded the same respect, or plays by the same rules, but we aren't, and don't. Adults may think they're stressing academics, but they're not. Instead, the adults of the system have colluded to set up its hidden rules; and its practices mirror the game that they play out in the "real world."

It was particularly telling that some of the people labeled "Preps," while agreeing that the Preps were dominant, insisted that they didn't belong there. "That's not me," they said. They literally could not see themselves as special to the system. But anyone standing a bit outside the circle could clearly see their influence. This phenomenon is known to social psychologists as the "hidden curriculum." In most institutions (and particularly in school systems), there is an unspoken message that one group of people fits in better than anyone else. Many, many stories of adolescence—from *Cinderella* to S. E. Hinton's *The Outsiders* to *Grease* to the Harry Potter novels—are grounded in the struggle to come to terms with the hidden curriculum. There is certainly an economic component—the Preps are those who dress better, who act in a more genteel way, or who have better family connections. But the primary factor that separates the favored from the unfavored in the hidden curriculum is knowledge—knowledge of the subtle forms of behavior that signal your membership in the elite. That's the kind of knowledge that is so important and so difficult that it takes six or seven hours a day to learn.

The phrase "hidden curriculum" was coined by Benson Snyder, dean for institute relations at the Massachusetts Institute of Technology (MIT) in the early 1960s. Learning that some intelligent students were dropping out, he began to explore why. At this time, MIT deliberately overpressured its students; those who did poorly in midterm physics exams, for instance, lost their scholarships. Students used military metaphors to describe their progress; they talked about having friends "shot down" or "going AWOL." The only people who could stand it were those who learned how to play the game, figuring out which dean wanted to see them wearing a tie, and which class work they could skip with impunity. That was the hidden curriculum at MIT—learning how to manipulate a large, machine-like institution by paying the right kinds of attention to both its culture and its core group.

Snyder also conducted research at Wellesley, the exclusive women's college just south of Boston. Wellesley had been designed as a kind of garden of human development, where students were "cultivated" and from which "bad seeds" were dismissed. While MIT students expected to be ignored in 300–400-person lecture halls, Wellesley students knew faculty members would take a direct, personal interest in them—and they were expected not to chafe at the attention.

In both cases, he concluded, the real purpose of school was to teach students to adapt to an overarching culture. Sociologists have found the same is true of all sorts of schools. For instance, in her ethnographic study of an inner-city high school in Detroit, anthropologist Penelope

Eckert found that the "jocks" (upper-middle-class students) were routinely groomed for success (or as Eckert called it, given a sense of being "in control") while the "burnouts" (working-class students) were subtly guided toward failure (or being "in the wrong"). Jocks took part in school activities, built close relationships with teacher mentors, and jealously guarded personal property (along with information about their family troubles that might be used against them). Burnouts stayed clear of adults (often including their parents), spent their free time outside school, and shared continuously; cigarettes were not just a regular form of currency but a continuously shared resource. Students in both groups learned to orient themselves to core groups by paying close attention to the people "who really mattered," both among the teachers and students. That was, arguably, the single most important thing they learned.

You could make a case that schools shouldn't play favorites this way, that they shouldn't have core groups among either faculty or students. But it's inevitable that they will, for schools are organizations. It may not be human nature to gravitate to core groups, but it's certainly organizational nature.

What we all thus need, in learning-oriented organizations like school systems, is to have better core groups that are diverse enough that every student can see him or herself reflected somewhere in one or more of them, and thus see examples of how powerful he or she could become. This might mean, for instance, inviting local business owners (including owners of working-class businesses like garages and beauty shops) to teach—not so that others will follow their example but so that students will have examples to emulate.

That would require a willingness to teach students how to build equity. That, in turn, might require schools to operate under open-book or transparency principles. "In every school I've worked in," says public-school educator and writer James Evers, "the budget is secret. The teachers will negotiate what they think is a piece of a limited pie. They hear 'there isn't funds for that.' About priorities that seem to be important. And then they find out that there are funds for the superintendent to go off on a trip or for a few favored teachers or administrators to take a workshop. There's no clear, open sense of which parts of the budget are discretionary and which are open to discussion."

Imagine if instead of teaching students to blindly accept the harshness of core groups, schools became places where students learned how to build a competent, fulfilling life in a world of core groups. There is so much to learn: how to respect authority without demeaning oneself before it; how to approach a core group to learn about it without challenging it unproductively; how to conduct oneself; how to cultivate all kinds of equity, from relationships to reputation to financial, with the purpose of creating a better life within or without organizations; how to look at systems not as a victim but as a learner; and, in the end, how to develop, design, and situate one's own core groups and one's own organizations.

Most schools pick out a few students (usually Preps) with "leadership potential" and let them learn about core-group dynamics through osmosis and a bit of practice. But schools could teach all their students how to start organizations and lead them. They can give all students the chance to create a core-group experience for themselves. Some might not use that chance, but everyone would have it. That in itself—the knowledge that an educator, once upon a time, trusted every person to create core groups for themselves—could make all the difference.

⓲

THE POWER OF AN IDEA: NEW AMERICAN SCHOOLS AND COMPREHENSIVE SCHOOL REFORM

David T. Kearns, John L. Anderson, and Nelson Smith

The creation of New American Schools (NAS) required the drive of CEOs and political leaders, the strategic skills of MBAs, the wisdom of educators, and the financial resources of public and private sectors.[1] We believe that it provides a good illustration of the ethical uses of various kinds of power. Yet we know that political and financial leverage would mean little without the power of the central idea NAS embodies— comprehensive school reform. We also know that NAS would never have appeared or persevered for more than a decade if its leaders and staff were not possessed of a passion to do the right thing for kids.

That passion has supported the notion that schools themselves, being closest to kids, should be the unit of reform, that classroom learning should be the paramount objective, and that systems should be organized around the goal of increasing student achievement.

Over time, this idea has taken many shapes. Today it can be seen in NAS's work with small high schools, charter schools, and in the redesign of district and state operations. But coherence has always been a watchword. To understand why, we first provide some background about the external factors that led to the organization's founding.

BACKGROUND

Following his campaign commitment to be "the education president," George H. W. Bush convened a summit in 1989 of all the nation's governors—the first since the Depression—to galvanize action around standards-based education reform. The Charlottesville, Virginia, meeting was an extraordinary convocation; the governors' work, supported by political, business, and education leaders, produced a national commitment to fulfillment of key education goals by the year 2000.

The summit capped years of activism ignited in large part by *A Nation at Risk*, the 1983 report of the National Commission on Excellence in Education, which galvanized reform by bluntly warning of a "rising tide of mediocrity" that would be viewed as an act of war if imposed by a hostile power. A raft of reports and conferences followed, perhaps most prominently the 1986 manifesto of the National Governors Association, *Time for Results*. This report set out the basic bargain that has come to characterize many subsequent initiatives: autonomy for accountability. "We'll regulate less," the governors said, "if schools and districts will produce better results."

The business community had also become increasingly active. Many mainline business leadership organizations adopted an education initiative, but the most far-reaching came from the Business Roundtable (BRT), composed of CEOs of major corporations. The BRT's program was grounded in nine "Essential Components of a Successful Education System" (The Business Roundtable, 1995), beginning with high academic standards and including performance assessment, accountability, school-level autonomy, and such supports as technology, parent involvement, and teacher professional development. The Essential Components provided a framework for significant state-by-state lobbying and technical assistance work, applying not only business leverage but also business skills to the equation.

Yet there was little actual change where it mattered most—within schools. You could walk into a classroom in 1991 and it would look pretty much the same as one would have in 1891. In a nation that prided itself on innovation, most of our schools were still trying to deliver knowledge via a teacher standing in front of a blackboard. We had made enormous strides in granting poor, minority, and disabled kids the right to an education—but the educations they were getting needed an overhaul.

But what could, or should, the federal government do about it? Having committed the nation to ambitious new goals, the administration faced constraints of law and tradition. Moreover, the nature of federal lawmaking had sometimes confused matters at the school level.

A TRADITION OF RESTRAINT

Education is not mentioned in the Constitution and thus is formally reserved to state jurisdiction. Indeed, the broad movement toward public education was inspired by the example of Massachusetts in the 1840s, when Horace Mann led its newly created State Board of Education in championing support for "common schools." Yet since the Founding, education has been a concern of national leaders, as reflected in comments by Thomas Jefferson: "A system of general education, which shall reach every description of our citizens from the richest to the poorest, as it was the earliest, so will it be the latest of all the public concerns in which I shall permit myself to take an interest."[2]

Never directly dictating programs or curricula, federal officials often sought to exercise their leverage either directly (as in the Northwest Ordinance of 1787, which made admission as a state contingent on setting aside land for schools) or by providing resources (from the Morrill Acts, which supported land-grant colleges after the Civil War, to the Smith-Hughes Act of 1917, which directly funded vocational education programs after 25% of World War I inductees were found to be illiterate, to $75 million in teacher salaries provided by the Reconstruction Finance Corporation during the Great Depression) (Cross, 2003).

The post-Sputnik National Defense Education Act of 1958 marked a clear turn toward "federalization" of education policy. The landmark Elementary and Secondary Education Act (ESEA) of 1965 cemented that stance by directing millions to school districts serving disadvantaged children. ESEA and the Supreme Court's 1954 decision in *Brown v. Board of Education* were the twin pillars of a federal commitment to education as an issue of equal opportunity, a commitment addressed later with respect to children of immigrants and those with disabilities.

With *A Nation at Risk*, the job of federal policy became far more complex. As difficult as it was to pry open the schoolhouse door, it was quite a different matter to ensure that every child who enters has access to a rich and well-rounded education that meets world-class standards of excellence. Meeting this challenge meant changing what happens *inside* classrooms, an area that for two centuries had been off limits to federal intervention.

Again, this was not completely terra incognita. Federal monies had been spent trying to improve reading and math skills or providing new kinds of professional development for teachers. The Elementary and Secondary Education Act had spawned numerous small program innovations that were later funded for national dissemination through the National Diffusion Network. The Department of Education sponsored networks of regional education laboratories whose mission was to spread innovation throughout their regions. Yet all these efforts worked within the existing paradigm of schooling and with traditional dissemination models, and by 1991 there was a clear sense that they were not doing much to hasten the torpid pace of reform.

In fact, the way programs were organized and funded may have helped impede progress by scattering focus at the local level. Federal grants were often aimed at a single subject, or a few grades, or a troubled student group. Administrators would chase after the funding and install the programs without reference to any broader vision of what should happen in each school. Far too often, commendable programs that had worked well in initial pilots would end up out of alignment with school and district goals and standards.

A DIFFERENT APPROACH

In 1991, a way was found to focus reform where it mattered most—in the classroom—and to do it through a national but not necessarily "federal" solution. Continuing its response to the challenge laid down in Charlottesville, the business community crafted a private-sector initiative christened the New American Schools Development Corporation (now known simply as New American Schools). Its formation was an-

nounced by President Bush along with other education initiatives in a
Rose Garden ceremony in April 1991.

One coauthor of this essay, David Kearns, left the chairmanship of
Xerox Corporation to begin serving as deputy secretary of education on
May 31, 1991, and there he took on the assignment of getting the corporation off the ground. He enlisted another coauthor, John Anderson,
a former IBM executive who had led the Business Roundtable's education initiative.

Apart from its sheer audacity—the idea of creating a private corporation for broad public purposes—what made NAS different was its
reengineering of the relationship between national policy and local
schools. While the Department of Education had funded a good deal of
research, mostly through university-based "centers," it could not
demonstrate much of a track record in turning the research into bottom-
line results. NAS sought to give innovation a foothold by moving the
"R&D" process out of government and into the private sector.

More important, housing the initiative in the private sector meant
freeing it from the whims of congressional appropriators and enabling it
to concentrate on whole-school designs. Its premise was that schools
themselves must change, from what the late RAND researcher Thomas
Glennan called "homes for a collection of activities and programs of var-
ied origins" to coherent, evidence-driven enterprises whose mission is to
advance student learning. This approach would break a mold cemented
by decades of federal, state, and philanthropic programs that attacked
discrete problems in teaching or administration or student motivation.
Instead, NAS sought "designs" that would shape and power every aspect
of a school, from its calendar to its classroom layouts.

In a sense, asking the private sector to lead this effort wasn't a radically
new idea. After all, it was commonplace for the federal government to
enlist universities, think tanks, and contractors to address specific issues
in education. However, asking the business community to fund and supervise the process—and to address the K–12 grade span—was new.
There was resistance. The head of the Council of Chief State School Officers said that he could not "comprehend why the Secretary and the
President consider a private research effort to be the centerpiece for system change for the most important function of government—education"

(William T. Grant Foundation & Institute for Educational Leadership, 1991).

Yet it also attracted strong support, and not for the usual political reasons. To be sure, there was a "sweetener" in the original legislative proposal, providing $1 million for implementation of a new school design in each congressional district; that was denied, however, and it turned out to be unneeded. And yes, the president pushed hard, as did his education secretary. What got the proposal adopted was the power of the idea itself.

Among policy makers, especially governors, the idea evoked strong support. Many had not only participated in the Charlottesville summit but had served on innumerable boards, conferences, seminars, town meetings—and had fought hard for reforms that proved agonizingly slow in showing results. If the challenge was not to give out more money but to produce real innovation, they were game.

The idea of seeing *schools themselves*, rather than districts or states, as the object of reform appealed mightily to educators. A decade earlier, pathbreaking research on "effective schools" had been developed by Harvard professor Ron Edmonds and others. The findings had been simple but powerful: that high-performing schools serving disadvantaged students shared such characteristics as clear missions, high expectations, strong instructional leadership, and frequent monitoring of student progress (Association for Effective Schools, 1996). These characteristics could be nurtured by district leadership but too often were pulled apart by conflicting funding streams and shifting priorities as administrators came and went. The school community itself—principal, teachers, parents, and students— had to own a school's mission and believe in its instructional strategies, or external support was moot. In effect, a school-based approach provided educators with a powerful vehicle for putting these findings to work.

Yet the idea of school-based reform would likely have waited another decade or two had it not been for the commitment of the business community. In retrospect, it is easy to see why the notion had such a galvanizing effect on corporate leadership. American industry had massively reengineered production processes in the prior decade, using information technology to put more decisions at the point of customer contact while monitoring companywide progress through intensive evaluation of feedback against goals. Why should schooling keep delivering a one-size-fits-all product?

At the same time, business had learned important lessons about how culture interacts with productivity; Xerox Corporation's Palo Alto Research Center (PARC), for example, had done landmark work on the notion of "learning communities," in which information about performance was avidly digested and interpreted across organizational boundaries to produce a next generation of innovation. It was high irony that our schools could hardly be called "learning communities" in this respect, emphasizing inputs over outcomes, running on agrarian calendars, and compensating tenure rather than accomplishment.

THE LAUNCH

Although congressional funding for "break the mold" schools was denied, the private corporation proceeded full steam ahead. The work would require an enormous amount of capital, and the prospect of obtaining it from private sources was daunting, but the response was immediate and impressive. $40 million was raised from corporations to finance the initial phase of the work. Then, at a White House ceremony in November 1993, Ambassador Walter Annenberg announced a contribution of $50 million, which gave the initiative immediate credibility among his colleagues and made it possible to gather another $40 million from various business and philanthropic sources over the next three years, for a total of $130 million.

This was certainly an exercise of "power," in that it steered needed funds to a worthwhile project, but it was more an example of leadership, particularly on Annenberg's part. Having created a vast communications empire, he was acutely aware of shortcomings in our educational system and had already contributed millions to less comprehensive causes. His determination to seek substantial improvements resulted, later in the decade, in the Annenberg Challenge, a $500 million contribution to school reform at 18 sites nationwide.

With initial funding assured, NAS moved onto the takeoff ramp. In order to invite the widest possible group of innovators, the corporation conducted a massive national request-for-proposals (RFP) process, grounded in three objectives, that proposed designs must

- Address the whole school
- Embody a belief in high standards for all children
- Cost no more to operate than existing schools.

The RFP brought in more than 700 proposals, the pool of applicants including researchers from RAND and other "think tanks," education and business leaders, universities, nonprofits, and individual citizens. NAS selected an initial set of 11 "design teams"[3] that had presented compelling visions of what schooling might look like in the next century. A substantial portion of the first year's funding was spent on direct technical assistance to the design teams, refining the initial proposals and using a variety of business tools and strategic planning support to help ready the designs for national dissemination.

As much imagination, creativity, and money as this phase required, the pace accelerated dramatically as the New American Schools designs went to market. We knew that getting designs widely adopted wouldn't resemble the cinematic "field of dreams"—if you build it they will come—but that it would require a careful process of identifying partner districts with the interest and capacity to implement designs, and then of building trust between the teams and the districts.

During this early period, the NAS board felt it important to have a clear mission and to clarify the organizational beliefs and principles that would distinguish this effort from less successful predecessors. We settled on six core values.

- *Quality:* NAS is committed to the ongoing identification and use of what works within the field of education. NAS and our affiliated partners set high expectations, and we are able to achieve demonstrated results.
- *Scale:* NAS is not content to let good ideas sit on the shelf or to operate in only a limited number of schools; rather, we are committed to the development and use of innovative dissemination strategies that enable what works to reach every child possible.

- *Sustainability:* NAS works to fulfill our long-term commitments with partner schools, districts, and states through fee-based partnerships. Ultimately, sustainability represents our commitment to build capacity for continuous improvement and learning at every level of the education system.
- *Choice:* NAS works to ensure that educators, parents, and community leaders have a diverse portfolio of high-quality options to choose from as they develop strategies for school improvement, including charter and contract schools.
- *Entrepreneurship:* NAS helps school, community, and business leaders apply creative and innovative approaches to helping all students reach high levels of learning. NAS seeks out and applies groundbreaking solutions to the challenge of improving schools.
- *Equity:* NAS and its partners are determined to ensure that No Child Left Behind (NCLB) is more than a slogan in America's schools and school districts. NAS and its partners believe that all children can learn to significantly higher levels, and our work seeks to close pervasive achievement gaps nationwide.

An example of how we enacted these values is found in how we defined "scale" to mean a willingness to implement NAS designs in at least 30% of its school sites. There was little science in this number, but we felt that it would create enough ripples to have some effect on the way the system itself did business.

Since there was not only a promise of innovation but substantial funding and technical assistance as part of the NAS package as well, communities around the country were eager to get on the bandwagon. We did a road tour that visited a dozen cities, showing off the new designs, talking about the need for a new generation of American schools, listening to what local folks were saying about the strengths and challenges of their existing systems. In some places we were greeted like Lindbergh returning from Paris. In one memorable case, Memphis hired the Coliseum, invited all the city's teachers, recruited school bands, and threw open the doors to parents and community leaders. It was quite an extravaganza.

By mid-1995, we had settled on the initial group of partner districts and created memoranda of understanding spelling out the mutual

responsibilities of the corporation, the teams, and the districts. Then
began the hard part. As the idea of "break the mold schools" had moved
from federal policy to corporate blueprint, to district alliances, it had remained somewhat hypothetical. The most difficult choices, and the
most important course corrections, happened—inevitably—once the
designs went to work in real schools, in real towns and cities.

To help communities organize their decision processes, we created a
set of analytical tools showing how a redesigned district would look and
providing indicators of readiness in key areas: leadership, resource allocation, professional development, evaluation, and community engagement (including educators and parents).[4] Yet much still depended on
the skill and tenacity of local leaders.

Some early adoptions proved enormously complex, in no small part
because the models themselves were evolving rapidly. At the Foshay
Learning Center, a 3,500-student K–12 school in South Central Los Angeles, getting Los Angeles Learning Centers[5] in place required extensive permissions from the district as well as support from the design
team, for such things as creating a K–12 school, developing health clin-
ics, and doing extensive work to empower parents. It took some time for
the model to mesh with the college-readiness theme that was central to
the school's mission under principal Howard Lappin. (Happily, the long-
term results have been stunningly positive. Foshay was to be named one
of the 100 best schools in the country by *Newsweek* magazine in 2000.)

There were many cases in which the good ideas met resistance, but it
would be misleading to say that resistance was overcome by the application of "power"—unless power is equated with endurance and a taste
for problem solving. The most predictable confrontations involved districts that had invested money and pride in their own professional development processes—which had to give way to external teams, with nationally sanctioned expertise and resources to back it up.

These early experiences produced two important alterations in strategy. First, we quickly realized that the most promising school design
could be defeated by a district administration that was either resistant to
innovation or too wedded to its own ways. Hence, we began creating a
range of systemic supports for reform. NAS commissioned scholars like
Allen Odden of the University of Wisconsin and Karen Hawley Miles
(now of Education Research Strategies) to produce road maps for dis-

tricts that needed to decentralize operations in order to give schools more leverage to implement the designs. We worked with pioneering superintendents like Gerry House in Memphis and Diana Lam in San Antonio, who were willing to innovate. The corporation added staff to work directly with districts on reallocation of their resources (financial and otherwise) so they would be better aligned with standards and reform goals. And we started working directly with states on how they, in turn, might support reforming districts.

It should be emphasized that NAS undertook these new levels of work because they were necessary to facilitate progress at the school level. We were not much interested in abstract arguments about system change or policy debates driven by any set of ideological commitments. We wanted schools to have the freedom and resources necessary to improve student performance, and that required untangling knots created at district and state levels.

Second, we came to understand that the change process was costly and that even if we could defray some of the costs of adoption, districts and schools would need a reliable way of financing the first critical years of implementation. This was not part of the original R&D conception of the enterprise. We had hoped that the designs would not only be appealing and effective but also relatively self-contained in terms of cost. Yet districts discovered that they had to hire substitutes for teachers being trained and acquire technology to support new software. The economics proved unsustainable, and our strategy required some rethinking.

So in 1997 we went to Congress and sought approval of the first Comprehensive School Reform Demonstration Program, which would provide direct grants for tasks related to adoption of schoolwide designs—and not only those sponsored by NAS. We were somewhat surprised by the relative ease with which the proposal was passed (becoming part of the FY 1998 Appropriations Act), since even at this point there was no broad or organized constituency for the idea of schoolwide designs. Again, it was less a question of exerting muscle and more a question of leadership—in this case coming principally from Wisconsin Democrat David Obey and Illinois Republican John Porter, who both made the CSRD cause their own and did a good job of bringing along their House colleagues in a bipartisan effort.

The program proved popular and made possible a rapid expansion in the number of schools adopting comprehensive designs. Over 1,800 schools received grants as part of the original 1998 cohort, and an additional 1,000 schools were funded through the FY 2000 funding increase. The Department of Education estimates that an additional 3,000 new schools are now receiving funds from the 2001 and 2002 allocations (U.S. Department of Education, 2004). More than $300 million was provided in the FY 2004 federal appropriation for comprehensive school reform.

Along the way, we continued to work with Congress as it refined the program—for example, providing information about the essential components of truly "comprehensive" programs during the FY 2000 funding cycle. We saw this as a way of making sure that even these public funds would promote the NAS core values of quality and sustainability.

It's gratifying that these efforts have been rewarded by good results. In 2002, RAND issued a study that summarized its key findings on over a decade of studies on the effectiveness of comprehensive school reform. With respect to student achievement in 163 schools, RAND found that 81 schools (50%) had made gains relative to district averages in mathematics and 76 schools (47%) made gains relative to district averages in reading (Berends, Bodilly, & Kirby, 2002).

It can also be argued that the Comprehensive School Reform movement inspired subsequent reforms ranging from the spread of charter schools to increased emphasis on "schoolwide" programs in Title I funding. These are both "systemic" initiatives that build in different ways on a belief that inspired the founding of NAS, that schools themselves must be the central unit of reform—driven by results and shaped by missions embraced by the entire school community.

LEAVING THE NEST

One marker of NAS's success is that most of the design teams themselves have become self-sustaining, nationally competitive enterprises, each active in multiple markets. This happy situation has required a shift in our relationship not unlike that faced by families when children reach adulthood. Our original model promised soup-to-nuts support, including infusions of capital, technical assistance, and advocacy. As the designs teams grew and prospered—and in many cases became important national voices on their own—NAS had to consider how and where it could continue adding value. This led to another set of fundamental shifts in the nature of our organization.

We took a new approach to supporting the financial needs of design teams. In place of sustaining grants, we moved toward an investment model, in which a reconfigured New American Schools Investment Fund would allow design teams and other education service providers to borrow on favorable terms—but with the expectation that operations would be self-sustaining. The fund's investments are subject to extensive due diligence on the borrower's financial position and program strengths, a provision that acts as a lever for maintaining quality in the market and protecting the fund's investments.

NAS has also helped create the Education Quality Institute, a new nonprofit dedicated to impartial evaluation of education programs (now housed at the American Institutes for Research). EQI can provide a clear, third-party picture of whether educational innovations actually work. This is critical information not only for our own investments and those of other funding sources but also for educators in search of programs backed by "scientifically based research," as required under the No Child Left Behind Act.

LOOKING FOR LEVERAGE

In recent years, NAS has faced a particularly fascinating dilemma: how to apply the power of our *experience* in new ways. There are organizations that advocate for school reform, others that provide seed capital for education ventures, and still others that provide various sorts of technical assistance to educators and policy makers. There is no other organization that does all of these things, and none that has come through the long process of helping implement redesign strategies in districts across the country. One recurring theme that emerged from this work is the extent to which transforming districts need direct, hands-on help in evaluating their current state and reengineering their processes to align resources with intended results.

Again, we reviewed the evidence. We knew that although change had to happen in schools and classrooms, they often existed within sluggish and outdated systems. We saw that there was a critical need for services, but we knew that direct delivery was highly capital-intensive. We saw that in a time of economic recession, state and district budgets were squeezed to the bone, making vast new investments unlikely.

NAS leadership decided that the organization should concentrate on engagements that could have critical impact beyond the immediate client. We turned the corner from being a grant-dependent organization to become what is now a nonprofit consulting firm, often working with and through organizations that have networks of schools (including traditional districts but also including charter authorizers).

Our relationship to the philanthropic sector has changed dramatically. In its early days, NAS collected contributions from foundations and then managed their distribution to design teams. Today, the foundations themselves are often our direct clients, with NAS using its field experience to bridge the gap between the intentions of funding sources and school-level implementation. For example, NAS is drawing on a decade of working with design-team scale-ups to help the Kellogg Foundation launch its Middle Start program, a middle school initiative originally operating only in one Michigan region, as a viable national program. In San Diego, NAS is acting both as fiscal agent and technical-assistance manager for a major grant from the Bill and Melinda Gates Foundation, creating 14 new small high schools from three traditional schools.

THE POWER OF LEARNING

Over time, NAS's business model and conceptual frame have shifted dramatically. Each phase of our development has been informed by a particular notion of how the power of capital, talent, and ideas might be deployed toward the goal of improving education. In the early stages, a centralized pool of funds and a core of technical expertise helped launch break-the-mold school designs. In the middle years, we put advocacy to use in finding sources of support that could sustain the designs, and we began working on "upstream" problems that kept states and school districts from realizing the potential of school-level innovations. Today, we deploy the skills of experienced educators and business consultants to identify and resolve "knots" in the design and administration of entire systems.

None of these shifts was undertaken casually. Rather, all arose from reflection upon the results of our work and the changing nature of the markets in which we operate. NAS is a learning organization that from the outset has enlisted the power of candid third-party evaluation—and then shared the results not only among ourselves but with the public at large. For a decade our principal evaluation partner was the RAND Corporation, and its publications on New American Schools tell the story of an organization that has learned from its missteps and adopted new strategies as circumstances demanded.

That is probably the most important lesson of all. Whatever millions NAS has been able to amass, however many CEOs and university presidents have sat on our board, we would never be able to use "power" in an absolute sense to change a huge and constantly evolving education marketplace. We have been able, however, to apply human, intellectual, financial, and political capital in different mixtures at different times, pay close attention to results, and, as Lincoln said, "think anew" when the time came.

NOTES

The authors dedicate this essay to the memory of Tom Glennan, whose insight, honesty, and diligence helped improve the education of America's children.

1. At the time this essay was written, New American Schools had not yet merged with the American Institutes for Research (AIR). That merger occurred on January 1, 2005.

2. Letter to Joseph C. Cabell, 1818.

3. Four of the original eleven eventually ceased operations or left the NAS portfolio.

4. These tools are included in the publication *Exploring Comprehensive School Reform* (New American Schools, Alexandria, VA, 2001).

5. Now called "urban learning centers."

REFERENCES

Association for Effective Schools. (1996). Correlates of effective schools. Retrieved on September 1, 2003, from www.mes.org/correlates.html.

Berends, M., Bodilly, S., & Kirby, S. (2002). *Facing the challenge of whole school reform: New American Schools after a decade.* Santa Monica, CA: RAND Corporation, p. 130.

The Business Roundtable. (1995). *Continuing the commitment: Essential components of a successful education system.* Washington DC: Author.

Cross, C. T. (2003). *Political education: National policy comes of age.* New York: Teachers College Press.

U.S. Department of Education. (2004 April 27). *Comprehensive school reform program.* Retrieved on April 27, 2004, from www.ed.gov/programs/compreform/ 2pager.html.

William T. Grant Foundation & Institute for Educational Leadership. (1991). *Voices from the field: 30 expert opinions on America 2000, the Bush Administration strategy to "reinvent" America's schools.* Washington, DC: Authors, pp. 39–40.

LESSONS IN POWER SHARING AND LEADERSHIP SHAPING WITHIN THE FORUMS OF CAMPUS GOVERNANCE: A CONCERTO IN C MINOR

William J. A. Marshall

To become great, it is first necessary to become little.

—St. Augustine, Bishop of Hippo, fifth century

INTRODUCTION

Effective dialogue gets a boost when all players agree on the relative accuracy of the facts at hand. Jason Miner—Democratic National Committee research director—put it succinctly: "Things don't stick unless there is a nugget of truth in [them] . . . [because truth] feeds into and helps build narrative . . . otherwise you're just throwing stuff against the wall, and that doesn't work" (Harris, 2004, A-21). Given this astute commentary, governance mavens may wonder whether the relative accuracy of the dialogues that happen or don't happen within their own campuses is like "throwing stuff against the wall," or more like "things . . . [that] feed into and help build [constructive] narrative."

While people may quibble about the accuracy of facts and about whether truth may be relative or absolute, there nevertheless exists an indispensable commodity vital to the effectiveness of all dialogue exchanges, namely, the perception of fairness. Fairness—a conspicuous feature of ethical leadership—is both an act of the intellect, ensuring accuracy of the facts perceived, and an act of the will, requiring the subordination of subjective preferences in the interests of objectivity.

This writer—not unlike Richard Dana's 1840 sea epic *Two Years Before the Mast*—has served 12 years before the mast of his own campus governance system as the elected chair of the University Faculty and University Faculty Senate. Such an extended tour of duty on the high seas of governance has driven home the premium roles that fairness, authenticity, and good will play when brokering agreements among the various players composing the faculty, administration, and board of trustees governance systems on campus. Forthrightly, the writer has made every effort to incorporate the principle feature of fairness in the design of this essay by balancing the perspectives of the issues being raised among all the players in governance.

The summer of the Olympics in Athens and national political conventions in Boston and New York provided an excellent opportunity for this writer to reflect on a series of musings over the triumphs and frustrations of the past decade-plus within the complexities of his own campus governance system. The Zen aphorism that best captures this opportunity for summer reflections states: "You cannot see the field you are standing in, until you first step outside of it." The reflections have produced a set of musings, arranged for purposes of convenience under two headings: (1) Musings on Arrogance, which are categorized so that the discussions (a) describe a governance behavior; (b) present a working hypothesis that attempts to explain the behavior; and (c) conclude with a shared governance principle that offers insights on lessons in sharing power and lessons in shaping leadership within collegiate governance forums; and (2) Musings on Antidotes, which are categorized as a set of governance axioms.

Such discussions of behaviors, hypotheses, and principles, and the attendant axioms that flow from them may contribute to our search for the commonalities existing among the Venn diagram–like alignments of faculty governance structures, administrative governance structures, and board governance structures. Because the DNA of shared governance resides in the combinatorial properties of these interactive structures, leaders must continually be asking themselves: "What happens, and what is prevented from happening, when Circles *A*, *B*, and *C* overlap or pull apart from each other?

MUSINGS ON ARROGANCE

Governance Behavior #1

President Harry Truman once mused at how frustrating his successor General Dwight D. Eisenhower would find the presidency. Ike, who having had all of his orders unquestioningly obeyed in the military, would soon find that almost nothing of any significance happened on short order in the White House. And in similar fashion, we also experience time and time again the moving of reputable and collegial members of the faculty into line officer positions, only to see them become impetuous, bewildered, and even belligerent when it dawns on them that their former colleagues do not reply "How high?" to their imperiously barked "Jump!"

Working Hypothesis #1   What causes such a Dr. Jekyll/Mr. Hyde transformation in our erstwhile colleagues? One hypothesis has it that the newly appointed administrators seem to be in a hurry. Why? Because they realize their tenure in office may be cut short, so they must do everything possible to impress their boss that mountains are being moved, and must do everything possible to impress their followers that their legacies as leaders will live on in the changes they are trying to promulgate—if only everyone would cooperate.

Shared Governance Principle #1   "Slowness. Slowness. Slowness." Newly appointed administrators tend to be obsessed with speedily produced outcomes. Why? Because insecurity breeds task orientation and overconcern with products—number of meetings attended, number of documents demanded from direct reports below, and number of assignments completed for the boss above. Excerpts from a child's poem "Slow Dance," of unknown origin, say it all:

Do you run through each day on the fly, when you ask: "How are you?"
Do you hear the reply? And when day is done do you lie in your bed,

With the next hundred chores running through your head?
You'd better slow down, don't dance so fast;
Time is short, and the music won't last. (Anonymous Works)

Working Hypothesis #2   Another hypothesis states that newly appointed administrators may be working for those dreaded Theory *X* bosses, who question everything and assume nothing positive of their hapless appointees. This circumstance becomes particularly vicious when the temperaments of the boss and subordinate administrator are also at loggerheads. Such commonly seen conflict is exacerbated when the boss is also left-brain dominant—that is, overly critical, overly accustomed to precision and to adherence to the rules of policy—as contrasted with the subordinate administrator who may be creatively right-brain dominant, open to big sky possibilities and therefore not obsessed with the specifics of onerous details.

What is unfortunate about this internecine proximity of personality interactions is that the subordinate administrators, even though they may have previously adopted the beneficial attributes of being Theory *Y* or even Theory *Z* in their positive assumptions about others, nevertheless must now of necessity adjust accordingly by adopting negative-oriented Theory *X* assumptions themselves. That is, they must now question the motives and work habits of the very people who report to them, in order to keep up with their boss's incessant demands. Regrettably, they now become so busy keeping their jobs that they have scant opportunity for actually doing their jobs. As the boss breathes down their necks for evidence of accomplishments and follow-through on myriad orders, so too do they in turn breathe down the necks of those below them, leaving no stone unturned in their mad efforts to impress the boss above.

Shared Governance Principle #2   "All line officers are ethically and morally responsible for ensuring the success of every subordinate administrator that they have appointed." Not to do so amounts to nonfeasance and a violation of their fiduciary roles as line officers of the institution. And subsumed under this principle is the requirement that this selfsame spirit of professional support and collegial cooperativeness from line officers also be extended to elected governance officers, who in carrying out their assigned duties to the body politic require sufficient budgetary resources, meeting facilities, and work space. For them not to do so would be an act of ill will.

Similarly, it also behooves governance officers, on their part, to operate in good faith by keeping line officers apprised of timely concerns long before they burgeon into full-blown campus issues. Quick and easy access, both ways, between governance officers and line officers is an integral ingredient for maintaining an effective governance climate on campus.

Special Corollary to Principle #2   "The communication interchanges between line officers and governance officers, as well as those occurring with trustees, must be characterized by authenticity, civility, and respect." While timely access among the key players is one thing, credibility of communication content is quite another, as is the manner of the tonal delivery of that content.

Governance officers are expected to demonstrate authenticity when meeting privately with the administration, as they convey the true pulse of their electorate. Never should they presume to promote their own private agendas or individual departmental concerns under the guise of representing the greater needs of the faculty, at large. Line officers for their part must refrain from "shooting the messenger" during such candid exchanges, but be willing and able to accept the feedback on campus conditions in the spirit that it has been given.

Governance officers and line officers alike are also expected to demonstrate civility—a rare commodity within some campus climates. When line officers rant and rave at the elected officers of the faculty and when governance officers themselves deliberately provoke their counterparts with "we vs. they" jeremiads, the quality of campus debate deteriorates dramatically.

Senator Mike Mansfield (D), former Senate majority leader from Montana, had been slated to deliver a speech on the floor of the Senate on that fateful Friday afternoon of November 22, 1963—the day President Kennedy was assassinated. It was not until 35 years later that another Senate majority leader, Senator Trent Lott (R) from Mississippi, invited the then 95-year-old Mansfield back to the floor to deliver that eclipsed speech—as relevant now as it was then. The topic? Civility. As excerpted: "Senators must embrace their collective duty to work on behalf of the Nation. This can prevail only when there is a high degree of accommodation, mutual restraint, and a measure of courage. Humility suggests that it is not the Senators or leaders [in the White House] who, as individuals, are of fundamental importance, but instead, it is the institution of the Senate, itself, [that is of fundamental importance]."

He inveighed against those who adopt a different persona when in power. "I shall not make myself look like a majority leader by donning my mandarin robes. . . . I am what I am, and no title, political act, or image maker can alter that! Leadership is not about twisting arms or playing the playground bully. Leadership lies in the ability to persuade others through reason to come around to their point of view and to move on" (Comity, 1998, A-19).

"And to move on," Yes! This message is as valid today, as it was when originally penned, almost a half-century ago. And, rhetorically speaking, what excuses do our line officers and our governance officers have to offer for not being civil with each other, for not listening to each other, and for not showing respect to each other?

Finally, as for respect, that's a class act! An excerpt from a poem of unknown date and provenance puts forth the matter most eloquently:

> Class knows that comity, good manners, and civility pay the lasting dividends of good will. Class never runs scared because it is sure-footed and confident—being able to handle anything that comes along. Class cannot be faked, because it is real; you know it when you see it. And finally, if you don't have class, then no matter what else you have, it really doesn't matter, because you won't live on in the memories of those you leave behind.

If governance officers and line officers experience personality conflicts or subscribe to disparate political philosophies, at the very minimum their professional code of decorum can and should demonstrate the respect that is owed to each other's office—be it the presidency of the campus, or the presidency of the Faculty Senate—if not to each other's person.

Governance Behavior #2

An even more pernicious variant of arrogance than that born of impetuousness and the arrogance born of the necessity to save one's own skin when under fire surfaces from within the depths of the Maslovian "need for esteem." One aspect of this esteem-based administrative malady appears frequently in the press under the headline "Potomac Fever." Although the designated name is unique to our Federal City (i.e., Washington, D.C.), it is by no means limited to the nation's capital; it is alive and well on our nation's campuses. For example, faculty members never cease to be amazed at how quickly and splendiferously draperies, furnishings, and the other trappings of "Look world, I have arrived" office decor appointments accrue to newly appointed administrators—no matter the condition of the budget, no matter the needs of the departments. Office space and office furnishings have continuously become the number-one priority of business for newly appointed panjandrums. Yet it takes but a glance at the road kill littering the funny farms of academe to show how the perpendicular pronoun—"I"—has impaled the insufferable egos of people who think of themselves first! Parenthetically, the term "funny farm" is not the author's choice but the actual term used by two deans on his campus who feared what people would say of them as they were about to leave their embattled positions.

While not all governance officers obviously succumb to this trappings-of-office version of the malady, some do, nonetheless, expect special treatment and recognition of a different kind, namely, special favors, special handling, or special invitations from on high—be they social, political, or professional. Yes, while governance officers need occasional access to such gatherings, how many of them have had the presence of mind to report back to their constituencies the results of such gatherings? And how many of them even took the time during such gatherings to share the campus Zeitgeist with the powers that be? If they have not done so, they also have probably been impaled on the politically perilous danger point of the perpendicular pronoun—"I."

Potomac fever is a fever of delusion, a fever that says: "I could be so successful if only I had more resources from my boss," or "I could be so successful if only I had better cooperation from my direct reports." It is a fever of grandiosity proclaiming loudly in word and action: "My agenda is more important than yours; therefore, I speak and you listen"; or, "My time is more important than yours; therefore, I attend to my business first and you will just have to wait until I get around to seeing you for that 3:00 appointment." Sound familiar?

Working Hypothesis #3   Benjamin Franklin once opined that if the whole world were blind except him, what need would he have of fine furniture or fine clothes? Since he was born before Maslow, we would say today that he was probably talking about prestige—that intangible something bestowed on us by others. Most people tend to seek prestige, until the drive is reasonably satisfied, then it loses its effectiveness to motivate behavior further in that direction. "Most people"—that is, people who have not succumbed to the delusions of potomac fever.

"Some people," however, do suffer from an exaggerated sense of self-importance. Such people usually experience their epiphanies when they come to fathom the all-important distinction that not all campus leadership positions are necessarily occupied by leaders! Believing that this just might also apply to themselves, they suddenly experience serious misgivings about their roles and even see their current perquisites of rank quickly paling into insignificance, as compared to how they looked at the time of their initial appointment as line officers or governance officers.

Because unmet needs drive behaviors, beleaguered occupants of leadership positions, holding onto whatever vestiges of prestige they can muster, now grasp for straws in the vaporous fogs of other peoples' heads. Other peoples' heads? Yes—because that is where the gratification of the esteem-based need for prestige exists, in the opinions that others have of our records of accomplishments and our competence as leaders. Prestige can only be granted to us by others—freely and of their own accord. How futile it is, then, for the occupants of leadership positions to attempt to control what is not theirs to control. And how foolish it is for them to allow their senses of accomplishment, their self-concepts, and their happiness to reside in the vaporous vagaries of other people's heads.

Yet there exists another aspect of this Maslovian need for esteem, though unlike prestige, it falls indeed directly under the occupant's control, namely, position power. The power motive drives behavior when recognition and prestige are perceived to be in short supply. To make up for this deficiency when performing in highly visible roles of campus leadership, such individuals begin to overcompensate their feelings of inadequacy by controlling and micromanaging others. The fuzzy logic at work here goes something like this: "If others will not willingly grant me, as the occupant of a leadership position, the recognition and prestige that I believe is rightfully mine by virtue of my rank and office, I will demand it by coming down hard on them with the full authority of my position, often to the refrain: 'That will show them who is the boss.'"

Power is the Janus-faced god of administration. On the one hand is the "engaging-faced" aspect that commits others to willingly follow a leader's initiatives; on the other hand is the "sobering-faced" aspect that compels others through their sense of obedience to lawful authority to comply with a leader's orders. The downside for others? Fear—fearing the consequences for not complying with a line officer's lawful order.

The downside for self? Pornography—reveling in the enjoyment of power for the sake of power while publicly protesting to the contrary. Such is power's pornographic pleasure—the secret enjoyment of its exercise coupled with the simultaneous denial of the act of its enjoyment, to both oneself and to others. Such perverted denial finds its example in the lament of line officers laying people off: "This hurts me more than it hurts you."

King Henry II's infamous soliloquy of 1170 about his nettlesome Archbishop Thomas à Becket, immortalized in T. S. Eliot's (1935) *Murder in the Cathedral*—"Who will rid me of this meddlesome priest?"—has become an object lesson for all line officers down to the present. Reportrayals of this "Henry II Phenomenon" drama occur whenever the holders of power profess public shock at what others have done on their putative behalf. Line officers know full well that their every wish becomes the sycophantic command of their insecure direct-reports who strive to please and to ingratiate themselves at the expense of others. Such is the abuse of position power in any organization, let alone campus governance circles.

Shared Governance Principle #2   "To become great, it is first necessary to become little." While an occasional piece of windy conceit is allowed to pass for everyone, it is modesty, especially for those in power, that endears leaders to the hearts of their followers. The humility born of modesty unlocks the conundrum of power, namely, leadership is influence that instills commitment in others, whereas management is control that breeds compliance from others.

It is recommended, therefore, that those who occupy leadership positions turn around from time to time to see if anyone is willingly following them. It is also recommended that they come to understand that it is the office that they occupy that gets them invitations to councils of the campus decision makers, that gets their phone calls returned, and that gets them invitations to the soirees of the multitudes. Not to understand these nuances is not to discover who they are as individuals and where they fall in the true scheme of things on campus and in life beyond.

Time magazine essayist Frank Trippett (1981, 81) was convinced "that boasting usually signals some pathetic private weaknesses . . . [because it's] the kind of thing that traps people into spiritual emptiness." Trippett, in his fascination with the "berserk egos" of America's media darlings and political leaders, cited Associate Director John Schimel of the William A. White Institute of Psychiatry: "[Braggadocio] is a way of denying some form of insecurity." Trippett then concluded his essay "On Leading Cheers for No. 1" with a bite: "The rule is simple: the louder and more prolonged the bragging, the more profound and painful the secret doubts and distances that are being masked. Given this pattern, the self-glorifier deserves less than applause and more than mockery. Pity is perhaps the more appropriate response" (p. 81).

Governance Behavior #3

Campus administrators fear who is saying what about them to their bosses. They fear that the faculty are continually looking for some impolitic imbroglio or policy infraction that may have been committed in their earnest efforts as line officers to govern campus change. They fear the reverberations within the governance systems on campus that follow almost any major policy decision they make. Finally, they fear that the faculty will pounce on the accumulation of their governance shortcomings— oblique or otherwise—while derisively deigning to accommodate them with a dismissive wave of the hand that says: "This too shall pass—off they go to the funny farm."

Working Hypothesis #3   And why is this? Perhaps it is the fear of loss and the fear of failure that fuels the insecurities plaguing the occupants of leadership positions on campus. Ironically, fear of possible loss is what defines risk, and risk is what defines leadership. Fear of loss of face, fear of loss of respect, fear of loss of position are all real and are all attendant to every act of leadership. Because leadership is taking people to where they have not been, leaders must assess the calculus of risk inherent in any significant undertaking—including reorganizing the administrative structure, realigning budget priorities pursuant to vision implementation, and appointing key line officers, with or without the faculty's blessings.

Such fear of loss afflicts the occupants of leadership positions even more so if they have brought with them to their positions their unresolved insecurities of the past. Uppermost, perhaps, is the fear of how they will appear to others—"I'll look stupid;" "I'll be ashamed, if I don't succeed."

Clearly, we have something of a paradox here. That is, if it is true that the higher up the flagpole the occupants of leadership positions go the more people will see their ass, why did they gravitate toward such exposed and public positions, especially given their fears of loss and failure? David Maraniss (2004, B-05), commenting on President Clinton's recent autobiography *My Life*, had similar misgivings: "One of the paradoxes of Bill Clinton is that he was drawn to a profession that promises constant tension and anxiety, conditions hardly conducive to keeping old demons at bay."

Siegelman (1983, 118) throws a brilliant light on this paradox by framing it in the form of a penetrating question followed by a sobering reflection. To wit: "If we were to fail at something without anyone else knowing about it, would it still bother us so much? Perhaps if we could shed this need to preserve a certain image, then perhaps we could look at [the fear of loss and] failure in another way."

Line officers and governance officers who are in touch with their psychological centers, accept the risks that come with leadership initiatives, being both willing and able to learn from the failures that inevitably result from their many efforts. Freedom from failure, therefore, is not the goal of leaders; dropping their public persona is the goal—à la Senator Mike Mansfield's "stop looking like a [Senate] majority leader . . . donning

[your] mandarin robes. . . . I am what I am and no title . . . can alter that."
That is the goal! So learn to let go!

Let go of what, you may ask? Let go of pretense, let go of the need
for prestige, and let go of the need for perfectionism. Siegelman (1983)
inspiringly sums it all, when she says, "Perhaps 'letting go' is the key
term here. Letting go of your zeal for perfection is letting go of a little
part of yourself. But that, in turn, requires a certain security about who
you are; and if you are uncertain about that, then you can't afford to re-
linquish anything. Letting go means having confidence that whatever
you do is 'good enough' and that 'good enough' is really all that fallible
human beings can aspire to" (p. 120).

Shared Governance Principle #3   "Humor humbles; it creates insights. That is what makes it such a powerful instrument for change"
(Coutu, 2004, 70). Humor, the shortest distance between a speaker and an
audience, bonds leaders to followers—all other things being equal. For
leaders, humor communicates that they do not take themselves as seriously
as they take their responsibilities. Humor is serious business and enjoying
humor does not mean that leaders are not serious people. If it means anything, it shows that they have no problem with being the butt of their own
self-deprecating piece of humor. People who laugh at themselves endear
themselves to others, which in turn promotes a certain comfort level with
them—forging bonds, and maybe even inducing eventual followership.

Because a defensive crouch creates a disabling posture, hidebound
line officers and governance officers would do well to take on the advice
of William James: "We don't laugh because we are happy; we are happy
because we laugh." Almost a century later, *Harvard Business Review*,
sharing the comments of TRW's chief executive officer, Frederick Crawford, echoed this Jamesian wit: "If everybody could agree to stop work
for three minutes every day to have a good belly laugh, and then go back
to work again, we would have fewer law suits, fewer hospital patients,
and business would be more prosperous" (Dyer, 1991, 126).

MUSINGS ON ANTIDOTES

While several antidotes to the arrogance of people occupying leadership
positions on campus have already been embedded within the aforemen-

tioned three principles of shared governance, there remains a final set of governance axioms for leaders and followers to ponder. These axioms—so self-evident that we often rush right by them in our haste to lead and to follow—provide leaders and followers, alike, with an opportunity for reflection and renewal, namely, Authenticity, Balance, and Forgiveness.

Axiom #1: Authenticity

Sham hypocrisy interferes with tuning in on the wavelengths of others. The worst possible place for an unauthentic person to be is in a position of leadership—where every mistake and foible goes off like a goalie's bell with every missed block of the puck on the frozen pond playing field. Contributing to part of this hypocrisy is the regrettable fact that the occupants of leadership positions tend to know more about others than they do about themselves. Leaders are either in touch with themselves or they are not. Followers resonate well with leaders who are comfortable with themselves and with others.

There's no faking in the leadership derby; we all know it when we see it. Just ask the janitors and secretaries in your buildings on campus—they know who the phonies are! The occupants of leadership positions within the governance systems on campus can hardly afford to postpone that much-awaited appointment with themselves, if they have not already found their psychological center. To do so would make them run the risk of succumbing to the impostor phenomenon.

The impostor phenomenon—described in succinct and behaviorally precise terms by Harvey and Katz (1985)—is a variation of "success anxiety," which preys on insecurities. At its core, "success anxiety" is that free-floating feeling of anxiousness brought on by self-doubts about one's performance capabilities and summed up in the sentiment: "Last month, I received a standing ovation for the speech I gave on my vision for the organization. Next month, I have to give a state-of-the-art update on that vision implementation, and am nervous about not receiving a comparable round of applause for my efforts." A touch of such anxiety is normal, except when it devolves into feelings that one is a fake, phony, or impostor who is about to be found out.

Prisoners of the impostor phenomenon share a variety of easily recognizable characteristics (cf. Harvey & Katz, 1985, 8). First and foremost of them is the "halo effect." The occupants of leadership positions—due to some projected charisma, or to some real or perceived past achievement—come to feel being trapped on the escalator of other peoples' expectations of their future performances. This discrepancy between leaders' own realistic self-assessments of their capabilities and their perceived assessments of what they think others are expecting of them will probably produce some considerable anxiety. Yet this characteristic by itself will not produce the impostor feeling. Three additional characteristics must accompany it.

One of these characteristics is a sense of denial. For whatever reason, such leaders refuse to accept the fact that they were appointed to their positions fair and square, or that they were truly instrumental to the success of some leadership event they had engineered within the organization. That is, they consistently attributed their success to some outside circumstance or fluke of fate, anything other than their own good work. The next characteristic is a sense of fear—fear of being exposed as a fake, fear of appearing incompetent, fear of being consigned to the ash heap of campus history. And the last characteristic cementing the impostor phenomenon firmly in place is the conscious effort of the leaders to hide their anxieties of fear, denial, and halo effect discrepancies under the guise of the workaholic syndrome.

The former Cincinnati Red Pete Rose double-timed everything—whether it was to and from the infield between innings, or to and from the bases, even on every pop-up foul ball. He recently explained the reason for this on a televised interview, stating that he never considered himself a gifted ballplayer and to make up for his self-perceived deficiencies had to work twice as hard, run twice as fast as the other players did—just to stay on the team roster.

This cult of hustle that covers for feelings of inadequacy is not limited to the baseball diamond—it pervades the playing fields of the leadership derby as well, under the managerial soubriquet of workaholism. "When in doubt, gallop," goes the adage of the French Foreign Legion. Workaholics just can't seem to "let go." They approach their tasks as if everything and everyone depended on them. Every *i* must be dotted, and every *t* must be perfectly crossed, or else the report, the event, or even the paltry dinner party will fail to impress others, thereby exposing them as frauds. Pell-mell do they move on to their next task—seldom, if ever, savoring the accomplishments of their last achievement.

Savoring requires a pause, which in turn requires the silence to enjoy that pause. By eschewing silence they rush to action, all the while reveling in the noise that prevents them from considering a much-needed appointment with themselves. Silence, after all, lies at the core of listening. And there exists perhaps no better listening laboratory for leaders in which to train than the sounds of silence from which come the stirrings of their own souls.

As Harvey and Katz (1985) so poignantly put it: "[The workaholic impostors] wonder if they can sustain the successful image of themselves that they have [so unwittingly] created. No one found them out this time . . . but maybe the next [time] they won't be able to put out such superhuman efforts [to succeed in the eyes of others, let alone themselves]" (p. 37). Thus does the absence of authenticity—with themselves, primarily, and with others, secondarily—contribute to the victim's perception of their success as being due, disproportionately, to hard work rather than to their innate competence and gifts of leadership.

Axiom #2: Balance

Sailboats and leaders have something in common—they have occasional moments of serene calm often punctuated by other moments of sheer terror! Both of them in bouts of rough weather show a tendency either to turn into the froth and fray of the wind, head on, or to turn away from it. Which one they pick usually depends on one of two alternatives, either (a) the shape of the sail or their courageous confidence in pursuing their current course of action, or (b) the balance of the boat or the balance of their political support for pursuing that current course of action—be it directed head on into the opposing forces or deflected away from those forces.

Nautically speaking, the force of the wind on a sail produces a center of effort, whereas, resistance to this force by the boat, especially the keel, produces a center of lateral resistance. Unless these two "centers" are in proper alignment, the boat will not survive the onslaughts of heavy weather. Politically speaking, unless the occupants of leadership positions are themselves psychologically centered, neither will they survive the tumult that comes with the turf of organizational leadership.

A comparable principle from the field of aerodynamics says as much. Namely, when an airplane is climbing too slowly in the sky, its aerodynamic drag builds up, because the nose of the plane is too high. If an altitude adjustment is not quickly made, the plane will arrive at such a point that even at full throttle it will not be able to climb any more and will begin falling back to earth. So the only solution available is to drop the nose and trade off some altitude to gain the necessary speed to climb again. How simple, you say! Yet, how infrequently do we see the occupants of leadership positions making their own necessary altitude/attitude adjustments when trying to regain the flagging respect of their followers—the very people who have the power to bring them down to earth again.

Speaking of earth and sky, Euclid discovered a geometric principle of proportion, balance, and beauty by observing nature and the structure of the galaxies. He had dissected a rose and found the positions of the petals always precisely arranged. He had also dissected an apple and found that the seeds arranged themselves into a five-pointed star pattern forming consecutive sets of isosceles triangles—wherein the ratio of the lengths of the longer sides to the shorter ones were aligned in the same ratio that governed the arrangements of the rose petals. This Golden Ratio of length to width was always equal to (phi) Φ = 1.6180339887 (cf. Livio, 2002).

The Milky Way Spiral Galaxy, the spiral flights of falcons zooming in on their prey, the spiral chambers of the nautilus—which influenced Frank Lloyd Wright's design of the Guggenheim Museum in New York City—the Great Pyramid of Khufu, Leonardo da Vinci's *Mona Lisa,* and Salvador Dali's *The Sacrament of the Last Supper* are all principled on the value of phi, the Golden Ratio.

And the relevance of all this? Our minds are attuned to symmetry and geometric beauty of form that obeys the laws of proportion and balance. Proportion—the size relationships of parts to each other and to the whole—is what contributes to aesthetically functional effectiveness. Beauty, therefore, is a recognition of the presence of perceived proportions in relationships—whether in nature, your own academic department and college, or in the relative proportions of time characterizing the balance pans of your personal and professional life.

Not everyone need be president, dean, director, or follower in the Venn diagram–like dynamic characterizing our governance structures on campus. What is important, and what contributes to the geometric beauty and effectiveness of the whole governance system, is that all the players perform their roles splendidly well. The Academy Award goes not to the prince or the pauper but to the players who performed their roles with grace and distinction.

Thus, perhaps the biggest challenge facing newly appointed line officers and governance officers is their acceptance of the fact that their need for esteem, need for achievement, need for acceptance, and need for power are indeed operative and at work driving their behaviors, and that these drives must be balanced through the fulcrum points of their psychological center. Once this awareness of needs and the acceptance of the struggle to balance such needs is brought to the forefront of their consciousness, they will be in excellent shape to control them. But if they deny their existence and operation in themselves, no control will be possible. Why? Because the occupants of leadership positions cannot control what they deny exists!

Axiom #3: Forgiveness

The final and most significant axiom of shared governance is the good will born of forgiveness. Without good will, nothing but strife and travail will prevail. Without good will, trust and confidence in relationships will fail. And without good will, all attempts at leadership and followership will come to naught. For good will at its very core is predicated on forgiveness.

Simon Wiesenthal (1969) has wrestled with the issue of forgiveness for the past six decades of his life, especially after liberation from the Mauthausen concentration camp in upper Austria in 1945. During his internment, he had been summoned to the deathbed of a dying SS officer, whose final efforts at confession and soul-cleansing contrition depended on Simon's forgiveness. The perplexed prisoner could not fathom the nature of the request and kept silent during his several visits to the officer's deathbed. Before he could unravel the unusual complexities of the dying man's request, death intervened.

While his conscience has bothered him ever since, it has been to our benefit that the withheld act of forgiveness had occurred. It has been to

our benefit that innumerable symposia have been convened, wherein
leaders from all walks of life and most continents on Earth debated the
ethics and morality of granting or withholding forgiveness. And it has
been to our advantage that we have had the benefit of their musings on
forgiveness (Wiesenthal, 1969), including:

- "Must we forget before we forgive?" (p. 103) (Sven Alkalaj, am-
  bassador of Republic of Bosnia and Herzegovina to the United
  States).
- "Forgiving and forgetting are two separate acts. One should forgive
  . . . from our need to be free and to get on with our life, but we
  ought not to forget . . . [because] by remembering, we choose forgiveness over retribution" (p. 148) (Matthew Fox, president of University of Creation Spirituality, Oakland, California).
- Recognition of repentance is a necessary first step in the absolution
  of forgiveness; i.e., forgiveness from me must be preceded by a
  recognition from you of the harm your action has caused (cf. 140)
  (Cf. Eva Fleischner, Office of Catholic/Jewish Relations, U.S.
  Catholic Conference).
- "A Tibetan monk, incarcerated for 18 years in a Chinese prison,
  came to see me after his escape to India. During the course of that
  meeting I asked him what he felt was the biggest threat or danger
  he had faced while in prison. [I was amazed and inspired at his extraordinary and inspiring answer.] He said that what he feared most
  was losing his compassion for [his] Chinese [captors] (p. 103) (Eu-
  gene J. Fisher, associate director of the National Conference of
  Catholic Bishops).

HOW PROFOUND! HOW HUMBLING!
HOW ENCOURAGING!

So often, leaders—in their haste to do what they think is right—lose
sight of what others may think is right. Umbrage is taken, conflict
mounts, and the "we vs. they" lines of battle are drawn. If the participants of campus governance debates kept in mind that famous line from
T. S. Eliot, "In the end is my beginning," perhaps the principles and ax-

ioms discussed in this brief treatise on governance, power sharing, and leadership shaping would take root.

Once leaders have left their campus positions and governance roles, all that remains is what lives on in the memories of their successors in leadership—final memories that will define the beginnings of their lasting legacies. All the symphonic compositions of governance are written in minor key, where the signature pattern of the music is based on the timing of the intervals between the notes. Governance, leadership, and power are timed to the unique intentions and masterful skills of an incredible cast of characters within the board, faculty, and administration. Would that all campuses be as blessed as mine has been!

REFERENCES

Anonymous Works. (n.d.). Slow dance: A child's poem. Retrieved June 30, 2004, from Poetry Archives at www.emule.com.

Comity hour with Senator Mike Mansfield. (1998 March 25). *Washington Post*, A-19.

Coutu, D. L. (2004). Putting leaders on the couch. *Harvard Business Review*, 82(01), 70.

Dyer, D. (1991). The voice of experience: An interview with TRW's CEO Frederick C. Crawford. *Harvard Business Review*, 69(06), 126.

Eliot, T. S. (1935). Murder in the cathedral. New York: Harcourt Brace.

Harris, J. F. (2004 June 29). A democratic attack dog with the manners of a Boy Scout. *The Washington Post*, A-21.

Harvey, J. C., & Katz, C. (1985). *If I'm so successful, why do I feel like a fake: The impostor phenomenon*. New York: St. Martin's.

Livio, M. (2002). *The Golden Ratio: The story of phi*. New York: Broadway Books.

Maraniss, D. (2004 July 4). The places beyond a biographers reach: Bill Clinton's interior monologue. *The Washington Post*, B-05.

Siegelman, E. (1983). *Personal risk*. New York: Harper & Row.

Trippett, F. (1981 June 8). On leading cheers for No. 1. *Time*, 81.

Wiesenthal, S. (1969). *The sunflower: On the possibilities and limits of forgiveness*. New York: Schoken.

INDEX

U.S. Department of Education, 162, 200, 226, 234

Vaill, P., 17
values, shared, 122, 127, 137
Vazonyi, B., 123
Velasquez, M., 87, 121
Von Bertalanffy, L., 3
Vroom, V., 153

Waldersee, R., 20
Waldman, D. A., 25
Waterman, R. H., 136
web of accountabilities, 57, 63, 94
Weisbord, M., 150
Wellesley College, 220
Wharton Executive Education, 159
Wharton School of Business, 159
Wheatley, M., 3, 16
White, L., 112
whole-system change: charting a course for, 119; a moral compass

for navigating, 111; using power and political behavior, 73
Wiesenthal, S., 255
Will, G., 198
William A. White Institute of Psychiatry, 248
William T. Grant Foundation and Institute for Educational Leadership, 228
Woodman, R. W., 132
Worley, C. G., 18, 19, 42, 52, 102, 112, 152, 153
Wright, F. L., 254

Xerox Corporation, 162, 227

Yammarino, F. J., 25
Yetton, P., 153
Yoffie, D., 87

Zeitgeist, 245
Zen, 240

ABOUT THE AUTHOR AND CONTRIBUTORS

Francis M. Duffy is a former high school teacher and certified school administrator and supervisor. He is a professor of change leadership in education at Gallaudet University in Washington, D.C. He held an honorary faculty position at Harvard Graduate School of Education, sponsored by Chris Argyris. He is also an organization improvement consultant specializing in whole-system change and a 2002–2003 Education Policy Fellow with the Institute for Educational Leadership in Washington, D.C. He has published six books on creating and sustaining whole-district school improvement, including *Moving Upward Together: Creating Strategic Alignment to Sustain Systemic School Improvement* (2004); *Courage, Passion, and Vision: A Guide to Leading Systemic School Improvement* (2003); and *Step-Up-to-Excellence: An Innovative Approach to Managing and Rewarding Performance in School Systems* (2002), all by Rowman & Littlefield Education.

Russell L. Ackoff is the Anheuser-Busch Professor Emeritus of management science at the Wharton School, University of Pennsylvania. He has authored 22 books: most recently *Redesigning Society* (2003) with Sheldon Rovin, *Re-Designing the Corporation* (1999), and *Ackoff's Best*

(1999). A former president of the Operations Research Society of America, vice president of the Institute of Management Sciences, and president of the Society for General Systems Research, he has received six honorary degrees and is a member of the Academy of Natural Sciences for the Russian Federation and The International Academy of Management.

John L. Anderson is vice chairman of New American Schools, having served as president for seven years. Prior to joining New American Schools, Anderson was an education consultant to corporations, state-based coalitions, and state governments. John began a 30-year business career with IBM after graduating from Yale University. He is a member of numerous boards and committees of education-related organizations, and he is active in the community of Durango, Colorado, where he resides.

Richard Farson has led several organizations noted for their innovative programs in human affairs. As president of the Western Behavioral Sciences Institute, which he helped found in 1958, he directs the institute's centerpiece program, The International Leadership Forum, an Internet-based think tank composed entirely of highly influential leaders addressing the critical policy issues of our time.

Long interested in the field of design, he was the founding dean of the School of Design at the California Institute of the Arts and a 30-year member of the board of directors of the International Design Conference in Aspen, of which he was president for seven years. In 1999 he was elected as the public director (nonarchitect) to the national Board of Directors of the American Institute of Architects.

A University of Chicago Ph.D. in psychology, he has been a naval officer, president of Esalen Institute, a faculty member of the Saybrook Graduate School and Research Center, and a member of the Human Relations Faculty of the Harvard Business School.

His books include *Science and Human Affairs; The Future of the Family; Birthrights;* the critically acclaimed best seller *Management of the Absurd: Paradoxes in Leadership,* now published in 11 languages; and *Whoever Makes the Most Mistakes Wins: The Paradox of Innovation,* coauthored by Ralph Keyes. An article based on this book won the McKinsey Award for the best *Harvard Business Review* article published in 2002, the one "most likely to have a major influence on managers worldwide."

Libia S. Gil recently joined the American Institutes for Research to continue her work as the former chief academic officer for New American Schools. Dr. Gil provides senior counsel on leadership development initiatives and assists states and districts in developing strategies for improving student achievement by bridging research evidence with practice evidence.

Dr. Gil was superintendent of the Chula Vista Elementary School District for over nine years. Under her leadership, which began in 1993, the district experienced continuous growth. She fostered the successful implementation of numerous school change models, including six charter schools and partnerships with Edison Schools Inc., School Futures Research Foundation, Accelerated Schools, Comer, MicroSociety, Standards-Based Instruction, and the Ball Foundation. Student academic performance and customer satisfaction survey results showed increasing gains. In 1998, the community passed a $95 million school bond with a 76% voter approval to support modernization of learning environments. Standard and Poor's has continued to give the district an A+ rating to reflect efficient district management with the lowest centralized administrative costs in the county.

In addition to multiple awards and honors, Gil received the 2002 Harold W. McGraw Jr. Prize in Education for her outstanding leadership as Chula Vista superintendent. The McGraw Prize is awarded annually to individuals who demonstrate exceptional contribution to the improvement of education systems. Dr. Gil is recognized for her work in redesigning central office roles and functions to serve and support teaching and learning in the classrooms. Accountability systems and performance standards were key vehicles institutionalized to increase student and adult learning outcomes.

Gil began her teaching career in the Los Angeles Unified School District and has taught in various programs, including English as a second language, bilingual education, and gifted and talented programs. As a teacher, she and her colleagues created a successful K–12 alternative school and numerous alternative classroom programs. She has held a variety of administrative positions including school principal and area administrator, supervising K–12 principals, and assistant superintendent for curriculum and instruction. Dr. Gil has a Ph.D. in curriculum and instruction with emphasis on bilingual and multicultural education from the University of Washington.

Michael E. Hickey is the Naomi Price Hentz Distinguished Professor and the director of the Center for Leadership in Education (CLE) in the College of Education, Towson University, Baltimore, Maryland. Prior to this appointment, Dr. Hickey served a distinguished career as superintendent of the Howard County Public School System in Maryland from 1984 to 2000. Before coming to Maryland, he served as superintendent in the St. Louis Park Schools, a suburb of Minneapolis, for eight years and as assistant superintendent and deputy superintendent in Seattle, Washington, for seven years.

Dr. Hickey's primary areas of academic interest are leadership, change, strategic planning, and human resource development, particularly the linkage between leadership and the teaching/learning process.

Mike is a dedicated cyclist as well as an art collector of eclectic tastes. His wife, Nichole, is a professional artist in residence at the Howard County Center for the Arts in Maryland.

David T. Kearns is chairman emeritus of the New American Schools Corporation, a private, nonprofit, bipartisan organization established by American corporate and foundation leaders in July 1991 to restore American public education to world preeminence.

Mr. Kearns, a Former Senior University Fellow at the Harvard Graduate School of Education from 1993 through April of 1995, currently serves on the Executive Committee for the Harvard Project on Schooling & Children. From 1991 until 1993, Mr. Kearns served as deputy secretary of the U.S. Department of Education. Prior to this appointment, Mr. Kearns held the position of chairman and chief executive officer of Xerox Corporation from 1982 until 1990. Through his leadership, Xerox Corporation demonstrated to the world that American business could reinvent itself and compete successfully in a global economy.

Prior to joining Xerox, Mr. Kearns served as a vice president in the data processing division of IBM. He has served as chairman of the board for the National Urban League, Junior Achievement, and the University of Rochester. Mr. Kearns is a former member of the Board of Directors of Ryder System, Inc., and a former director of the Chase Manhattan Bank and Time Warner, Inc. In addition, he serves as a trustee of the University of Rochester and a former trustee of the Ford Foundation. Mr. Kearns is a member of the Business Council and the American Philosophical Society.

Mr. Kearns has written three books. *Winning the Brain Race*, coauthored with Denis P. Doyle, outlines a bold plan to make our nation's schools competitive; *Prophets in the Dark*, coauthored with David A. Nadler, explains how Xerox reinvented itself in order to become a worldwide industry leader. Mr. Kearns's most recent book *A Legacy of Learning*, coauthored with James Harvey, analyzes the difficulty of transforming American schools and calls for a new definition of "public education."

Mr. Kearns graduated from the University of Rochester in 1952 with a degree in business administration. He has served in the U.S. Navy. Mr. Kearns and his wife Shirley reside in New Canaan, Connecticut.

Art Kleiner is a writer, partner in the consulting firm Reflection Learning Associates, and cofounder of MIT's Learning History Research Project. Art's writing and projects focus on evolving territories education; organizational learning and change; cultural change; scenario planning; interactive media role and methods of learning in organizations; and business and society. They have included collaborations with the leading business thinkers, from Peter Senge to Peter Schwartz. His award-winning books include *The Age of Heretics*, a history of the movement to change corporations for the better, from Kurt Lewin to Tom Peters, and *Who Really Matters*, an examination of power in organizations. He is also the coauthor of *The Fifth Discipline Fieldbook*, a frequent magazine writer, and a former editor of *The Whole Earth Catalog*. He teaches a course on the future of the telecommunications and media infrastructure, using scenario planning methodologies, at New York University's interactive telecommunications program.

William J. A. Marshall is a professor and chair of the Department of Administration and Supervision at Gallaudet University in Washington, D.C., having served at the helm of the University Faculty Senate for almost ten years and recently completed an unprecedented third three-year term as the chair of the university faculty and university faculty senate. He trains doctoral and master's degree students in special-education administration. He was awarded the President's Distinguished University Faculty award in 1990. He formerly taught at the University of Washington at Seattle and the University of Illinois at Champaign. He is the former administrative director of the Whitney Young Magnet High School in Chicago and the dean/director of the Model Secondary School for the Deaf on the campus of Gallaudet University.

Sheldon Rovin is emeritus professor of health care systems at the Wharton School of Business and former director of Healthcare Executive Management Programs at Wharton Executive Education and the Leonard Davis Institute of Health Economics, all at the University of Pennsylvania. Dr. Rovin's publications include over 90 journal articles and book chapters and eight books. His latest book is *Redesigning Society* (2003), written with Russell Ackoff. Dr. Rovin's principle consulting and teaching interests are the application of systems thinking; idealized design; interactive planning; and creative thinking to the design, management, and leadership of organizations. He was the dean of the University of Washington, College of Dentistry, from 1973 to 1977.

Nelson Smith became the first president of the Charter School Leadership Council (CSLC), a national organization representing all sectors of the charter movement, on December 1, 2004.

He was previously vice president of policy and governance at New American Schools (NAS), a national nonprofit founded in 1991 to pursue systemic education reform. There his client practice focused on the management and governance of public charter schools and their role in catalyzing reform in traditional systems.

Mr. Smith served for three years as the first executive director of the District of Columbia Public Charter School Board. From 1985 to 1992, in the U.S. Department of Education, he oversaw numerous programs devoted to improving education through research-based methods. In the early 1990s he was Vice President for Education and Workforce Development at the New York City Partnership, where he developed school-leadership and school-to-work programs, as well as organizing a business-led study of the governance of New York City's million-student public school system.

In 2002, he was appointed by the U.S. secretary of education, Rod Paige, as one of 21 negotiators who developed federal regulations for the No Child Left Behind Act. He has written numerous papers and articles on the impact of NCLB on the charter sector and served as chair of the Federal Policy strand of the U.S. Department of Education's 2004 National Charter Schools Conference.

For the Progressive Policy Institute, Mr. Smith has authored studies of the charter school movements in California and Texas. For the Education Commission of the States he wrote *The New Central Office*, an exploration of how central-office functions change as schools move toward contract-based accountability. He also advised the Buffalo, New York, Board of Education in its effort to create a new network of district-sponsored charter schools.

A 1972 graduate of Georgetown University's School of Foreign Service, he is a resident of the District of Columbia, where he is active in civic and arts organizations.